A Pictorial G
to the
Nepal Himalaya

Siân Pritchard-Jones

Bob Gibbons

First edition: November 2020; ISBN: 9798679024687
Published by Expedition World; www.expeditionworld.com; sianpj@hotmail.com

Front cover photo: Himalchuli from Nauban Kharka, Ganesh Himal
Back cover photo: Braka monastery near Manang
Cham mask at Jang monastery, Limi
Title page photo: Annapurna II and Lamjung from Naudanda

A Pictorial Guide
to the
Nepal Himalaya

Siân Pritchard-Jones
Bob Gibbons

About the authors

Siân Pritchard-Jones and Bob Gibbons met in 1983, on a trek from Kashmir to Ladakh. By then Bob had already driven an ancient Land Rover from England to Kathmandu (in 1974), and overland trucks across Asia, Africa and South America. He had also lived in Kathmandu for two years, employed as a trekking company manager. Before they met, Siân worked in computer programming and systems analysis. Since they met they have been leading and organising treks in the Alps, Nepal and the Sahara, as well as driving a bus overland to Nepal. Journeys by a less ancient (only 31-year-old) Land Rover from England to South Africa provided the basis for several editions of the Bradt guide **Africa Overland**, including the sixth edition published in April 2014 and the seventh coming soon.

In 2007 they wrote the Cicerone guide to **Mount Kailash** and Western Tibet, as well updating the **Grand Canyon** guide. Their **Annapurna** trekking guide was first published by Cicerone in January 2013, with the 2nd edition in 2017. In 2015 they were in Nepal during the earthquakes and published **Earthquake Diaries: Nepal 2015**. A Pictorial Guide to the **Horn of Africa** (Djibouti, Eritrea, Ethiopia and Somaliland), **Australia: Red Centre Treks** and **In Search of the Green-Eyed Yellow Idol**, a 40-year travelogue & autobiography, are published by Expedition World. See also **Saudi Arabia**, **Chad Sahara**, **Ladakh**, **Lebanon** and **Karakoram K2 treks**.

For Himalayan Map House they are writing a new series of trekking guidebooks: **Himalayan Travel Guides**. **Kanchi's Tale** is a new series of books covering various expeditions as seen through the eyes of a young Nepalese mountain dog – an educational doggie travelogue!

See back page for titles so far published. All books are also available on Amazon.

Authors below Ganesh V and Ganesh I

Please send your comments and updates to sianpj@hotmail.com

Acknowledgements

So many people have inadvertently contributed to this collection of our images from across Nepal. Thanks to Exodus Expeditions during the heady days of overland and to Sherpa Expeditions, whom we worked for as trek leaders in the 1980s (and the Alps until today). To Ravi Chandra, Chris and Tashi Lachman and all the team at Ama Dablam Trekking in Kathmandu for inviting us to lead group treks in Nepal for many years. Also to Rama Tiwari and the team at Pilgrims Book House for encouraging our enthusiasm to delve more deeply into the culture of the region.

Very special thanks to Pawan Shakya, Udyog R Singh and the team at Himalayan Map House, who invited us to research the treks for their Himalayan Travel Guides series; thanks for the map of Nepal at the back of the book. Great thanks to Jitendra Jhakri Tarali Magar, Jag Budha Magar, Kul Bahadur Gurung, Pasang Dawa, Purna Thapa Magar, Rajendra B Lama, Sanjib Gurung, Chhewang Lama and all the other guides and porters who have enabled us to produce our series of Himalayan trekking guides.

Thanks to Karna, Sunil and Rajan Sakya at the Kathmandu Guest House for many happy stays and memories. To Sunil Shrestha and Uttam Phuyal at the Hotel Moonlight for their superb hospitality. Thanks also to Sohan Shrestha at Hotel Pilgrims and to Mingma Sherpa of The Everest Equipment Shop for the great sleeping bags and jackets. Also to KC, Bhandari's Photo Shop and Northfield Café for the scrumptious enchiladas and chocolate brownies. Last but not least, to David Durkan of Mountain People, Ian Wall, Tony Jones, Steven Stamp and Ade Summers. For the additional photos as listed, thanks to Kev Reynolds, Paulo Grobel, Sanjib Gurung and Sir Crispin Agnew.

Contents

Kanchenjunga 14
Makalu 31
Everest 45
Rowaling 64
Langtang 78
Ganesh Himal 92
Manaslu & Tsum 102
Annapurna 128
Dhaulagiri 150
Mustang 153
Nar Phu 168
Dolpo 177
West Nepal 196
Map of Nepal 213
Other books by the authors 214
List of trekking areas 215

Preface

Nepal was made for adventure; its fabulous mountains, nature, culture, religious mix and people are the cornerstones of its attraction. High, remote valleys and deep impenetrable gorges hide secret places of mystical charm, enticing explorers and climbers even to the point of risking death. Early visitors defied its forbidden status to sneak into the region, just reaching the mostly forbidden city of Kathmandu being the aim of some of these adventurous souls. Others, often from British India, came as traders, clandestine geographers and colonial agents. When the country opened in 1950, the floodgates opened; travellers, climbers, self-appointed mystics, hippies and traders poured in. The lure of Nepal and the Himalaya became almost insatiable as its wonders and mysteries became known to the inquisitive world outside. Everest was finally conquered in 1953, after many decades of failures from the Tibetan side since the 1920s. Today Nepal is a travellers' and trekkers' paradise, with untold wonders to discover.

In this series of Pictorial Guides, some of the countries are globally well known, but not all the destinations are familiar to visitors. Nepal is no exception. Most travellers today arrive by plane, but a significant proportion still travel overland from India or Tibet/China. This book is divided into sections covering the major trekking routes, splashed with some of the cultural attractions. Nepal remains a timeless haven of peace and tranquillity, with scenic wonders all around. Despite some creaking bones we still find ourselves drawn to these mountains, time and time again. It is an addiction that is hard to shed, so beware – you too may find that the 'once-in-a-lifetime' trek becomes habit-forming!

This pictorial book aims to bring together our photographic collection from 1974 to the present. Hopefully it will provide inspiration to would-be explorers and inquisitive armchair travellers. The new challenge is how to learn more without the adverse issues of global climate change – a challenge more difficult today than for those of us who were able to experience the world in quieter times. The spirit of adventure lurks within, a spirit that poses new questions, sometimes with no answers...

It's a dangerous business, Frodo, going out your door. You step on to the road, and if you don't keep your feet, there's no knowing where you might be swept off to.
***The Lord of the Rings,* J R R Tolkien**

Chenresig image in the Tsum Valley

Introduction

This pictorial guide is essentially an introduction to trekking in Nepal through pictures; it is in no way aiming to be a true guide. For those details there is a plethora of guidebooks on offer. It's a sad fact that travelling to such places is much harder today and likely to become even more so in future. Health, security and safety concerns are more widespread, and global issues temper freedoms; all of this means less understanding of peoples and cultures far removed from our own daily lives. How this clash of interests plays out will be for future generations to discover.

Nepal is a very diverse country, ranging from the semitropical lowlands bordering the Ganges plains of North India, through the middle hills and up to the highest peaks on earth. Every geographical and natural habitat is found here. It's a wonderland for botanists, bird watchers and naturalists, as well as adventurers, walkers and climbers.

As diverse as the geography are the people who call this place home. Nepalese have long learnt the art of survival in remote and desolate places. Farmers till the life-giving fertile meadows of the middle hills and herders use the bounty of nature to eke out a living amid glorious scenery. Across the arid plains of the high country below the crags, cliffs and soaring buttresses of the Himalaya, the ingenuity and stoicism of the populations is amazing. Hindu temples and devotees characterise the lower slopes and central hills, while esoteric Buddhism and quaint monasteries dominate the rugged domains below the peaks.

Nepal is changing fast; industrious farmers, informative guides, wild-eyed nomads, traditional villagers, modern city men and women, and well-heeled elites are all found here. Much of the region has a rapidly growing economy, while other areas are still quiet backwaters where life remains little changed. Some images date back to the 1970 and 1990s, an era of great explorations and adventure; others are from more recent years. The Himalayan treks of Nepal are all magical; scenically sensational, culturally captivating and inherently inspirational. There is no better place than the high mountains to regain a sense of hope for the future.

Welcome to Nepal!

General information

Getting there
The main overland routes are from India and China, through Tibet. There are many entry points along the southern Nepal frontier. Land borders between Nepal and India include Sonauli/Belahiya near Bhairahawa; Raxaul/Birgunj; Nepalganj; Mahendranagar; and Kakarvitta. The Sonauli/Belahiya border north of Gorakhpur is the most-used entry point from India. Buses connect Bhairahawa to Kathmandu and Pokhara. A long journey by local transport links Nepal to Delhi in the west, through Mahendranagar/Banbasa. Those travelling between Kathmandu and Darjeeling or Sikkim can cross the eastern border at Kakarvitta.

Kathmandu is also linked to Lhasa in Tibet by the new highway through the border at Rasuwa/Kyirong. The road is generally tarred to Lhasa but poor on the Nepalese side near Dhunche in the Langtang area. The 5–6 day journey to Lhasa will blow your mind. It climbs over a number of spectacular 5000m passes through Lhatse, Shigatse and Gyangtse to Tibet's once-forbidden capital, Lhasa. The original route from Kathmandu to Tibet via Barahbise, Zhangmu and Nyalam was badly affected by the 2015 earthquake and has not yet reopened; it remains to be seen if overland travel will restart on this route.

The following airlines serve Nepal from Europe, Southeast Asia, the Pacific, Australia and North America:

Air Arabia and Fly Dubai from The Gulf; Air Asia budget flights from Kuala Lumpur; Air India via Delhi, Kolkata (Calcutta) and Varanasi; Bangladesh Biman for budget travellers with time to kill via Dhaka; Chinese airlines link Kathmandu with Lhasa, Chengdu, Kunming and Guangzhou (Canton); Dragon Air from Hong Kong; Druk Air from Paro, Bhutan, to Kathmandu and on to Delhi; Etihad Airways via Abu Dhabi from Europe; Indigo a budget Indian carrier; Korean Airlines from the Far East; Nepal Airlines flies from Delhi, Bombay, Dubai and Hong Kong – for those with bags of time; Oman Airways and Salaam Air via Muscat; Jazeera Airways via Kuwait; Silk Air from Singapore; SpiceJet and Indigo are low-cost Indian carrier; Thai Airways via Bangkok, from Europe and Australia/New Zealand; Qatar Airways via Doha from Europe; Turkish Airlines via Istanbul from Europe; plus Virgin, BA and other airlines to Delhi, then one of the Indian carriers to Kathmandu. This information is subject to change.

Landscapes
For a region with so many high mountains, Nepal is still surprisingly accessible to most trekkers and travellers. Almost every type of vegetation, fauna and flora can be experienced on the trails heading north from the southern border to the Tibetan plateau. Ricefields dominate the lowland strip of the Terai. Almost immediately the Siwalik Hills rise up, with dry forest and meandering rivers. Farms and villages cling to the soaring but fragile slopes of the Middle Hills, where most of the rural population lives. Deep gorges and wild rivers cut through these hills.

On the northern horizon the Himalayan peaks glisten in the clear sunlight of sunrise, watching over the villages, terraced fields, deep canyons, high meadows and eerie forests. The arid and mostly treeless uplands of the Tibetan plateau host high valleys, where glacial rivers and rudimentary agriculture support life. The mountains are fantastic: a range of rugged, sublime panoramas, soaring spires, jagged ridges and picture-postcard lakes and glaciers.

Climate

The best season for trekkers to visit is just after the Indian monsoon season from mid-October to late December, before the cold mist and cloud of winter roll in through January and February. Skies are crystal clear for trekkers and the luminescent light wonderful for photography. Winter can have some clear but exceedingly crisp days in late December and January. There is a certain charm visiting a quieter Nepal in winter, but disruption with snow and cold is very likely. Most lodges close in mid-December, except on the most popular routes like Everest and Annapurna. The spring season – March, April and for higher areas May – is also popular, although more cloud is likely.

Money matters

Changing money is easy in the tourist towns, with exchange booths. Banks tend to take hours and are not generally used by tourists. ATMs are available in all urban areas, but step into the mountains and there are only a few in the most popular trekking regions. Outside these areas, carrying extra cash is advised. The Nepalese Rupee is the currency.

Religion

> *Holy places never had any beginning. They have been holy from the time they were discovered...*
> **The Land of Snows,** Giuseppe Tucci

Life across Nepal is still significantly influenced by religious and traditional beliefs. Everywhere, from a hilltop monastery to the back alleys of Kathmandu, people follow cultural traditions through daily rituals and frequent festivals. The main religion of the country is Hinduism, which is found in the lowlands, Middle Hills and in the central valleys. Buddhism is the religion of the high Himalaya and the Tibetan plateau. Much of the country has some connections to Shamanism, with beliefs often intermingled. There are a few Tibetan Bon centres in the remote, high areas close to Tibet, while Sikhs, Christians, Muslims and others are in a minority.

Health and safety

Healthwise Nepal has a mix of poor and excellent facilities; it's a question of who can afford it. The hospitals and health infrastructures in the cities are quite good. Most of the regions away from urban centres have local clinics with limited facilities. Traditional medicines have long been popular with Nepalese.

The diseases of the hot lowlands, like dengue, malaria and other menaces, are absent in the high country generally above 1200m. Check with medical experts, though, as things are changing with global warming. Food hygiene has improved dramatically but can still be mixed. The more comfortable hotels and popular restaurants are pretty good. Beware any empty lunchtime spots.

Crime in the cities is rare and out in the rural areas the level of honesty is pretty amazing. Apart from the remote chance of a political incident, few visitors feel threatened.

Any venture into untamed and wild places presents some risks and dangers. A trek to the remote Himalayan regions needs careful preparation and informed planning by any prospective visitor. See our series of detailed trekking guidebooks listed in the back of this book.

Visas

Most foreign nationals require a visa. Normally visas are available from embassies and at land borders, as well as at Tribhuvan International Airport in Kathmandu (check for any changes before arrival). Entering or exiting the country at the remoter crossing points and from Tibet may be subject to change, so always check the latest requirements in all cases. Applying in your own country will cost more. Remember to apply well ahead of travel, in case there are any holidays at the embassy due to festival periods in Nepal.

Obtaining a visa on arrival is normally the easiest option, but check in case of any new restrictions. To save time at the airport, fill in the preliminary form online at home and print off the bar code. The maximum length of stay in Nepal is five months in one calendar year; the fifth month is not always possible. Tourist visas are available for 15, 30 or 90 days, at a fee of $30, $50 and $125 (payment in cash) respectively.

Extensions in Kathmandu are obtained at the Immigration Department at a cost of $US45 (the minimum fee, for 15 days) or for a daily charge of $US3 per day. Anyone requiring a visa extension in Kathmandu must go online and fill in the forms in advance, uploading a passport-style photo. Using the machine in the immigration hall is free of charge.

All visas are currently multiple-entry, making visits to places like Bhutan, Tibet or India much easier than before.

Check the up-to-date fees at www.nepalimmigration.gov.np
For comprehensive embassy listings, see: www.mofa.gov.np

Travelling around

Travel within Nepal is possible either by road or by air.

Bus and jeep

Road transport can be on a noisy, crowded public bus, a so-called 'tourist bus', or in a privately hired jeep or car. It's a compromise between comfort, safety, time taken and money spent. Road travel to places further afield can be long and tiring. Routes go via the Terai lowlands to the trekking areas of Kanchenjunga and Makalu to the east, and West Nepal and Dolpo to the west. Jeep dirt roads are pushing into previously remote areas, even into the high Himalaya, with amazing speed. Don't expect a comfortable ride; tracks are often dreadful.

Internal flights

Operated by a few local airlines, the main routes are to Pokhara, Nepalganj, Bhadrapur and Biratnagar. The main mountain routes are to Lukla (for Everest) and Jomsom (for Mustang and the Annapurna Circuit). Other sectors with less frequent services are to Tumlingtar (for Makalu and the Arun Valley route to Everest) and Taplejung/Suketar (for Kanchenjunga).

Further away flights head to Juphal/Dunai (for Dolpo), Jumla (for Rara Lake and Dolpo) and Simikot (for Saipal, Limi Valley and Kailash). Flights are subject to delays caused by weather and occasionally by other 'Nepalese' factors.

Helicopters are becoming quite common for sightseeing charters as well as rescue missions. Across the popular areas, Everest and Annapurna groups are using helicopters to cut the length of the treks. With ever-higher costs per day for trekking, this is not as surprising as it seems.

Flying into a restricted area needs a special permit for the flight, which could take up to five days to obtain, so forward planning is necessary. For a 5–6 seater helicopter, the weight limit is around 450kg of passengers, baggage and supplies.

Budgeting

There is no way to generalise about the exact costings, as trekking itineraries in Nepal vary in length, comfort and remoteness. Some areas have added restrictions and higher fees; others are relaxed and allow independent hiking. The cheapest areas for independent trekking are Langtang, Annapurna and Manaslu. Everest is more costly, with flights to Lukla and higher living costs above 3500m. Rolwaling, Kanchenjunga and Makalu have enough lodges for a lower cost trek. Ganesh Himal is surprisingly lacking in much tourist infrastructure. Mustang and Dolpo require permits and guides, while most of West Nepal has logistical issues, with camping often the only option. Of course most trekkers have guides, cooks and porters or beasts of burden for more comfort. A few posh hotels now exist in the Everest region, plus a limited number in the Annapurna foothills.

Conclusion

Unlike so many places in the world where the freedom of the road is a misnomer these days, trekking in Nepal remains a fabulous option for exploring the Himalaya. Getting fit for a trek is recommended and, for first timers, making arrangements through a foreign or local agent is advised.

The trekking routes are set out from east to west, with brief descriptions of the trails, degree of difficulty and factors that define the specific routes of the areas.

The main aim of this picture book is to inspire its readers to go beyond the familiar, to discover the treasures of Nepal – its mountains, its people and its culture. That 'once-in-a-lifetime' trek to Nepal is likely to be life-changing and habit-forming!

Mandala during a festival in **Bungamati, Kathmandu Valley**

Kathmandu

Kathmandu – the classic architecture of **Durbar Square**

Despite the urbanisation of the valley, Kathmandu still has many magical corners where life remains traditional and enticing. History and culture abound, the sights are stunning, and the melting pot of people is welcoming

Kathmandu Valley hosts amazing places like **Boudhanath Stupa**

Pokhara

Another centre for trekkers, **Pokhara** in 1979 was little more than a village near the side of **Phewa Tal lake**. Today it's a bustling town and the base for many treks in the Annapurna and Dhaulagiri regions

Fishtail (Machhapuchhre) towers high above

Kanchenjunga

Kanchenjunga North Base Camp from **Pang Pema**

Kanchenjunga is the third highest mountain in the world, after Everest and K2. It's a massive complex of peaks with huge glaciers draining from all sides. The Kanchenjunga region is remoter than most trekking areas, requiring a longer taking from 3 to 4 weeks.

Kanchenjunga Trek
There are two approaches to the north and south base camps but ideally spend longer to accomplish both by crossing the Selele La pass to link the routes. The usual trailhead is Taplejung, which has an on/off airfield, or is more reliably reached by a long bus or jeep trip from Bhadrapur airstrip. Before reaching Taplejung, the road passes through **Ilam,** famed for its **tea gardens**. The **road journey** to **Taplejung** from **Ilam** takes over **7hrs**. Exit points are back at Taplejung or the shorter option to Khebang and Hapu, where new dirt tracks have bus services for Ilam. The treks here are long, with three weeks being the minimum for a relaxed adventure. Lodges and food are adequate to avoid camping.

Kanchenjunga North Base Camp Trek
The northern trek heads to the myriad of glaciers adjacent to Pang Pema, following the route taken by climbers along the Kanchenjunga Glacier. The route is shadowed by a vast array of soaring peaks and spires – beauty beyond belief.

Kanchenjunga South Base Camp Trek
The southern approach crosses high ridges and worms its way to the Yalung Glacier, where the stupendous South West Face of Kanchenjunga dominates the approach. The South Base Camp is along the Yalung Glacier, with views from Oktang being the easiest to access. Two approaches to Kanchenjunga from Sikkim offered the only window on all that was known about the great mountain before Nepal opened in 1950.

llam tea gardens   **Taplejung**

The trail passes **traditional houses** of the Limbu people along the **Tamur Kosi** river

People create local handicrafts and worship at a monastery (**Sankha Deksheling Gompa**) on the alternative high trail between Taplejung and Chiruwa

The route crosses many side streams of the Tamur Kosi on **exciting bridges** to Chiruwa and Tapletok, where there is a checkpost. The lower trek spends a lot of time in dense forest, where birdsong and the shady canopy ameliorates the hotter temperatures at lower elevations

Sukethum has a **lone lodge** overlooking the Ghunsa Khola river, just after the confluence of the Tamur and Ghunsa rivers. Following the Tamur, the route leads to Olangchun Gola and the Lumbasumba pass, a wild trek where only camping is possible. The lodge offers free spiders, **informative wallpaper**, a lively host and good food

The trails are quite demanding, with **landslips** and overgrown areas; the route climbs steadily along the **Ghunsa Khola** valley

Some of the bridges on this landslide-prone route are rather **precarious** – some would say exciting, others might use expletives to attempt to explain the adrenalin rush!

The route climbs along the Ghunsa Khola to **Amjilosa** and then up a steep stretch to **Gyabla** village, with a quite OK lodge and some local entertainment

The trail climbs above the forests of the valleys to the open meadows of **Phole**, where the monastery is worth a visit. The people here are Tibetan refugees but have been in the settlement for many years

The **wispy forest trail** is a delight to Ghunsa, a major centre on the Kanchenjunga trail

A day of rest is on the menu at **Ghunsa**. **Tashi Choling** monastery, said to be over 1000 years old, hosts **21 Taras** and an ancient image of **Guru Rinpoche**

Dawn over **Ghunsa** and another exciting day ahead – on the trail to **Kambachen**

Fabulous scenery on the trail to **Kambachen**

Yak attack near **Rampuk Kharka**

Bridge before **Kambachen** camp

Sunset on **Jannu**, **Sobje** and **Thonje**

Sobje and **Thonje** peaks from **Kambachen** camp

Breakfast before a side trip to **Jannu** (now Kumbhakarna) viewpoint east of camp

Sunset from **Kambachen** camp

Merra Peak avalanches seen from the trail to **Ramtang**

Bharal (blue sheep) near the camp at **Ramtang**

Fabulous sunset on **Kambachen** Peak

21

Views north on the 'landslide' **trail to Lhonak** with the **Kanchenjunga Glacier**, Tengkoma Peak, Drohma Peak and the **Mojka 'piton tower'** ahead

Kanchenjunga Glacier   **Yaks** below **Pathibhara Chuli**

Lhonak is a good place for a two-night stop; those with limited time can make a day trip to **Pang Pema**. **Wedge Peak** is a major peak on the trail to Pang Pema. The trail climbs steadily, but with the altitude, it's a slow walk. From Lhonak (4780m) the trail follows the northern ablation valley beside the Kanchenjunga Glacier to Pang Pema (5143m). From here are the best views of Kanchenjunga's massive north faces and glaciers.

A higher viewpoint around the northern side valley is tricky following landslides; it's best checked out by camping at Pang Pema or using the basic shelter in season.

Pang Pema with **new landslides** ahead on the trail

Views from **Pang Pema** are of **Kirat Chuli**, **Nepal Peak** and **Kanchenjunga** (right)

The trek back to Ghunsa from Lhonak is easy, apart from the landslides and passing the **Khandunchan Falls** noted by **Sarat Chandra Das** during his explorations of the valley

Back in **Ghunsa**, the authors with **Ian Wall**

Climbing from **Ghunsa** to **Selele Camp**

Views west up the trail to the **Nango Laptse** pass, one access route to the Lumbasumba trail

The views of **Jannu** from the **Selele La Pass** are amazing and en route is the strange **'cat' outcrop**

View of **Everest** and **Makalu** from the **Selele La trail**

25

There are four passes on the trail from **Ghunsa to Tseram**, although the last three are much less demanding. Kabru and Rathong are superb from the last rocky col

The steep descent to Tseram passes **Tsho Chhung Donka lake** to reach **Tseram**

The trail north is spectacular, passing small lakes below **Rathong Peak** and the massive **Yalung Glacier** en route to **Oktang** and **Kanchenjunga South Base Camp**

The ridge trail to **Oktang** has great views of Kanchenjunga

The **Yalung Glacier** is followed by climbers to an advance camp, but it's a rugged and dangerous route for trekkers

Trekkers can visit **Oktang** on a day trip from Tseram or Ramche before returning to Tseram after lunch at Ramche. The trail back to Tseram needs care due to unstable cliffs in a side ravine. There are now a couple of OK lodges at Tseram and the 'foodings' are sustaining before the long exit trek to Ilam

Heading south, the trail passes **Andi Kharka**, the side valley leading to the Kang La and Sikkim. The route heads through **Tortong** and climbs the rugged **Laisiya Bhanjyang** with views of Jannu before a big descent to **Yamphudin**

From **Yamphudin**, where the monastery is worth a visit, the route heads through **Ghatichhinne Bhanjyang** to Khebang. The trail for Taplejung heads through Mamanke and Lali Kharka on a different trail. The shorter trail drops to Khebang and then steeply down to the river and on through **cardamon plantations**

The trail descends very steeply to the **Hapu Khola** and on to the roadhead at **Hapu**, where our crew prepare our last night's dinner

Sunset on **Kabru** and **Rathong** from **Ramche**

Makalu

Makalu from the ridges east of Base Camp

Considering that Makalu is the fifth highest peak in the world, it sees surprisingly few trekkers. Perhaps this is one of its appeals. However, it has many magnetic and hypnotic aspects: soaring cliffs, snowclad defences, inspiring glaciers, subtropical forest-clad hills and passes to conquer.

Makalu Base Camp Trek
Being more of a wilderness trek, it will attract those eager for a temporary respite from the madness of the 21st century. It can be done as a lodge trek in season, but in winter after mid-December most lodges will be closed. Currently most trekkers retreat the same way over the Shipton La pass; the route outlined below is a more 'adventurous' option.

Yeti Foot Trail – Barun Valley
The beguiling, tangled but deserted forested Barun Nadi Valley has, until now, been the preserve of woodcutters and wildlife. Almost totally undiscovered, this alternative route from Makalu Base Camp could become a popular choice in future. However, for now the trail is wild, unused and occasionally dangerous. Ideally use this valley for the exit from Makalu Base Camp. Camps along the valley are at Bagare, Chamlingma, Tutin and Dhumjang. The route continues south along the upper Arun River to Num.

Lumbasumba Trek
Increasingly on adventurous trekkers' radar, the Lumbasumba Trek is the newly designated link along the Great Himalaya Trail between Kanchenjunga and Makalu. It allows trekkers to penetrate deep into unknown country south of the Tibetan border – an area so remote that only herders know its true secrets. The trek is long and tough, but full of surprises en route. Hidden peaks, delightful forests, quiet babbling streams and often-deserted hillsides greet those who venture here. Camping with occasional teahouses/homestays is the only way to trek and the rhythms of caravan life soon dispel notions of modernity.

Jaljale Milke Danda Trek
Probably to be called the Rhododendron Heritage Trail, this newly proposed trek is sure to be a winner for those who don't enjoy high altitude and the extra cold weather of the icy peaks. The main attraction is the cultural life of the villages, but there are also airy panoramic views and colourful rhododendron forest on the upper slopes. It's not a trek that claims to be very easy, but that's a relative statement. Expect the usual steep ups and downs through a section of wild country; be prepared for anything once the remote trail is fully functional. Camping for now is the only option, but the southern areas are sure to become dotted with enthusiastically run homestays.

Makalu Base Camp Trek

The monastery in **Yangle Kharka**

The easiest access to the trek is to **fly to Tumlingtar**. A rough road heads through **Chichila** and on up to **Num** (and now further along the Arun Valley)

Num is the usual village the first night. The trail descends steeply through **terracing** to the **bridge** over the **Arun River** before a big climb, some in **bamboo** forest, to Seduwa

From **Tashigaon** a forest trail climbs steeply through **Dhara Kharka** and **Unshisa** to the **Khongma Danda** lodge. It's an airy place with superb panoramic views over the lowlands

The route climbs along a **knife-edge ridge**, with views of the Lumbasumba region, up to some chortens, where a stunning **view of Chamlang** appears to the west. Trails into the Chamlang valley are poor and rarely used, even by herders

Chamlang (7321m) lies at the head of the steep-sided Isuwa Khola valley

Sano Pokhari lake is higher up, with views east to the Lumbasumba peaks

The Shipton La pass (4125m) is the highest on the trail from Khongma to Dobato

The trail continues to the **Thulo Kalo Pokhari** lake and then climbs to the **Keke La** pass. Views of the **Chhochenphu Himal** loom large to the northeast on the Tibetan border

A steep descent leads to the lone rustic lodge at **Dobato**

Views of **Chhochenphu Himal** loom large to the northeast on the Tibetan border

The trail plunges from **Dobato lodge** into wispy forest through **Mumbuk** to join the **Barun Khola River Valley**

Following the river, the route crosses landslips to **Yangle Kharka**, with a good lodge and monastery. The images are **Chenresig**, **Gampo** and **Guru Rinpoche**

After **Yangle Kharka** the trail passes the **cave sanctuaries** of **Shiva** and **Parvati**

The peak of **Tutse** dominates the route as the trail climbs past the **'Pregnant Rock'** outcrop to **Merek**

Looking back, **Tutse** is still dominant   Higher up, so is **Yaupa Peak**

The route climbs under the **Merek** cliffs into open but steep meadows to reach the beautiful campsite and rustic lodge at **Langmale** (4410m). Dominating the view ahead to the west is the superb fluting of **Chamlang**

The trail above Langmale climbs, with views of Chamlang, Hongu and the still unnamed Peak 4 to **Shershong**, where a large rock provides a good lunch spot. Turning north, the last steady climb brings the trekker to **Makalu Base Camp**, where four basic lodges can host those who venture this far in season. Out of season, camping is also possible. Views are even more spectacular above the base camp area

Sunsets at **Makalu Base Camp** are sensational, with almost 4000m of sheer buttresses to the summit of Makalu

Ideally spend a day or so
hiking along
the **Barun Glacier** to
Swiss Camp,
with views of Lhotse, Pole
and the Barun wall.
Those with time can
try the trip towards
Sherpani Col

East of Base Camp
a ridge offers views of
Lhotse
and the eastern
Kangshung Face
of **Everest**

Icy trails and side streams are a hazard in winter along the **Barun Khola**. The dense forest is a delight, although the overgrown trail is not, in some stages. The camp at **Bagare** is set in dense, eerie forest with 'interesting' nocturnal audio!

The **fabulous forest trail** continues past waterfalls and refreshing pools with some heart-stopping drops and dodgy sections to a camp at **Dhav Khola**

The trail keeps trekkers entertained. Our trek dog, **Kanchi**, is amused, especially when she came to the Barun Valley via Base Camp from Tashigaon and needed to share our sparse provisions. She abandoned us in Syaksila when a 'suitable boy' dog appeared

After days of wilderness, the newly-named Barun Valley – **Yeti Foot Trail** – reaches the sultry Arun Valley that drains from Tibet. **Syaksila** is the first settlement of note, with curious people. The **Lhomi** people are found along this valley, as well as in the Lumbasumba region to the east

A new dirt road is pushing north along the dramatic **Arun Valley** to the Tibetan border, cutting into once very remote areas

Sunset on Makalu from Base Camp

Everest

The summit of Everest taken from **Tengboche** with a telephoto lens

The Everest region is magical. Sometimes visible from the Kathmandu Valley rim, much of the region is still amazingly peaceful and life goes on serenely, ignoring the frenetic pace of the cities. It consists of two distinct areas: Solu (southwest of Lukla) and Khumbu (north of Lukla). Of all the trekking regions in the Nepal Himalaya, it is to the Khumbu that those seeking a peek at the highest peak on earth come. But this region also holds added delights apart from Mount Everest, for the wealth of the culture is as fascinating and varied as the many mountains on display.

The region is Buddhist – quite different from the middle hills and the major areas of Nepal, which are mainly Hindu. These northern valleys host Buddhist communities whose ancestry can be traced back to Tibet. Here are quaint, mystical monasteries with vibrant art, devout monks and colourful festivals, an understanding of which will enhance any trek.

The Everest region's trails are now being integrated into the Great Himalaya Trail network. The byways of Everest still remain some of the most sought-after trails in the country. Fit and adventurous trekkers can bag a couple of demanding lesser summits for a grander perspective.

Treks include the Everest Base Camp Trek, Everest Panorama Trek, Everest Gokyo Trek, Three High Passes Trek, Classic Everest Trek, Arun Valley Trek and four short new escapes from the busier trails. With fabulous lodges and varied food, few trekkers camp in the region. The Lukla airstrip services most trekkers, although buses do head for Jiri and beyond, as well as to the Phaphlu area.

Everest Base Camp Trek
The most popular trek in the Khumbu region, variations all head to the famous Base Camp or the stunning viewpoint of Kala Pattar. Ideally allow at least 2 weeks to allow for good acclimatisation and time to savour the side trips on offer. The flight to Lukla is an adventure in itself. Many trekkers take side trips to Thame monastery in the valley that leads to the Nangpa La into Tibet. Other options go to Chukkung from Dingboche, and some head to Ama Dablam Base Camp from Pangboche.

Everest Panorama Trek
For those wanting a shorter trek, this is the classic route taking in the highlights of the region – Namche, Tengboche and the Dudh Kosi valley approach. Flying to Lukla, the basic route takes just over a week, although longer is always better if time allows.

Everest Gokyo Trek
Some trekkers rate the views of Everest from Gokyo Ri, above Gokyo village, better than those from Kala Pattar. From Namche the trek heads towards Cho Oyu via Khumjung and Phortse Teng to Dole, Machhermo and finally to the series of lakes at Gokyo. Well acclimatised trekkers can climb Gokyo Ri for stunning views; other trekkers with more time head towards Cho Oyu along the moraines of the Ngozumba Glacier. The return route is usually via Thare to Phortse, Pangboche, Tengboche, Namche and back to Lukla.

Three High Passes Trek
Rapidly becoming a popular though tough option, this trek takes in three high passes below Everest. Most begin from Chukkung, crossing the Kongma La to Lobuche before heading for the Cho La pass between Dughla and Gokyo. It's partially on ice, although in good weather not particularly daunting. The Renjo La has a fantastic panoramic view of Everest and most of the peaks in the Khumbu, before trekkers descend to Lungden in the Thame Valley. Three weeks are needed for this superb route.

Classic Everest Trek
Following the original 1953 walk-in trail, this much shortened route now begins east of Jiri, wherever the roadhead has reached. The dirt road is expected to go close to Lukla eventually. The classic route crosses the Deurali pass after Shivalaya, then the higher Lamjura Pass to Junbesi, a great village. After Ringmo and Trakshindu monastery, a long descent through Manidingma reaches the Dudh Kosi at Jubing. The last stage, no less arduous, climbs along the Dudh Kosi through Khari Khola and Puiyan to Lukla. As the usable road snakes east, the length of the trek is reducing; ideally allow 10 days to reach Lukla from Jiri and take in side trips as the road extends, or trek for fewer days.

Arun Valley
Quite popular years ago, this route starts from Tumlingtar airstrip (or for masochists from Kathmandu by bus to Tumlingtar via the Terai and middle hills). It crosses some stiff passes like the Salpa, Surkhe La and Narkung La, with some arduous descents and ascents to cross rivers that drain north/south. After Pangom the route joins the classic route to Lukla and Everest.

Other treks/peaks
All these relatively newly developed treks require camping crews so far, and all add several days to any normal route. The **Numbur Cheese Circuit Trek** (6–8 days), **Pikey Peak Trek** (2–5 days,) **Dudh Kund Trek** (4–6 days) and **Monastery Circuit Trek** (12–14 days) are accessed from the Classic Everest route. Trekkers with climbing experience head for Island Peak and Mera Peak for high adventure.

Everest Base Camp Trek

Lukla in 1975 (note the Afghan-coated trekker!)   The landing strip has now been sealed

The trail heads down to **Chaurikharka** and along to the monastery of **Ghat**, passing mani walls to reach **Phakding**

From Phakding the trail follows the Dudh Kosi River with some **exciting bridges** (1985, now replaced). After the park entrance at Monjo and Jorsale, the route crosses a **high bridge** (right) and begins the climb to Namche Bazaar

Namche Bazaar is the main centre for the Sherpas. Today the children are well dressed and educated. These kids greeted us in 1975. The atmosphere remains as exciting as ever, with climbers, trekkers, 'philosophers', yaks and people thronging the streets

Namche has grown considerably since **1975** (left) and **2017** (right)

Everest is on view from the ridge-top

Namche Monastery hosts icons like **Chenresig** and the demonic **Mahakala**

Tengboche (Thyangboche) is a top destination a day's march above Namche. Seen here in 1975 (with Ama Dablam), 1985, 1989 and 2017. The museum is a mine of information about the Sherpa people, the culture and the monastery. Everest can be seen from here, as well as the Nuptse-Lhotse wall, Taboche, Ama Dablam and Kangteiga

Tengboche hosts the famous **Mani Rimdu** festival during the autumn trekking season, generally in November

Everest from **Tengboche**

Lodge in **Deboche in 1975**

Lunch below **Pangboche** monastery and the village houses

Thar on the trail to **Dingboche** below Taboche (Tawache peak). Breakfast in 1989 before a side trip to **Chukkung** below the **fluted cirque** and the **Amphu Laptsa** pass

Makalu from the side trip above Dingboche   **Trail to Pheriche**

Yaks at Pheriche   **Tshola Lake** above Dughla

Sunset on the **Nuptse-Lhotse wall** from Lobuche

Everest Base Camp and the **Khumbu Icefall**

Pumori and **Kala Pattar**

Everest and **Nuptse**

Everest summit

—

Top of the World

Everest Gokyo Trek

Some trekkers prefer the views of Everest from Gokyo Ri on the Gokyo Trek. It also has great views of Cho Oyu and the turquoise lakes of the Ngozumba Glacier

Kangteiga from **Khumjung**

Views of **Ama Dablam** from **near Kunde**

Mong La

Sherpa wedding party on the trail to Phortse

Trail to the Mong La

54

Forest trail to Dole from **Phortse Teng**

Local Rai porter

Phortse is a traditional village below the **trail to Dole, Machermo and Gokyo**

Ama Dablam

Cho Oyu from **Gokyo**

Cho Oyu
from
Gokyo

Panoramic views of **Gyachung Kang, Cholatse, Taboche** and the **Ngozumba Glacier**

Everest
from
Gokyo Ri
above
Gokyo

Everest Thame Valley

Often overlooked is the Thame Valley, which leads to Tibet on the ancient trade routes over the Nangpa La pass. En route is **Thomo**, with a **new monastery**.

Thame village has good lodges and a **historic monastery**

The peaks of **Kangteiga** and **Tramserku** dominate the views from Namche, Tengboche and, below, from Thame. **Sherpani ladies** head off to the market in Namche

From **Thame** with its luxury lodge, the trail climbs through **Thyangbo** to the **Tashi Laptsa** pass and over into **Rolwaling**, a rugged mountaineering route

The peak of **Malungpalung** can be seen well from Thyanbo. Higher up the Thame valley passing through Maralung to Lungden and beyond, the Upper Rolwaling peaks of **Singkorab**, **Dragnag Ri** and **Pangbuk** appear. From the same viewpoint, **Cho Oyu**, **Pasang Lamu Peak** offer sublime sights towards the Nangpa La pass. Beyond Lungden there is one more lodge at **Arye**, but after this only camping is possible towards the Nangpa pass. Getting to the pass is discouraged, as it marks the Tibetan China border. Another high pass links the upper Thame Valley with the upper Gokyo Valley, but it's a dangerous and difficult option requiring some mountaineering skills

From **Lungden**, which has four lodges, a trail links with **Gokyo** via the **Renjo La pass** (above left). Ideally cross it from east to west; the views of Everest from the Renjo La are stunning. Returning to Namche brings good lodges and good food

Classic Everest Trek

This route was used by the first expeditions to Everest from Kathmandu, being a 3-week walk-in from the capital. Later a Swiss-engineered road (we drove on it in 2010) was constructed to **Jiri** (right), cutting the time by half. It's still a full day's drive to Jiri from Kathmandu, crossing high passes offering views of the **Rolwaling** peaks, **Gauri Shankar** and **Menlungtse** in Tibet. Today a dirt road snakes towards Jubing/Kharikhola and perhaps soon to Lukla

From **Jiri** the route heads to **Shivalaya** and up to the **Deorali Pass** via **Buldanda** and on to **Bhandar**. Camping crews used to service groups on this trail to Everest. These days most trekkers fly to **Lukla**, making this trail a delightfully quiet option, while having good lodges and food

An alternative trek used to head north from **Chisopani** near Janakpur through **Okhaldhunga** to **Salleri** and **Phaphlu** to link with the classic route at **Ringmo**. Today it's a drivable alternative to the Jiri route. Phaphlu has an airstrip with some flights

On the classic route from Bhandar, the trail descends to Kenja. During the Dasain festival **makeshift wheels** are often seen. After crossing the Likhu Khola the trail climbs again through Sete and rhodendron forest to the **Lamjura Pass** (3530m), the highest before Namche. Continuing east beyong Lamjura is the picturesque village of **Junbesi**, with **Thupten Choling** monastery on a side trail above to the north

Above **Thupten Choling** the peaks of **Numbur** and **Karyolung** are spectacular

From **Ringmo** the trail crosses a pass to **Trakshindu** monastery

The route drops steeply through **Manidingma**, with superb terracing en route

The cook crew climbing from **Jubing** through **Kharikhola** towards **Puiyan** and on along the **Dudh Kosi Valley** to **Lukla** with its **airstrip** (seen just on the right above)

Everest can also be reached from **Tingri** on the Tibetan side on a trail (and dirt road) via **Rongbuk Monastery** to the **North Base Camp**

Rolwaling

Gauri Shankar seen from **Simi** is just one of the peaks seen on this route that reaches a high point overlooking **Tsho Rolpa Lake** below **Pigpherago Peak**

Rolwaling Trek

Although only one pass separates it from its more famous neighbour, the Khumbu, Rolwaling is a forgotten, mysterious land. It remains an amazingly peaceful destination; life plods on serenely, ignoring the frenetic rush of city life. Gauri Shankar is the crowning star of Rolwaling, but a superb array of sentinels guard the Tibetan frontier, such as Chobo Bamare, Chekigo, Kang Nachugo, Dragnag Ri, Chukyima Go, Parchamo and Pigpherago. These northern valleys host Buddhist communities whose ancestry can be traced back to Tibet. Mystical monasteries grace the landscape, blending into the majestic visions all around.

Lapche Valley Trek

For decades a restricted area and inaccessible to all but a few herders and Buddhist hermits, the Lapche Valley north of Lamabagar is a dream come true for those who want to be among the first outsiders to visit a forbidden land. This deeply cut canyon drains the mountains of Chobo Bamare and Ama Bamare. The valley hosts one of the most famed cave retreats of Buddhism. Tibetan sage and poet Milarepa spent some time meditating and seeking the path to nirvana here; it's no Shangri-La of comfort for any visitor today.

The trail clings and climbs along the valley, from the very start on a precarious series of dodgy wooden platforms sticking out of the rockface. Later, as nature attempts to hide the valley's secrets, the only way ahead is by even more daunting and often dangerous trails with vertiginous drops. This stairway to heaven offers well-equipped trekkers a chance to penetrate the hidden corners of Milarepa's domain. The demons are lurking here to catch the unwary and those who set out ill-prepared. The gods of the Himalaya do not let those who venture into their domain go without some penance. Be careful!

Bigu Gompa Trek

Formerly the main highway to Rolwaling, this region is now a peaceful backwater crowned by the Tinsang La pass views and the treasure house of Bigu Gompa. The farming hills could not be more typical or interesting, with picturesque houses among lush terraces of rice and millet. Throw in the intriguing mix of colourful ethnic groups, and it's a winner.

Tashi Lapcha (Laptsa) Expedition

This 'trek' rates as one of the most potentially dangerous Himalayan crossings and really is a haunt of mountaineers. Dogged by rock fall and snow avalanches, the pass has been used by locals for centuries to link Rolwaling to the Everest Khumbu region. It should only be attempted by well-led, well-equipped and experienced mountaineering parties. Therein lies its most attractive attribute, and mountaineers flock to the fabulous peaks in the vicinity of the pass.

Rolwaling Trek

Most trekkers begin by climbing from the road at **Chhetchhet** to **Simi**, where the monastery hosted fabulous paintings before the earthquakes of 2015

A beguiling forested trail climbs from Simi to **Surmuche**; the local children are curious when trekkers arrive at their lodge

The quiet forest hosts prolific bird and animal life with few people. Once the trail begins to emerge from the dense forest, there are views of the superb, fluted **Chekigo Peak** ahead and later at **sunset**

The rugged, wild trail reaches **Dongang** before a climb to the main settlement of the deeply cut Rolwaling Valley, **Beding**

Beding monastery should not be missed, with **Guru Rinpoche** a prominent icon. Higher above is a cave retreat to explore

Climbing on from Beding, the trail passes a **cave monastery devoted to Guru Rinpoche** before reaching the monastery at **Na**, a herders' settlement often visited by climbers

The **East Face of Gauri Shankar** is spectacular, as is the long ridge of **Chekigo**, **Bamongo** and **Kang Nachugo** above **Na**. It's particularly spectacular at sunset

From Na the scenery is sensational all the way to **Tsho Rolpa Lake**. To the north are the peaks of the Upper Rolwaling Glacier valley. Peaks like **Ripimoche** and **Dragnag Ri** float above the vast **Rolwaling Glacier**. There are rough trails into this great cirque of little known or trodden peaks, but some rope skills are advised. Dragnag Ri is perhaps the most noted peak for climbers here

To the south there are views of the climbing peaks of **Ramdung** and **Chukyima Go** accessed from Na and popular with so-called 'Trekking Peak' climbers. A new but untried trail is supposed to be developed leading south from Ramdung to link with the Classic Everest Trek but …

Kang Nachugo peak from **Tsho Rolpa** lake   **Tabayabyum** from **Na**

The **lodge at Beding** is a welcoming spot as **kids play in the sun**

Sunset on **Gauri Shankar**

Lapche Valley Trek

Lapche monastery can only be reached following a wild and sometimes treacherous trail that clings to cliffs and steep-sided slopes. The trail begins at **Lamabagar**, where a new dam is under construction beside the small monastic community

The small settlement of **Lumnan** hosts a monastery below the dramatic peaks of Jugal Himal. The gorge is spectacular all the way to Lapche

The rugged trail continues to **Lapche**, where the monastery reveres the **Buddha**, **Dorje Phagmo** and, most of all, the poet sage **Milarepa**, whose meditation retreat is here

Milarepa
at
Lapche

Outcrop above Lapche

Gauri Shankar from the north

Monk
on the
densely
forested
trail

Bigu Gompa Trek

The main prayer hall (lhakang) of **Bigu Gompa** nunnery

Dolakha is the regional centre, with its **Hindu temples**. The trail to Bigu climbs from Chhetchhet on a steep path through traditional villages. **Sag (spinach)** is the staple diet

House near **Orang**, where there is a large school. **Bulung**, **Laduk** and **Loting** are the main villages before reaching Bigu

Superb flowers line the trails here. The soaring spire of **Chobo Bamare** is the main peak overlooking the valleys and hills of Bigu. From Bigu Gompa and its large nunnery, the trail crosses the airy Tinsang La, with a new dirt road snaking down 1500m to the Bhote Khola and the main road at Barahbise. Before the earthquakes of 2015, this road linked Kathmandu with Lhasa, Tibet, and is due for repair. It's a superb route passing through Tingri, Shigatse, Gyangtse and the dazzling turquoise Yamdrok Lake.

Langtang and Jugal Himal

Langtang at sunset from above **Dhunche**

Langtang Trek

Langtang Himal is a magical and mysterious land. This area, close to and visible from the Kathmandu Valley, is amazingly peaceful; life plods on serenely, ignoring the frenetic rush of city life. The main peak of Langtang Lirung is surrounded by a superb array of sentinels guarding the Tibetan frontier, such as Pemthang Karpo Ri, Langshisa Ri, Dorje Lhakpa and Gangchenpo. Trekkers can bag a couple of demanding viewpoint summits for a grand perspective. These northern valleys host mystical monasteries and Buddhist communities whose ancestry can be traced back to Tibet.

Gosainkund

North of Kathmandu is the great brooding ridge of Gosainkund, where soaring ridges hide the sacred lakes. The wild amphitheatre of the Hindu god Shiva allows passage from Langtang to Helambu by way of the Laurebina pass and the Gosainkund lakes. The Ganja La pass and the harder mountaineering Tilman Pass are crossed occasionally. The god of destruction (Shiva) does not let those who venture into his domain go without penance.

Helambu

Almost in the backyard of the Kathmandu Valley, the ridges and hills of the Helambu region are often bypassed without a glance. The south-facing, sunny aspects of Helambu offer a warmth and hospitality to be welcomed by those itching to get away from it all without enduring weeks of discomfort. Welcoming people make any sojourn along these less frequented trekking routes a delight. Hindu farmers work the fields, living a way of life little changed over the centuries. (We will ignore the most obvious sign of modernity – mobile phones – for this gushing introduction for just a few indulgent minutes!).Trekkers, however, can do themselves a big favour by entering or exiting the Langtang region along its pleasant and well-endowed (with lodges) routes.

Mountain lovers can observe the Jugal Himal range – the equal of any – from a number of vantage points.

Langtang Trek

Trekkers ascending **Tsergo Ri** with **Langtang Lirung** behind

The trail begins in **Syabrubesi** and climbs steadily along the Langtang Khola through quiet forest to lodges at **Bamboo** and **Lama Hotel**

Through **Lama Hotel** the route climbs to **Ghoretabela** before reaching **Langtang** village

Yaks love watching trekkers, but don't get too close!

During the **2015 earthquakes**, the trail was obliterated by a vast rockfall from Langtang Lirung (photo: Sanjib Gurung)

Chortens grace the trail before Langtang village

Views above **Langtang** village in **1984** and **2014**

After Langtang village,
the trail continues to
Kyanjin Gompa
with a spectacular
view of the
Ganja La pass
to the south

Most trekkers stay in **Kyanjin** for a couple of days to explore the upper valley and climb **Tsergo Ri** or **Yalung Peak**. **Kyanjin Gompa** hosts a great collection of icons, with **Guru Rinpoche** and his consorts prominent

North of **Kyanjin Gompa** is a **secretive lake** and the **Yabru Glacier**

Langshisa Peak

The fluted
Gangchenpo

Shishapangma (photo: Sanjib Gurung) and **Langshisa Peak** are seen from **Tsergo Ri**

Beyond **Langshisa Kharka** views include the Tibetan border peak, **Pemthang Karpo Ri**

83

Gosainkund to Helambu Trek

Linking Helambu with Langtang, a steep trail climbs from near **Pairo** through forest, **Syabru** village (seen in **1984** and **2014**) and upland meadows to **Sing Gompa**

The **dense forest** around Sing Gompa hosts **Red Pandas**, but seeing one is rare. Near Sing Gompa is **Phulung Monastery**, a little-visited place with unusual artwork. Images of the four guardian icons adorn the outer area

Superb views of
Ganesh Himal
to the west
from
Phulung Gompa

From **Sing Gompa**
the route climbs
along a ridge to a
chorten, where the
trail becomes
steeper after
Laurebina (3910m)

The climb to the
often ice-covered
Gosainkund lake
offers panoramic
views of
Langtang, the
Tibetan peaks and
Ganesh Himal

From the **Hindu shrines of Gosainkund**, the trail descends steeply to **Phedi**. Our porter **Kiran** heads down to **Ghopte**. Lower down are the villages & terracing of **Helambu**

The undulating trail from **Tharepati** passes through **Mangangoth**, **Kutumsang**, **Gul Bhanjyang**, **Thodung**, **Pati Bhanjyang** and **Chisopani**. New 'escape' dirt roads from Pati Bhanjyang allow variations in the trek now. Chisopani has become a weekend retreat for Kathmandu residents, as the road network has extended. The **Jugal Himal** peaks dominate the northern horizon all along the Helambu ridges. The main peaks including **Dorje Lhakpa** and **Phurbichyachu** glisten in the dawn light

Shivapuri (above right) overlooking Kathmandu is one final high point on the Helambu route. Another more common choice is to descend from **Chisopani** on a steep trail through **Mul Kharka** to **Sundarijal** near **Sankhu**

Historic **Nuwakot** is another attraction of the Langtang region, not far from Trisuli village. It hosts Newari architecture; nearby is the **Famous Farm**, a wonderful rural retreat

Tamang Heritage Trail

Sunset on **Ganesh V** from **Nagthali**

Nestling between Ganesh Himal and Langtang in the shadow of Tibet is the Tamang region of the upper Rasuwa district. It's the Tamang people who grab the limelight here; their colourful, ancient and traditional Tibetan-influenced culture is unique. Although predominantly Buddhist, they have a surprising number of Hindu traditions and some have found Christianity. Their ancient shamanism ancestry has not quite vanished, either.

The fabulous viewpoint of Taruche above Nagthali is a stunner, revealing the shy peak of Ganesh I, the elephantine Ganesh V, as well as the long-forbidden ancient trading post of Kyirong in Tibet. Topping it all off is Langtang to the east, watching at close quarters.

The Tamang Heritage Trail is accessed from the Ganesh Himal region via Gatlang or from the main Dhunche–Langtang road. New lodges and well-developed homestays give the trekker a wide choice of accommodation, as well as the advantages of planning long or shorter day hikes.

The main villages are Gatlang, Tatopani, Brimdang, Nagthali, Thuman and Briddhim. Some trekkers head to Langtang from the Tamang Heritage Trail on a high trail from Briddhim directly to the lodges at Bamboo.

A trek here is just the ticket for a short but stylish introduction to the thrills of trekking in Nepal.

The traditional village of **Gatlang** was sadly damaged during the 2015 earthquakes but the people are resilient and have rebuilt. Festivals are a big part of the Tamang culture

Views of
Chilime
from the trail to
Tatopani, as the
harvest is
in full swing

The lodges of
Tatopani
are excellent

Tamang **traditional dress**   **Nagthali** viewpoint, with lodges and monastery

The monastery has an impressive image   **Nagthali** lodge
of **Guru Rinpoche**

A good trail climbs from **Nagthali** to the **Taruche** viewpoint, but watch out for goblins!

Looking north into Tibet over **Kyirong**   **Ganesh III** seen from Taruche

Ganesh I is superb from Taruche   Traditional village of **Thuman** on the trail down

Briddhim monastery hosts a curious image of **Mahakala**

A **crumbling chorten** appears near the trail end before **Syabrubesi**

Ganesh Himal

Ganesh IV from **Phyangchet** monastery above **Shertung**

Ganesh Himal is protected by the benevolence and good luck of its mentor – the Hindu god Ganesh. This area, so close to and visible from the Kathmandu Valley, is amazingly little-trodden and remote. Few have trekked into its enchanting dense forests; high pastures grace the lower ramparts of the snowy wonders. Its wild and rugged valleys shelter secret gems of infinite wealth. The western parts below Ganesh IV (Pabil) and Ganesh III (Salasungo), north of the Ankhu Khola, actually do hide rubies, minerals and metallic wealth.

Ganesh Himal Trek

The trek is sometimes referred to as the Ruby Valley Trek. The trails are steep, lonely and often poorly maintained, yet very enticing to those willing to sacrifice familiarity for adventure. Lower down are the industrious farming villages of Borang, Chalis, Shertung (Sertung) and Tipling, where Gurung, Tamang and Ghale people utilise the rich soils and natural wealth.

The trail climbs from **Arughat** through **Manbu** and on along a ridge high above the **Budhi Gandaki** valley. Schoolkids play in **Dhunchet** village as women gather in the street below

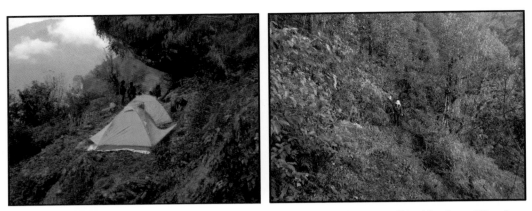

The overhang camp at **Lhamodhunga** before the dense forest trail to **Nauban Kharka**

Myangal pass
(2975m)
heralds a view of
Ganesh IV

Khading is the first settlement after the **Magne Goth** pass (2936m), with a homestay

Young and old come out to greet the trekkers, such a visit is so rare in **Khading**

In **Lapchet** village the local Christian church is used as a homestay

Rachyat village has shady banana trees in a lush farming setting

The trail from **Rachyat** has great views and later some testing stages on a well-engineered pathway. The route descends to the **Tatopani hot springs**

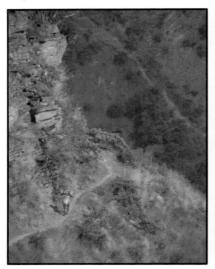

Ganesh III from **Neber**

Sunrise on **Ganesh IV**

Ankhu Khola from near **Tikkas Danda**

It's a warm welcome in **Chalis**, with its **school** and **cultural show** for visitors

Above **Chalis** is **Shertung** village

Above that is **Phyangchet** monastery

The village of **Tipling** (below) is a significant settlement

From **Tipling** the trail climbs through **Laptung** and on to **Phuktung Kharka**. Higher up from **Marmelung Kharka** (a good tea stop) and the **Pangsang La** pass there are great views of **Ganesh IV**

The climb up to the **Pangsang La** pass through forest and meadows is relentless, but the **views over Central Nepal** are sensational, as are the peaks of the Annapurnas, Baudha, Himalchuli, Manaslu and Langtang to the east (below right). It's worth **camping** on the Pangsang La; a basic lodge has been set up with an eye for the future. A narrow rough dirt track is being pushed through to Tipling, but with only a couple of jeeps or trucks a week, it's hardly an issue so far

Looking north to the **unclimbed peaks of Tibet above Kyirong** glowing at sunset

The trail descends, with **Langtang** ahead, to good lodges at **Somdang** in sight of **Paldor**, a popular climbing peak (below right)

A dirt road connects Somdang to Syabrubesi now, but the walking trail is a delight over the **Khurphudanda Pass** to the **Parvati Kund** shrine and lake

Sunset on **Ganesh IV** from the **Pangsang La**

101

Manaslu

Manaslu east faces from **Gumba Lungdang**

The Manaslu Circuit offers stunning views of the great peaks of Himalchuli, Ngadi Chuli, Manaslu and the Larkya Himal, as well as the eastern giants of the Annapurnas – Lamjung, Annapurna II and Kang Guru. A myriad of lesser known, but equally spectacular, peaks add to the fiesta of snowy summits. The name 'Manaslu' derives from the Sanskrit word *manasa,* meaning 'mountain of the soul'. The region has an amazing variety of geographical landscapes and cultural differences. The higher valleys sing only to the tunes of soaring predatory vultures.

Manaslu Circuit Trek

Passing through sheer-sided gorges, the deep rivers of the Budhi (Buri) Gandaki and Marsyangdi provide vital access to the Himalayan peaks. Hikers can luxuriate in the warmth of the low riverside trail along the Budhi Gandaki river. Beyond Jagat, the exuberant, colourful Hindu culture is replaced by the more contemplative Buddhism. Mani walls, kani gates and chortens dot the byways. Heading northwest from Philim through Deng, the Manaslu Circuit trail continues its relentless climb to the upper reaches of the Budhi Gandaki and the villages of Lihi, Sho, Lho and Shyala to Samagaon. The arid uplands of the Tibetan plateau take hold beyond Samagaon and Samdo. The Larkya La, the highest point of the trek at 5160m, offers a fabulous panorama of Cheo Himal, Larkya Peak, Himlung, Kang Guru, Nemjung and Annapurna II. Down the other side in Bimthang, the exquisite meadows provide a welcome respite from the high altitude. A paradise of elegant peaks, quiet forests and bubbling streams lead the way further down to Dharapani, Tal and Besisahar.

Tsum Valley Trek and Ganesh North Base Camp

The Tsum Valley is a unique region with Buddhist traditions. Monasteries, quiet villages, and soaring peaks dominate this hidden land adjacent to Tibet. Tsum can be combined with the Manaslu Circuit or visited separately. A wild side valley also climbs to the enticing Gumba Lungdang nunnery and Ganesh North Base Camp.

Manaslu Circuit Trek

Travel in Nepal is always colourful, whether by bus or jeep. **Arughat** is the usual trek starting point. Another choice is to begin from **Gorkha** with its historic palace

The new road is shortening the approach march along the **Budhi Gandaki**

The route heads from **Arughat** to **Soti** and **Machha Khola** before snaking along to **Tatopani**. Where the road is being built, there are some rather **adventurous stages**, but these mau be completed by now! Beyond Tatopani steeper trails climb to Yaruphant and Jagat, with views of **Shringi Himal** through the trees

A short climb allows some great views of **Shringi Himal**

Sirdibas is a picturesque village, where local crafts are still practiced. **Philim** has great lodges and an unusual monastery with amazing icons, **Opagme** and **Chenresig**

From **Philim** the trail enters a **narrow gorge** to reach **Deng**

The drama
of the
Budhi Gandaki
gorge
continues
through
Bihi
and on to
Ghap

The trail climbs
through
Namrung to
Lho
with views of
Shringi Himal
and **Ganesh**
to the east

Sho kani gate
is typical of most
along the route

Lho is a major stop on the circuit, with great views of **Manaslu** and a fascinating, very active monastery

Manaslu and **Manaslu North** are seen from **Lho**

Shyala is higher up and a good place from which to explore **Pungyen** monastery valley.
Kutang Peak (above) is prominent from the monastery and its noted chorten

Children on the trail to Samagaon   **More chortens**

Samagaon is a traditional village

Festivals are colourful affairs

The **houses are built from stone**, with various levels for livestock, living and prayers. Good lodges are found here – a legacy of the many mountaineering expeditions who use it as a logistics base when climbing Manaslu

The monastery is worth a visit, if the keys can be found

Manaslu from **Samagaon**

The **Manaslu Glacier** from the trail

Himalchuli from above **Samdo**

Samdo village and school

Yak attack above **Samdo**   Trail from **Samdo** to **Dharamsala**

Manaslu North   Trail to **Dharamsala (Larkya Phedi)**

Dharamsala Lodge is a cold but necessary place to overnight before the **Larkya La** pass. Views above the lodge are fabulous, but the altitude makes it tough going

Near the pass the **lake** is often frozen, with **Pang Puchi** behind east

Reaching the **Larkya La** pass is a definite high at 5160m

Views
on the
descent
are
out of this
world

Himlung
&
Cheo
Himal
dwarf
a trekker
on the
trail

Kang Guru & **Nemjung** are mighty

Descending to **Bimthang**, submerged beneath the clouds at sunset

The trail down is enchanting, with a view of **Manaslu West** (above left). Lower down, the forest is idyllic and village life enlivens the hike

Our porter **Tenzing**   Looking down to **Dharapani** on the **Annapurna Circuit** trail

The valley, with a scary new dirt road from **Dharapani**, is narrow down to **Tal**

Sunset on **Cheo Himal** from **Bimthang**

Tsum Valley Trek

Part of the Manaslu region, the wild, rugged and exotic little-known Tsum Valley is located north of Ganesh Himal and east of Manaslu. The landscapes and mountain vistas can only be described as superlative, as befits another real Shangri-La of the Himalaya. It hosts Buddhist communities living secluded lives, devoted to their traditional way of life and their iconic Buddhist deities. Picturesque monasteries are the focus of the communities. Dominating the whole Tsum region are the stupendous faces of Ganesh Himal, Shringi Himal and their spectacular glaciers.

Ganesh II from upper Tsum near Chule

The **Tsum Valley** trail begins near Chisopani and climbs to **Lokpa** before heading into the **Siyar Khola canyon**. Much of the route is on a **new metal pathway** up the sheer cliffs between Lokpa and Chumling

117

Vultures and predators soar above the old trail to the bridge below **Chumling**, a picture-postcard village of traditional houses, with chortens and a monastery above the lodges. **Kitchen areas** are sacred; visitors should avoid throwing scraps in the fireplaces

The Tsum region is famed for the number of **chortens** that 'guard' the trails. From Chumling it's more level through Tanju to Domje, before a big climb through Gho to Chokkang Paro. **Churke Himal** is adjacent to the Ganesh Himal knot of peaks high above the trail to Chokkang Paro

A fabulous glimpse of **Ganesh I (Yangra)** is on offer up from **Domje**. A local newborn sleeps; the children have seen it all before

Chokkang Paro is the main settlement in Tsum; Buddhist images in **Jong Gompa**

Mani stones are common

View of **Ganesh** from above **Chokkang Paro**

On the trail to **Ngakyu-Leru** and a welcoming homestay. Further north is the cave retreat of **Piren Phu** (meaning pigeon cave), which was used by the sage **Milarepa**

Gonhgye monastery above **Pangdun** before Chule hosts colourful **Cham dance masks**

Chule village has an unusual **kani** gate   … and an **impressive chorten**

Across the valley from Chule, **Nile** has a good lodge, where yaks are often in charge.
Further north is the famed **Mu Gompa**, a great side trip or stop on the trail towards Tibet

Guru Rinpoche in **Mu Gompa**　　　　along with **religious books and tablets**

Local child　　　　**Dhephyudonma Gompa** up a dodgy trail near Mu

Guru Rinpoche　　　　and **Chenresig** take centre stage here

Upper Tsum
towards **Tibet**

Lhasa Beer

Rachen Nunnery is an important religious centre in Tsum

Ganesh North Base Camp Trek

Above Domje, a deeply incised side valley leads up to the great Torogompo Glacier that gives access to the wonderland of Ganesh Himal's rarely seen northwest faces. Also up here is Gumba Lungdang Nunnery and the spectacular amphitheatre of the Ganesh peaks. This is a land of adventure, rarely visited and secretive, with untouched forest and undisturbed wildlife. Basic accommodation can be found at the monastery but above only trekkers with camping backup can stay higher – the great cirque of Ganesh I, Ganesh III, Ganesh IV and Ganesh II is sublime.

The valley is dominated by the ramparts and spire of **Ganesh II**

The good but steep trail for **Gumba Lungdang** leaves the Tsum Valley route just after Domje, where the quaint monastery is worth a detour. The trail climbs for almost 1000m through beguiling forest, passing chortens to reach Gumba Lungdang

Gumba Lungdang nunnery, with a ferocious protector and a **smiling nun** in residence

Beyond the Gompa is **Langdang Kharka**, with views of **Ganesh I** and **Himalchuli** (north)

Manaslu from above **Langdang Kharka**

Ganesh II from near **Torogompo Kharka**

Beyond Base Camp, below **Ganesh I**
(photo: Sanjib Gurung)

Looking towards **Ganesh III** & **Ganesh IV**

Himalchuli from **Gumba Lungdang**

Annapurna

Braka (Braga) monastery near Manang

After Everest, the Annapurna region is perhaps the most well-known and certainly the most popular trekking area in Nepal. With so much variety in landscapes and people – from lush semi-tropical forests to high altitude deserts, from short day hikes to multi-week extreme expeditions, with Buddhists and Hindus and a mix of other local religions, luxury lodges and more simple guesthouses – there's a trek to suit almost everyone here.

Fabulous high-altitude experiences include the Annapurna Circuit, first opened to trekkers in 1982, the Annapurna Sanctuary, Nar Phu, Mustang and Dhaulagiri. Lower down the hillsides trekkers can enjoy close contact with local people and their villages; eco-friendly, cultural homestay treks are the new thing. West of Poon Hill on the sunny slopes above the Kali Gandaki River, the Parbat Myagdi routes link Ghorepani with Beni. With enthusiastic road building in the foothills around Pokhara, things are changing. The Siklis Trek has been modified to become a destination rather than a trek: a place to enjoy a different experience, while remaining in a peaceful area. The Lamjung foothills – around Chowk Chisopani–Riepe and Tandrangkot–Puranokot – are still homestay destinations, but the trekking is now limited with dirt roads Similarly a little further north, the Gurung Heritage Trail is much shorter and seen as a village experience.

Annapurna Circuit
This remains the classic trek in Nepal and is still a top trekking destination. Roads may change it, but will not destroy it (after all, Switzerland has both side by side). Some previously neglected side trips are now popular and new alternatives to walking on or close to the new 'roads' have been developed.

Annapurna Sanctuary
Another classic favourite where little change, other than ever-improving comfort, has occurred. The views from this cloud-bubbling cauldron are still hard to beat.

Ghorepani Circuit

Affectionately known as the Poon Hill Expedition, this has all the ingredients for a short, spell-binding adventure in the foothills. Terraced hillsides, fairytale forests and soaring snow-covered spires contrive to make any visit memorable.

Annapurna Dhaulagiri

Once a hidden treasure, this route has become more popular. No longer solely a camping option, its high isolated ridges have seen an influx of trekkers, as lodges and community homestays have opened along its lower reaches. The airy belvederes of the Kopra Danda ridge are sensational; even the most experienced trekking hand will be blown away.

Mardi Himal

Long overlooked are two routes below Machhapuchhre: the Mardi Himal Trek and Machhapuchhre Trek. Both climb above the tree line to the base camps of Mardi Himal.

Restricted areas

Many would-be explorers are drawn to the captivating Tibetan culture and fantastic scenery. In these remote mountains, specialist trekkers can delve into the natural world, capturing magnificent predators like lammergeyer on camera, tracking the bashful Himalayan bear, sniffing out the elusive snow leopard and even yearning for the yeti.

Mustang

Upper Mustang, with its extraordinary walled city of Lo Manthang, has long been considered the fabled Shangri-La but changes comes to every corner of the globe. Getting there is every bit as fascinating and inspiring. Where in the world can you find such unbelievable variation – the highest peaks of the Himalaya, deep canyons, legend-filled settlements, staggering geology and contorted natural landscapes?

Nar-Phu

Perhaps the most astonishing region of all the Annapurnas, Nar-Phu is as barely known as it is difficult to access. Cut off for centuries by the highest passes and the most impenetrable, sheer-sided canyon in Nepal, the mediaeval villages of Nar and Phu are some of the country's most closely guarded secrets. Trekking here takes one to a new level of adventure and wonder.

The contrast between the **lush semitropical southern slopes** and the **arid northern side** of the range makes for classic trekking anywhere across the Annapurna region

Annapurna Circuit Trek

Mountain views from a day hike high above **Manang**

From **Besisahar** the dirt road heads below **Himalchuli** to **Chamje**, **Tal** and **Dharapani**, while the old trail heads past waterfalls to **Bahundanda**, **Jagat** and then **Tal**

The **beautiful trail** up to Tal avoids…   the **scary new road**

Porters have a tough time on narrow trails   **Tal waterfall**

The old trail climbs from Tal around the cliffs to Dharapani and **Tilje**, whose monastery hosts a much-revered **Sakyamuni Buddha**. The trail and road climb past Bagarchhap and on up to Timang

The route to **Timang** and the traditional village of **Thanchok** are on the way to **Chame**, the regional headquarters

Buddhist kani gates mark the village entries from here up to **Manang**. Views of Annapurna II are sensational from **Chame**, as is **Manaslu at sunset**

Old and young follow trekkers through **Koto** and **Chame**. The trail climbs to **Bratang** and then negotiates its way under overhangs and across bridges to the stunning **Paungda** rock wall below **Pisang**

Pisang is divided into two: most lodges are found in the lower area. Above on a hill is **Upper Pisang** and the **old and new monasteries**. There are a couple of lodges up here too. Trekkers have a choice of taking the lower trail from Lower Pisang to Manang via **Hongde** or the more scenic but higher trail via **Ghyaru** and **Ngawal** to **Braka** and **Manang**. The high route has superb views of **Annapurna II**, **Annapurna III** and **Gangapurna**

Upper Pisang is an atmospheric spot, with superb **views towards Manang**

The upper trail climbs past the green lake of **Mring Tso** to reach **Ghyaru**. Further along is **Ngawal** and, if lucky, wild **Thar**. A trail from Ngawal climbs steeply to the **Kang La** pass, which is used by trekkers to exit the Nar-Phu Valley. From Ngawal the trail climbs around the hillside below Chulu and drops to Braka. The **monastery** here should not be missed – be sure to hunt out the man with the key to see this ancient gompa

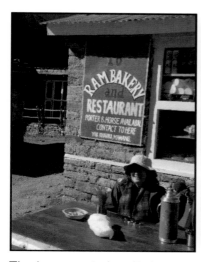

The lower route has its bonuses, like tea and cake at **Hongde**; the views of **Tilicho** are pretty tasty as well

Braka is a superb place below **Gangapurna**   **Annapurna III** dominates the valley

Manang is a great place for a few days' exploration, including a side trip to **Khangsar** and maybe Tilicho Lake. The Gangapurna Glacier is another option, as is a climb above Manang to the east, below Chulu. Various local monasteries are also worth a detour

The smoke of fires above **Manang at dawn**   On the trail to **Lattar** below **Chulu**

Superb **sunset on Chulu** from Lattar before the trail heads to **Phedi**, where porters prepare for the **Thorong La** pass. **Thorong Phedi** used to be a desolate camping spot before the new lodge complex was built. The trail for the pass begins steeply from Phedi; most depart at dawn or earlier

It's a long slog up to the **Thorong La** pass, even in good weather. Be careful if it's snowing and take heed of advice from the lodge owners at Phedi. Trekkers do die on this pass in bad weather. There are a couple of refreshment shacks after High Camp before the pass (and pony men if desperate)

There are fabulous views of **Gangapurna**, **Chulu** and **Putrun Himal** peaks on the climb

Hard to believe we've reached the **Thorong La pass**!

It's still a **long trek down to Muktinath**, so don't enjoy the views for too long!

It's almost 1600m down to **Muktinath**, a knee-crunching hike. **Blue sheep (Bharal)** can sometimes be seen on the descent. Old Muktinath has modernised since the road reached the settlement, whose **temple** is popular with Hindu pilgrims. **Ritual bathings** are common in the freezing air. Others, including Buddhists, revere the **eternal flame**

Jhong and **Putak** are historic settlements on the **northern trail** between Muktinath and Kagbeni, with ancient monasteries to explore

The **trail to Kagbeni** gives a last glimpse of the **Thorong La** pass. Kagbeni has grown since 1989, when camping was the norm. **Kagbeni monastery** hosts some great imagery

The quadrangle of **old Kagbeni** was little changed even in 2015, but the lodge area has mushroomed, with **Yakdonalds** and others serving tasty food. Kagbeni can now be reached by jeep from Jomsom, but the old centre remains as mysterious as ever

Lubra village   **Dumba Lake**

Jeeps ply from **Kagbeni to Muktinath** via Jharkot; **buses** also run to **Jomsom**

Trekkers can still follow a superb trail between Jomsom and Tatopani without meeting the new road. **Marpha** (with a **monastery** and **picture-postcard streets**), Tukuche and Larjung have retained their historic monasteries and typical Thakali houses, despite the road, and should not be missed. Lower down, Kalopani has good lodges and a fabulous view of Fang and Annapurna I (one of the rare glimpses of the highest peak of the massif)

Astonishingly beautiful artwork is everywhere in the monasteries

Tukuche Lodge

Tukuche main street

Dhaulagiri

Stairway to heaven

141

Guru Rinpoche

Kalopani school's out

Annapurna
and
**Fang
(Baraha Shikha)**
from
Kalopani

Ghasa kani gate

Rupse Chhara waterfall

Dana is a **picturesque village**   **Tatopani** is famed for its hot springs

Hanuman temple near Tatopani

The **trail climbs to Ghorepani** with views of **Dhaulagiri** from **Poon Hill** before descending to Birethanti and Pokhara

Annapurna Sanctuary (Annapurna Base Camp) Trek

Machhapuchhre (Fishtail) at sunset

One of the most popular treks, the Annapurna Sanctuary (also known as Annapurna Base Camp) takes visitors into a cirque of ice giants, including Annapurna South, Fang, Annapurna I, Annapurna II and Machhapuchhre. Ideally taking 9–12 days, it's a fabulous introduction to Nepal trekking near Pokhara.

Annapurna II from Pokhara   **Hyenja** in 1980 before the road was built

Hiunchuli and **Machhapuchhre** from near **Ghandruk**   Camping near **Chandrakot**

144

Ghandruk is a typical village en route

Children gather in winter   Festive **ferris wheel** in autumn

Annapurna South and **Hiunchuli** are companions on the approach to the Sanctuary

Above **Chhomrong**, the trail is in cloud rainforest through a camp/lodges at **Bamboo**; the trail emerges from the dense forest near **Bagar** and climbs to **Machhapuchhre Base Camp**, where porters used to sleep under rocky outcrops

Sunset on Machhapuchhre is sensational. Most trekkers head up to Annapurna Base Camp, but it's also possible to visit the base camp as a day trip from the lower lodges of Machhapuchhre Base Camp. Staying at Annapurna Base Camp offers super sunsets and sunrise over the fabulous south face of **Annapurna I**; hike up the moraine ridges of **Annapurna South** to watch the glaciers tumbling from the faces. **Fang (Baraha Shikha)** is also visible from here at close quarters

Views east of **Annapurna III** & **Gandharba Chuli** from **Annapurna Base Camp**

Gandharba Chuli & **Annapurna I** from Annapurna Base Camp. Great sunsets on **Machhapuchhre** are seen as the afternoon clouds dissipate

After leaving the Sanctuary, many trekkers head to **Ghorepani** via **Tadapani**, with wonderfuly views and a delighful forest trail. Another newly developed trek follows the long ridge in the picture above to a high point under **Mardi Himal** and **Machhapuchhre**:

Mardi Himal trek

The forest route climbs from **Dhampus** or **Australian Camp** through **Pothana**, **Deurali** and **Forest Camp** (above) to **High Camp**, with amazing sunsets. A steep climb continues to the foot of **Mardi Himal**, an outlier peak below **Machhapuchhre**

Annapurna Dhaulagiri Trek

With superb views of **Annapurna South** and **Dhaulagiri** (above right), the route is from **Tadapani** through pristine forest to herders' meadows and up on to **Kopra Ridge**. New lodges have replaced the cold nights of camping here. **Khairetal Lake** is the objective

Dhaulagiri Sanctuary Trek

This newly developed route is a mix of homestays and camping. The route begins from **Beni** by jeep to **Jhi**. The houses are still typical of the Magar people here. Dhaulagiri is on view night and day for much of the trek

The trail heads north along the west of the **Raughat Khola Valley** from **Jhi** through **Rayakhor** and **Ghyasikharka** to **Phedi**, where camping kicks in. It's all wild untrodden forest from here to the **South Base Camp**. The last 2km of the trail should be finished by now!

Sunrise over the rice fields of **Rayakhor** before the harvest. **Ghyasikharka** is another overnight stop before the trail climbs into virgin forest and a glorious sunset at **Phedi**

The new trail heads for **Dhaulagiri South Base Camp** but wasn't quite finished when we went. Returning along the east bank of the Raughat Khola the route passes through colourful forest to **Chimkhota**. The trek is ideal for those wishing to enjoy the culture of village life at close quarters

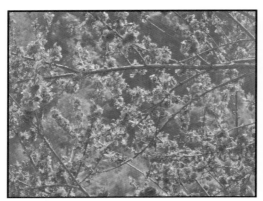 

The grand, if scary, finale is the exciting **Dragon Cliffs** path

Mustang

Harvest time in **Lo Manthang**

Mustang trek

The usual Mustang Trek encapsulates everything that defines the region. As short as 10–12 days, the route climbs steadily from the northern ramparts of the Annapurnas, from Jomsom to the wild, windswept hills of Lo Manthang. En route a variety of settlements host lively people, quaint monasteries and spellbinding scenery, dotted with atmospheric chortens. The climax of the trek is the first tantalising panoramic view of the fabled walled city of Lo Manthang, as picture-postcard today as it was to the first explorers. Most trekkers linger a day or two to soak up the charms of the city and visit some of the nearby cave monastery retreats. The return route can be varied, taking part of the wild route east of the Mustang Khola (Kali Gandaki). Being a relatively short trek that does not reach any too-dizzying altitudes, it is a very popular choice. New dirt roads enable shorter options.

Classic Mustang Trek

The Classic Mustang Trek includes all the popular sights, plus the scenery and geological grandeur on the eastern side of the Mustang Khola, which is about as unimaginable as anyone can – well – imagine! Added options are little-known treasures like Chungsi Ranchung Cave, the panoramic viewpoint above Syangmochen, Drakmar and Ghar Gompa (Lo Gekar). North of Lo Manthang, don't miss the isolated and astonishing cave gompa at Konchok Ling. Heading south from Lo Manthang, the trail is sensational, with cultural interest everywhere in places like Dhi, Yara, Luri, Tange and Tetang. The mind-blowing and wind-blown scenery will remain etched in the memory as deeply as nature's hand has left its astonishing marks on the physical landscape.

Monastery Cave Circuit Trek

Not on most trekkers' radar, the harder-to-reach monasteries and canyons east of Lo Manthang are amazingly remote. Places like Samdzong, Chodzong and Sakau Danda were generally ignored by the first trekkers, who had only limited time. As with any off-beat destination, only campers can truly get under the skin of these remote attractions.

Mustang High & Wild Expedition

In eastern Mustang, this is long and tough, with hidden peaks, delightful canyons, babbling streams and often-deserted hillsides. The inspirational peaks of Saribung, Bhrikuti, Khumjungar and Gaugiri dominate the route. Hidden deep in the chasms and gullies of the region are the holy lakes of Damodar. Camping is the only way to trek here, much as ancient caravans did long ago.

Damodar Kund / Saribung Expedition

The Damodar trek is a tough route, mainly for trekkers with mountaineering experience. It links the wilds of Eastern Upper Mustang with the stupendous mountains that dominate the hidden valleys of Phu and Nar. Hardy pilgrims come to the lake to be cleansed of their sins, often in the summer months. Crossing the 6100m Saribung Pass needs well-equipped crews and high-altitude mountaineering experience; it is no walk in the park. Peaks such as Bhrikuti, Khumjungar and Saribung guard the pass, but down in the mysterious Nar-Phu region it is Himlung, Cheo Himal, Kang Guru and Lamjung that capture all the attention.

Teri La Pass Expedition

A virtually unknown pass, it is not always successfully crossed. The Teri La pass links Tange in Upper Mustang with the lower valley of Nar below Phu. It's a wild, lonely, inhospitable, uninhabited region, where cliffs, rocky spires and dried-up meadows dominate the route. Choose the season carefully (maybe drier November); it is notorious for keeping foreign devils out of the region through snowfall and landslides.

The wild country of the **Damodar and Khumjungar Himal** is for rugged camping trekkers who relish the remote mountains of the Tibetan border in the Mustang and Nar-Phu region

Upper Mustang begins in **Kagbeni**, where the strange **Keni** image guards the gates of this once forbidden land. Following the **Kali Gandaki**, the route passes the cave monastery at **Mentsi** and, optionally, the amazing fortified village of **Tetang**

Tetang has two parts divided by a small canyon. Each is fortified with mud-walled ramparts, dark alleys and mysterious doorways. The local monastery can be visited when the **man with the key** is around. Tetang is on the trail between Tange and Muktinath for those taking the eastern route, or as a diversion from the main trail on the inbound trek

155

The trail climbs through **Chele** on a cliff trail to **Samar**, although the new dirt road snakes around on a long route. A superb detour involving some steep trails goes to **Chungsi Ranchung Cave,** a Buddhist shrine with over a hundred images of **Guru Rinpoche**

The route heads on to **Syangmochen**, where a short hike heads up to a viewpoint of **Upper Mustang** and the **Damodar** peaks to the east, like **Khumjungar**

The trail continues to **Geling** and **Ghami**, where a choice must be made. The main route is via historic **Tsarang**; a variation is via dramatic cliffs of **Drakmar** and **Lo Gekar**

The long mani wall en route to **Tsarang** (below)

Drakmar is set below fabulous multi-coloured cliffs riddled with **Buddhist cave retreats**. A pass leads to **Lo Gekar**, an historic monastery with a great lodge

After sustenance, the route heads on passing a stony-faced 'politician'. The first glimpse of Lo Manthang is amazing (1992); even today it retains an aura of exotic mediaeval unworldliness. The gates of **Lo Manthang** hide narrow alleys and mysterious corners

The people of **Lo Manthang** have lived by trade for centuries. The **masked Cham dance** festival is a highlight. There are **four monasteries** and the **Royal Palace** within the walls

North of Lo Manthang are the **troglodyte caves** of **Narphu** and **Chosar** with extensive tunnels and shrines

Trekkers should be sure to have a few days in and around Lo Manthang to explore the staggering sights.

Opposite page: East of Lo Manthang, en route to remote Chodzong, passing the **Sakar Danda** white mountain, is the Bon citadel of **Mardzong**.

Northeast of Lo Manthang is one of the strangest Buddhist retreats in Nepal; with the incredible fairytale eroded hilly approach to **Konchok Ling**, it could not be more sensational. The cave paintings are only accessible by a precarious cable route

A dramatic ridge trail leads from Lo Manthang high above the Mustang Khola to **Dhi**. With a couple of lodges, Dhi is a good spot to stay or take lunch. Across the river the trail climbs past the stunning cliffs of **Yara**

Yara is a great place to stay a couple of nights to explore the nearby **Luri Cave** with its amazing art and **Luri Gompa** nearby. **Tashi Kumbum** (below) is another site

From **Yara** a pass leads over to the **Dhechyang Khola** valley and further to the gullies that lead down to **Tange**. Views of Dhaulagiri and the Annapurnas are on offer

Tange is the village of chortens and a Shangri-La of dramatic landscapes

Tange hosts a small monastery; nearby are more well-hidden Buddhist cave shrines

The golden glow of sunset is magical in **Tange**. High above Tange, trails lead to the remote holy lake at **Damodar** and also to the **Teri La** pass into the **Nar-Phu region**. The main trail climbs from Tange to the **Soye La** (4300m) and follows the dramatic **Siyarko ridge** (overleaf) to **Tetang**. It's an unworldly hike, with deep canyons, snow peaks and strange eroded organ pipe features

Looking east above the **Tetang Khola** canyon to the **Damodar peaks**

The descent into **Tetang** is equally stunning

The pass south of Tetang offers superb views of **Annapurna**, **Tilicho** and **Dhaulagiri**. **Lubra Bon monastery** is a great detour before Jomsom

Nar-Phu

Kang Guru and **Phu** village from **Tashi Monastery**

The Nar-Phu region is one of the most mysterious and extraordinary destinations in the Nepal Himalaya and the Annapurna region. Far, far removed from modern times, these hidden valleys nudging the northern border have retained their ancient Tibetan-orientated culture. Pisang Peak and Kang Guru dominate the horizons. With so few inhabitants, the Nar-Phu region is a paradise for patient naturalists. The whole trek is characterised by remote, challenging and sometimes airy trails that most will enjoy. Mediaeval Phu has an amazing setting and the nearby Tashi monastery is a 'must see' close to Tibet.

Nar-Phu Trek
The trail begins in Koto, where a narrow canyon hides the gems to come. From Koto to Meta is a long hike, with a height gain of around 900m. Ideally from Meta head for Phu first to aid acclimatisation. The altitude gain to Nar is excessive at this stage.

For Phu an intermediate stop in Kyang is necessary, with only basic accommodation or camping. It's perfectly possible to descend from Phu to Nar Phedi or Meta in one long day. Beyond Nar, the Kang La is often snowbound and very steep down to Ngawal and on to the Annapurna Circuit route.

Phu to Damodar Lake Trek
As mentioned above and requiring some basic mountaineering skills, the trek from Phu into Upper Mustang via the holy Damodar Kund Lake crosses the Saribung Pass at over 6000m. This is a magical region adjacent to Tibet, with tiny hidden settlements like Chodzong and Samdzong nearer Lo Manthang.

A haunting defile hides the Nar-Phu region from the **Annapurna Circuit**; the trail leaves from **Koto**. The path is exciting, with sheer drops, narrow cliff stages and quieter forest

Lamjung is spectacular from **Meta** at sunset

Meta has good lodges

Weaving on the side of the trail near **Chyk**

Vultures circle in front of **Pisang Peak**

Quarrelsome yaks object to heavy loads

Views towards **Himlung** from the **Kyang** trail　　　　**Chyako**, a half-abandoned settlement

Do-it-yourself cooking and rough lodgings or camping may be required at **Kyang**

Annapurna II has a strange shape when viewed from the **Kyang** trail

More dodgy trails are encountered between **Kyang** and the **monolithic entrance tower** of **Phu** (below right)

A stiff climb follows to the **Phu Valley**, with mani walls, chortens and the **kani gate** of the village. Phu is around 800 years old and has retained its amazing style. There are four basic lodges and a rather unstable fortress area to explore. Phu could hardly have a more dramatic setting.

Phu village on a glorious morning

From **Tashi monastery**: views of **Kang Guru** peak and **Phu**

Tashi monastery

Guru Rinpoche takes centre stage

Mani stones and chortens decorate the hill

Cosy kitchen in the lodge

Views towards the **Saribung Pass** include **Bhrikuti Peak** and, closer, **Karjung Kang**

Blue sheep near the monastery

The trail down from Phu is **steep**

Entrance to the valley that leads to the **Teri La**, a wild route

Nar is a superb atmospheric village reached after a steep climb from **Meta Phedi**

Nar has four small monasteries (often closed)

There are great
views towards
the
Kang La
pass to the west

and
Kang Guru
to the east

Farewell to **Annapurna II** and Nar Phu

Dolpo

Entrance to the secretive **Panzang Valley**

Dolpo is a large area of western Nepal, a high and wild upland plateau with a sparse population but abundant cultural interest. The choice of trekking is almost unlimited. Access makes a trek expensive here, but for those willing to rough it camping, Dolpo is a treasure-house of wonders, like **Yangtsher monastery** (below)

Lower Dolpo

Most treks can be completed in two weeks, giving a great introduction to the mysteries of Dolpo. Treks combine the typical middle hills and culture with a touch of the true high Dolpo, and suit those less inclined to spend weeks at high altitude.

Phoksundo Lake Trek
The shortest option, taking 10 days, soon enough this trek will be the domain of lodge/homestay trekkers. The highlight naturally is the turquoise lake and Ringmo village, all set below sheer, towering cliffs and peaks.

Phoksundo – Kagmara Trek
This route takes in the wild and spectacular Kagmara pass, as well as delving into the traders' trails to Jumla, once a great kingdom of West Nepal.

Lower Dolpo Circuit Trek
Taking in Tarakot and then Dho Tarap, this trek is always a highlight, with the culture and the monasteries and the way of life of the people. It crosses two rugged high passes, the Baga La (5169m) and Numa La South (5309m). The trek drops to Ringmo village and the incomparable Phoksundo (locally called Phoksumdo) Lake. Descending the Suli Gad River concludes this great introduction to Dolpo. Snow blankets the region for many months, so timing is vital.

Upper Dolpo

Upper Dolpo Circuit Trek
Nestling between Lower Dolpo and the Tibetan border, this is the classic choice, with a culture that one might imagine lives only in the dreams of film producers. The route encapsulates everything of a visit to Dolpo – sheer-sided cliffs, exposed and challenging paths, glittering ice-cool lakes, beautiful mountain vistas. Reaching mystical Shey Gompa rewards all the toil and hardship (even that hefty permit fee will seem well spent!). Saldang and Yangtsher Monastery are jewels, all but unknown outside Dolpo. Being predominantly Buddhist, but with many pockets of Bon, the region is one of the last places in the world where ancient rituals, fervent beliefs and animistic traditions reflect the mystique of old Tibet. With more time it's good to explore the lost Panzang Valley, hosting monasteries and isolated communities of Shimen and Tinje.

Dolpo High and Wild Trek
Completed by very few but found inspiring, exhausting and exhilarating in equal measure by those who have done it, this trek from Dolpo to Jomsom is surely soon destined to be the talk of many more intrepid hikers seeking remote areas. The trails are steep, lonely and often poorly maintained, yet enticing to those willing to sacrifice familiarity for adventure. The trek usually includes Phoksundo Lake, Shey Gompa and Saldang before diverting east. North of Dhaulagiri for most of the way, the route climbs from Dho Tarap into countryside as wild as the Sahara. The last week is a kaleidoscope of scintillating exploration – barren landscapes inhabited by blue sheep and hidden snow leopards. The village of Chharka Bhot is the only real settlement before Tiri and Kagbeni, bordering Upper Mustang. The trek concludes in Jomsom, where transport options are now plentiful, unlike Dunai!

Dolpo to Mugu
Hardly ever visited, the region well north and northwest of Shey Gompa is beginning to delight in its newfound fame. Trekkers find the remote and rugged passes close to Tibet a challenge, while climbers are focused on Danphesail Peak, about as remote as it gets in the Himalaya. Of course traders, herders and the few people of the region see it as home, but for 'outsiders' like trekkers it is probably the last great frontier.

Masinechaur is a typical village of the region   **Dunai** is the regional headquarters

The trail to Phoksundo follows the Suligad Valley via **Rechi**   Even here people have **mobile** connectivity

The trail climbs to **Ringmo**, passing the **famous waterfall**   to reach **Phoksundo Lake**

179

Ringmo is a picture-postcard village on the shores of **Phoksundo Lake**. Nearby, be sure to visit the **Bon monastery**. The trail climbs around high above the lake on a narrow path that was once a death trap for yaks (as portrayed in the film Himalaya/Caravan)

Traders gather at our camp before the treacherous climb to the notorious **Kang La** pass. Bedevilled by snow, the Kang La (opposite) is always a weather-prone adventure

Blizzard conditions on the **Kang La** (5350m)   … a welcome arrival down in **Shey**

Tsakang Monastery retreat near Shey

Tsakang Monastery above Shey   View north towards Samling and Bhijer

The sometimes-exposed trail follows the ridges   with views of the Crystal Mountain

Sunset on Crystal Mountain, a revered peak in Dolpo

Kanjiroba Himal from camp near **Samling** with its **Bon monastery** and **friendly abbot**

Bhijer is a very remote village with a **monastery** and **curious children**

Leaving Bhijer on the **long climb** to the **Neng La** (5368m). Riding a horse might be considered cheating by some foreign devils, but the locals know all the tricks!

Kanjiroba peak looking west from the **Neng La camp**, a rather cold spot until the warming sight of sunrise

Saldang
is a
superb spot
high above the
Nagaon Khola
river

Saldang Gompa

with an exquisite image of **Mahakala**

The **lodge in Saldang** has seen some illustrious explorers, high lamas and a few badly dressed trekkers

Saldang is a great base for exploring the lower **Panzang Valley** and **Yangtsher Gompa**

The **Panzang Valley** is virtually impossible to navigate higher up and a big detour is required to access the main settlements of **Tinje** and **Shimen**. They are usually reached from across the **Khoma La** pass or from Chharka. Tinje once had a functioning airstrip in the good old days! Beware of getting into the dead-end Devil's Ravine to Margom. Bob took it – that's what you get for going ahead of your guide!

Icons in **Yangtsher Monastery**

The trail south from Saldang heads through wild canyons to **Sal Gompa**, **Tsa** and **Namdo**, where the harvest is in full swing   **Chorten** below **Hrap Monastery**

Hrap monastery is high above the trail on a side trip   **Chorten** before **Cha**

Cha settlement guards the canyons before the **Jyanta La** ascent

Camping below the pass is bitterly cold

Dhaulagiri and **Churen Himal** from the **Jyanta La** (5220m). The trail descends steeply from the pass, with continuing panoramic views to **Tokyu**, with a locally significant monastery. Nearby the settlement of **Kakar** also hosts a small gompa

Beware the **yak** attack   **New clinic** near **Dho Tarap**

The trail continues down to the main settlement of Dho Tarap, where a couple of good lodges have opened – a relief from camping, perhaps. Most trekkers head south from Dho along the Tarap Khola valley to the ancient former trading post of Taklakot and then to Dunai, hopefully for a flight to Nepalganj and Kathmandu.

Those seeking a wilder experience can head east through Shipchok and climb the Jharkoi La Pass that leads to Upper Panzang and over the Mo La pass to Chharka.

Chenresig (Avalokiteshvara) in **Champa Gompa** before **Dho**

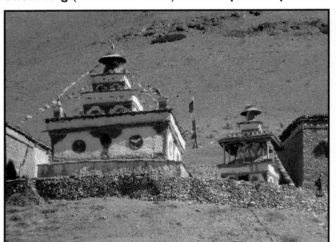

Dho Ribo Bumpa monastery near Dho Tarap hosts a superb image of **Guru Rinpoche**

Dho village

Shipchok Bon monastery

Harvest time at **Shipchok Bon village**

Another day, another high pass… this time the **Jhyarkoi La** (5360m), followed by a camp
in the **Upper Panzang Valley**

Crossing the **Mo La** (5030m) with our mules   View of **Dhaulagiri II** before Chharka

191

Approaching the fortified village of **Chharka**. The monastery, as always, is up a hill

A **Cham dance mask** in **Chharka Monastery** – don't come here after dark!

The trail from Chharka is remote, high and wild. The route heads through the isolated **Nulungsumda Kharka** camp to the easy **Niwas La** across a plain with views of the **Sandachhe peaks** (that hide the famed **Hidden Valley** of the **Dhaulagiri Circuit** trek) and on up the **Jungben La** (5550m). The pass rewards grim determination with euphoric pleasure. The descent isn't much easier – it's steep and loose underfoot!

Mukut Himal and **Dhaulagiri** shine from the pass   The **path down** does not!

There are superb panoramic views across to the **Thorong La** on the **Annapurna Circuit** and to **Upper Mustang** while descending through Ghalden Ghuldun to **Santa** (below)

A rare view of the cloud-blown northern flanks of **Annapurna I**

The long descent past **Tiri Gompa** to **Kagbeni** and the **Kali Gandaki** is relentless but rewarding, with superb views of Mustang – a fitting conclusion to trekking in Dolpo

Sunset on **Norbung Kang** from **Ringmo**

West Nepal

The peaks of remote and unknown **Phuparka Himal** east of **Jang**

Remote and virtually unvisited villages are the norm across **West Nepal**

West Nepal is a vast area that few trekkers ever get to – it's a time-consuming enterprise, but worth all the effort. The trekking choices are unrivalled, unusual and unknown, as well as varied. Access is via airstrips at Nepalganj, Jumla and Simikot. Increasing numbers of dirt roads are being pushed into the region.

Limi Valley trek
For many trekkers, the Limi Valley Trek and the Karnali valley route to Mount Kailash in Tibet are the main attractions of the western area. Today, despite the intrusion of currently unusable dirt roads from Tibet, the magnetic draw and stunning potential of the region is undimmed. Limi Valley remains untouched, with its mediaeval culture, fortress-style villages, crumbling citadels and magical monasteries. The return route is equally amazing, through high summer pastures on the Tibetan border and across the Nyalu La pass into quiet canyons, rugged ridges and lost valleys.

Saipal Base Camp Treks
Treks to Saipal will satisfy most mountain lovers. Close enough to the Simikot airstrip for routes of around two weeks, the area offers a glimpse of the wild, forested western uplands. Saipal (7100m) is an isolated peak that dominates its surroundings in stunning style. Diligent explorers can access its east and north faces.

Mount Kailash Kora Trek and the Guge Kingdom
Covered in our Tibet pictorial guidebook, this trek and the incredible former Guge kingdom in Tibet are amazing and can be accessed from Simikot and Hilsa. Both foreign trekkers and Indian pilgrims are drawn to the sacred Mount Kailash and the holy waters of Lake Manasarovar. Some combine the Limi Valley with a trip to Mount Kailash.

Ning Valley trek
Among those seeking the most remote spots in the Himalaya, the Ning Valley gets some tongues wagging. This lost frontier of West Nepal is wild and far off the radar, devoid of all but yak herder camps. These valleys might perhaps become the new Shangri-La of the west. Peaks like **Changwathang** (6030m) and **Changla** (6563m) will surely attract adventurous climbers very soon.

Rara Lake Trek and Mugu
Rara Lake is the largest body of fresh water in Nepal, surrounded by pine-scented forests. It is accessed from the airfield at Jumla and also now by bumpy bus. The lake is noted for its changing moods and colours, a veritable haven for photographers and nature lovers. Part of the Great Himalaya Trail in the western region routes run from Dolpo to Rara Lake via Mugu and from Rara Lake to Simikot.

Mount Api Treks
Api is almost the most isolated peak in West Nepal, sitting close to the Indian border. It could more easily be accessed from that part of India. From the Nepalese side it's a long haul north from Dadeldhura, Baitadi and the long Chamaliya Khola valley to Api South Base Camp. Those wanting to discover Api North Base Camp need to follow the border north from Baitadi via Darchula. Continuing yet further north is the strange peak of Om Parbat, sacred to Hindus, tucked up on the border of Tibet and India.

Kanjiroba Sanctuary Expedition
Unknown to all but a few climbers, this rugged expedition requires mountaineering experience to explore the higher reaches. Apart from the lower trails between Juphal and Jumla, the country is wild and uninhabited. Very few areas of Nepal are this isolated, making the lonely approach routes and ultimate mountain vistas a sparkling treasure.

Other treks in West Nepal

Increasingly followed by domestic trekkers, the route from **Rara Lake to Khaptad National Park** is a totally different experience. The route follows the GHT Cultural Trail, visiting the farming countryside of the middle hills. The Khaptad plateau is a unique place in Nepal, with ecosystems, fauna and flora to match. A new option is the **Patarasi Himal Trek** to dramatic snow-capped peaks west of Kanjiroba. The **Thakurji Lakes Trek** has so far been the domain of domestic pilgrims visiting the high lakes near Jumla. Lost Buddhist monuments and Hindu shrines are sure to find more appreciation in future. Outsiders are just discovering places like the Hindu ruins of Bhurti near Dailekh, Kankrebihar temple near Surkhet and the newly designated **Badimalika Cultural Trail**. For now the curious visitor will have to plan well and trudge some wild trails on the path to exploration. **Bardiya** and **Suklaphanta** National Parks have seen a steady stream of wildlife enthusiasts; the untouched forests yield sightings of common animals and tigers.

In the remote valleys along the Tibetan border across Nepal, like Limi in the west, Buddhist festivals invariably involve the **colourful masks** of the sacred Cham Dances. They generally celebrate the icons of **Buddhism**, with a couple of dances noting the vanquishing of the older **Bon** faith by Buddhism. The Bon also have Cham dances, which can be seen at Triten Norbutse monastery in Kathmandu near Swayambhunath

The airstrip at **Simikot** gives access to much of northwest Nepal

Old Simikot is a community of traditional flat-roofed mud houses adjacent to the tin roofing of the newer buildings. Tourists are not a very common sight for **village kids**

South of Simikot the village of **Barkhang** is a traditional **Nyinba** community

A cultural route explores the **Nyinba** area southeast of Simikot. It takes up to 4–6 days, depending on the time planned for village homestays. Most visitors use this route for acclimatisation before proceeding to higher country. The villages of **Limatang** (above) and **Burasya** are typical settlements

Raling Gompa is the high point of the circuit, hosting images of **Milarepa** (left) and **Manjushri**

Raling has an unusual (happy-looking) image of **Guru Rinpoche** and more familiar art

The sacred peak of **Shelmo Kang** watches over the Nyinba region

There are great views of the **Chotang** range, looking west from the trail that passes the **Bibug Cave** retreat heading back to Simikot

Limi Valley Trek

From **Simikot** the route drops steeply to **Dharapori**, then follows the **Karnali** to **Yalbang**

Yalbang monastery is the main religious centre of the area

Higher up the valley is **Tumkot**, with an image of **Samantabhadra** and a **snow lion**

After a camp at **Yari** the route climbs over the **Nara La** and descends, with views from Taklakot to the Tibetan border at **Hilsa** seen far below. **Mount Kailash in Tibet**, reached from this border, is the attraction for some trekkers and many Indian pilgrims

Gurla Mandhata and **Lake Manasarovar** are highlights of a visit to this rugged region

From **Hilsa** the **Limi** trek climbs steeply above the **Karnali River** to a camp at **Manepeme**

It continues on a rugged trail around the cliffs to the **Namka Cave** shrine

The route
continues to
climb and descend
wildly around to
Til monastery

Tiljung Camp below Til   **Nalakankar** peak above camp

Halji Rinchen Ling is an important gompa in Limi belonging to the **Drigung** sect

Along the valley is **Jang** and another historic monastery. From Jang the route heads north towards Tibet to a camp at **Traktse**. There are good options from Traktse in good weather. It's possible to climb north to the border, where a **view of Mount Kailash** is possible in clement weather. West of the trail are valleys used by herders in summer. Going east from below Traktse on the trail to **Tshomo lake** is the very remote **Ning Valley**; a high pass at the eastern end leads into the Dojam valley. Along the northern border is a high trail passing north of **Changwatang** Peak

The route to Tibet in poor conditions   The lower slopes of the **Ning Valley**

Views of the **peaks above the Ning Valley** (3 photos: Paulo Grobel)

Tshomo Lake and **Takyon Karpo** peak on the trail to the **Nyalu La** pass

Climbing the last stage to the **Nyalu La** (5001m)

From the pass it's a long drop to the **camp** at **Tshongsa meadows**

The next day the trail enters **wispy forests**, a delight after the high windy plateau

Lower down at **Singjungma** (3794m), the herders produce **chirpi**, a dried cheese. The ladies wear their **traditional turquoise jewellery**

On the trail to **Chadog**, herders are descending to warmer climes for the winter

From a camp at **Chadog** the route climbs   to the **Sechi La** pass

The peaks above the **Ning Valley** from the **Sechi La** have yet to be named or climbed. Saipal might be visible from the Sechi La before the trail descends into deep canyons and traverses the hillside through **Ohkreni** back to **Simikot**

Other treks in West Nepal

North of **Jumla**, a major transport hub with its airstrip and soon a new dirt road
(photo: Kev Reynolds)

Rara Lake

On the trails to **Mugu** and out via **Mandara**

Gamghadi

(6 photos: Kev Reynolds)

Exploring
the

**Kanjiroba
Sanctuary**

(photo:
Paulo Grobel)

211

Bob driving the **British Army expedition** to Api in 1980   **Api** (photo: Sir Crispin Agnew)

On top of **Saipal** in good weather (photo: Paulo Grobel/HMH)

The authors after so many treks!

Of course, any venture into untamed and wild places presents some risks and dangers. A trek to the Himalayan regions needs careful preparation and informed planning by any prospective visitor. That 'once-in-a-lifetime' trek to Nepal is likely to be life-changing and habit-forming! The aim of this picture book is to inspire readers to go beyond the familiar, to discover the treasures of Nepal – its mountains, its people and its culture.

Map of Nepal (© Himalayan Map House, Kathmandu)

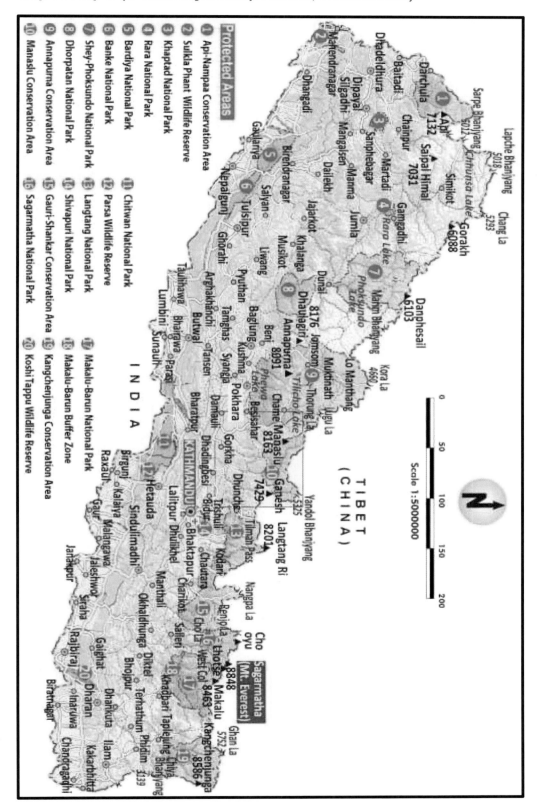

If you've enjoyed this book, or been inspired to find out more, please see our other books:

Bradt (www.bradtguides.com)
Africa Overland --- 2005, 2009, 2014, new edition due 2021

Cicerone (www.cicerone.co.uk)
The Mount Kailash Trek --- 2007
Annapurna: A Trekker's Guide --- 2013, 2017

Amazon / Kindle (www.amazon.com)
In Search of the Green-Eyed Yellow Idol --- 2015, 2016, 2019, 2020
(an autobiography)
Earthquake Diaries: Nepal 2015 --- 2015
The Horn of Africa: A Pictorial Guide --- 2016, 2020
Australia: Red Centre Treks --- 2016
Kanchi's Tale: **Kanchi goes to Makalu Base Camp** --- 2017
Kanchi goes to the Tibesti, Chad --- 2017
Chad: Tibesti, Ennedi & Borkou --- 2017, 2020
Karakoram: The Highway of History --- 2018
Ladakh: A Land of Mystical Monasteries --- 2018
Lebanon: A Brief Guide --- 2019
Karakoram & K2 Concordia (trekking guide) --- 2019
Saudi Arabia: A Traveller's Guide --- 2020
Saudi Arabia: A Pictorial Guide --- 2020
Africa Overland: A Pictorial Guide --- 2020
South America: A Pictorial Guide --- 2020
Asia Overland: A Pictorial Guide --- 2020
Tibet: A Pictorial Guide --- 2020
Nepal Himalaya: A Pictorial Guide --- 2020

Himalayan Map House (HMH) (www.himalayanmaphouse.com)
Himalayan Travel Guides (HTG) (www.himalayantravelguides.com)
& Amazon worldwide (www.amazon.com)
Manaslu & Tsum Valley --- 2013, 2016, 2019, 2020
Dolpo --- 2014, 2019, 2020; **Ganesh Himal** --- 2014
Langtang --- 2014, 2018, 2020; **Everest** --- 2014, 2018
Rolwaling --- 2015; **Mustang** --- 2016, 2019, 2020
Kanchenjunga --- 2017, 2020; **Makalu** --- 2017, 2020
West Nepal --- 2017; **Dhaulagiri** --- 2018
Nepal Himalaya --- 2015, 2017, 2019, 2020

Pilgrims (www.pilgrimsonlineshop.com)
Kathmandu: Valley of the Green-Eyed Yellow Idol --- 2005
Ladakh: Land of Magical Monasteries --- 2006
Kailash & Guge: Land of the Tantric Mountain --- 2006

List of trekking areas in order of appearance

Kanchenjunga 14
   Kanchenjunga North/South Trek ... 14
Makalu 31
   Makalu Base Camp Trek 32
   Yeti Foot Trail 41
Everest 45
   Everest Base Camp 47
   Everest Gokyo Trek 54
   Everest Thame Valley 57
   Classic Everest Trek 60
Rolwaling 64
   Rolwaling Trek 66
   Lapche Valley Trek 72
   Bigu Gompa Trek 76
Langtang 78
   Langtang Trek 79
   Gosainkund to Helambu Trek 84
Tamang Heritage Trail 88
Ganesh Himal 92

Manaslu 102
   Manaslu Circuit Trek 103
   Tsum Valley Trek 117
   Ganesh North Base Camp Trek .. 125
Annapurna 128
   Annapurna Circuit Trek 130
   Annapurna Sanctuary Trek 144
   Mardi Himal Trek 148
   Annapurna-Dhaulagiri Trek 149
   Dhaulagiri Sanctuary Trek 150
Mustang 153
Nar Phu 168
Dolpo 177
West Nepal 196
   Limi Valley Trek 202
   Other treks in West Nepal 210
Map of Nepal 213
Other books by the authors 214
List of trekking areas 215

Damodar Himal, Upper Mustang

Trekking anywhere in Nepal is an unforgettable experience – go soon!

Printed in Great Britain
by Amazon

1997 GRAND PRIX YEAR
HAZLETON PUBLISHING LIMITED

grand prix year 1997

PUBLISHER
RICHARD POULTER

EDITOR
SIMON ARRON

WRITTEN BY
ROB AHERNE & SIMON ARRON

ART EDITOR
RYAN BAPTISTE

PRODUCTION MANAGER
STEVEN PALMER

PUBLISHING DEVELOPMENT MANAGER
SIMON MAURICE

BUSINESS DEVELOPMENT MANAGER
SIMON SANDERSON

SALES PROMOTION
CLARE KRISTENSEN

PHOTOGRAPHY
LAT PHOTOGRAPHIC

GRAND PRIX YEAR
is published by
Hazleton Publishing Ltd.,
3 Richmond Hill,
Richmond, Surrey
TW10 6RE, England.

Colour reproduction by
Vision Reprographics Ltd., Milton Keynes, England.

Printed in England by
Ebenezer Baylis & Son (Printers) Ltd., Worcester.

ISBN: 1-874557-82-9

DISTRIBUTORS

UNITED KINGDOM
Biblios Ltd.
Star Road
Partridge Green
West Sussex RH13 8LD
Telephone: 01403 710971
Fax: 01403 711143

NORTH AMERICA
Motorbooks International
PO Box 1
729 Prospect Ave., Osceola
Wisconsin 54020, USA
Telephone: (1) 715 294 3345
Fax: (1) 715 294 4448

AUSTRALIA
Technical Book and
Magazine Co. Pty.
295 Swanston Street
Melbourne, Victoria 3000
Telephone: (03) 9663 3951
Fax: (03) 9663 2094

NEW ZEALAND
David Bateman Ltd.
P.O. Box 100-242
North Shore Mail Centre
Auckland 1330
Telephone: (9) 415 7664
Fax: (9) 415 8892

SOUTH AFRICA
Motorbooks
341 Jan Smuts Avenue
Craighall Park
Johannesburg
Telephone: (011) 325 4458/60
Fax: (011) 325 4146

Features

Foreword **4**
Team by team **6**
Girl torque **22**
Picture this **30**
F1 fanatics **38**
Murray Walker interview **4**
David Coulthard interview **7**
F1's lost teams **90**
1997's anniversaries **108**
Olivier Panis interview **12**
Drivers to watch **132**
1997 summary **142**

1997 FIA Formula One World Championship

1 Qantas Australian Grand Prix **10**
2 Grande Premio do Brasil **16**
3 Gran Premio Marlboro de Argentina **24**
4 17 Gran Premio San Marino **32**
5 Grand Prix de Monaco **40**
6 Gran Premio Marlboro de Espana **50**
7 Grand Prix Player's du Canada **56**
8 Grand Prix de France **62**
9 RAC British Grand Prix **68**
10 Mobil 1 Grösser Preis von Deutschland **78**
11 Marlboro Magyar Nagyij **84**
12 Belgian Grand Prix **96**
13 68 Gran Premio Campari d'Italia **102**
14 Grösser Preis von Osterreich **112**
15 Grösser Preis von Luxemburg **118**
16 Fuji Television Japanese Grand Prix **126**
17 Grand Prix of Europe **136**

foreword

by Murray Walker

Welcome to Grand Prix Year 1997. Of all the Formula One seasons I have followed from the TV commentary booth I can't think of a single one which hasn't given me a great deal of excitement – and this was one of the finest of all.

It had everything. Ferrari launched its most serious bid in years to lift the world drivers' championship. Williams found that life was just a little bit harder without Damon Hill. McLaren won for the first time since the days of Senna. Damon came within an ace of giving Arrows its first grand prix success. There were new faces on the podium, new race winners and even a new tyre war. Some great young stars were given a chance to show their colours and to top it all we had that pulsating finale. Truly, this was a year to cherish.

So pour yourself a drink, sit back and absorb some of the highlights of a mesmerising season of top-class motor racing. Then I'm sure you will join with me in looking forward to more of the same in 1998.

Ours is a great sport. Enjoy it.

grand prix year 1997

WILLIAMS-RENAULT
Jacques Villeneuve (left). Age: 26. F1 experience: Debuted with Williams in 1996 (four wins). Distinguishing marks: Son of legendary Gilles; tendency to change hairstyle radically; pre-season title favourite
Heinz-Harald Frentzen. Age: 30. F1 experience: Three years as Sauber team leader, 1994/96. Distinguishing marks: Son of an undertaker; great expectations – signed to take place of 1996 world champion Damon Hill

McLAREN-MERCEDES
David Coulthard (left). Age: 26. F1 experience: Williams 1994/95 (one win); joined McLaren in 1996. Distinguishing marks: Dropped by Williams just as he proved to be a match for Hill; once accidentally barbecued himself at Hogmanay
Mika Hakkinen. Age: 29. F1 experience: Lotus 1991/92; joined McLaren in 1993. Distinguishing marks: Won at everything he's ever done – apart from F1; accomplished monocycle rider

BENETTON-RENAULT
Jean Alesi (left). Age: 33. F1 experience: Tyrrell 1989/90; Ferrari 1991/95 (one win); joined Benetton in 1996. Distinguishing marks: Started racing in a Renault 5; of Sicilian descent; tendency to be described by media as 'smouldering', 'sultry', 'moody' and similar adjectives; should have won more races.
Gerhard Berger. Age: 38. F1 experience: ATS 1984; Arrows 1985; Benetton 1986 (one win); Ferrari 1987/89 (four wins); McLaren 1990/92 (three wins); Ferrari 1993/95 (one win); rejoined Benetton in 1996. Distinguishing marks: Tall; old; most experienced man in field with 196 grands prix completed before start of season
Alexander Wurz (inset). Age: 23. F1 experience: Nominated Benetton test driver for 1997. Distinguishing marks: Former mountain bike world champion drafted in as substitute for unwell Berger mid-season; son of rallycross ace Franz

the class

JORDAN-PEUGEOT
Ralf Schumacher (right). Age: 22. F1 experience: Watching elder brother Michael win races/championships. Distinguishing marks: Reigning Formula Nippon champion; fast surname; endlessly compared to big brother
Giancarlo Fisichella. Age: 24. F1 experience: Eight races for Minardi in 1996. Distinguishing marks: Italian passport, of which there have been ever fewer in F1 recently

FERRARI
Michael Schumacher (left). Age: 28. F1 experience: Jordan 1991; Benetton 1991/95 (19 wins, two world titles); joined Ferrari in 1996 (three wins). Distinguishing marks: Perceived to be the fastest man in the world; says Ferrari is not yet ready to challenge for championship; few believe him
Eddie Irvine. Age: 32. F1 experience: Jordan 1993/95; joined Ferrari in 1996. Distinguishing marks: Thumped by late, great Ayrton Senna after F1 debut in 1993 Japanese GP; says Schumacher (M) is the greatest; outqualified him on his Ferrari debut

of 1997

grand prix year 1997

STEWART-FORD

Rubens Barrichello (left). Age: 27. F1 experience: Jordan 1993/96; joined fledgling Stewart team for 1997. Distinguishing marks: In need of kick-start after initially promising F1 career turned stale

Jan Magnussen. Age: 24. F1 experience: One race for McLaren, 1995. Distinguishing marks: Dane with most successful British F3 record of all time; erstwhile fondness for cigarettes frowned upon by team management

SAUBER-PETRONAS

Johnny Herbert (above). Age: 33. F1 experience: Benetton 1989; Tyrrell 1989; Lotus 1990/94; Ligier 1994; Benetton 1994/95 (two wins); Sauber 1996.

Distinguishing marks: Tendency to change teams a lot circa 1994; smiles a lot; ridiculously underrated

Nicola Larini (left). Age: 33. F1 experience: Coloni 1987; Osella 1988/89; Ligier 1990; Modena 1991; Ferrari (occasionally) 1992 & 1994; new to Sauber. Distinguishing marks: But not for long

Gianni Morbidelli (right). Age: 29. F1 experience: Scuderia Italia 1990; Minardi 1990/91; Ferrari 1991; Minardi 1992; Footwork 1994/95; Sauber substitute 1997. Distinguishing marks: Brought in to replace underperforming Larini but swiftly broke arm in

testing shunt and had himself to be replaced for a while **Norberto Fontana** (left). Age: 24. F1 experience: Sauber test driver since 1996. Distinguishing marks: Habitual runner in Japan's Formula Nippon series thrown in at deep end

MINARDI-HART

Jarno Trulli (right). Age: 23. F1 experience: Explosive testing pace for Benetton at end of 1996 Distinguishing marks: Named after Finnish bike racing legend Jarno Saarinen, of whom his dad was a big fan

Ukyo Katayama (centre). Age: 34. F1 experience: Larrousse 1992; Tyrrell 1993/96; new to Minardi. Distinguishing marks: Aspirant mountaineer – wants to climb K2; used to buy his clothes from the children's department at Tesco in Redhill, Surrey

Tarso Marques (left). Age: 21. F1 experience: Brace of races for Minardi in 1996. Distinguishing marks: Young; won first car race aged 16; scored FIA F3000 win when still a teenager; contracted to Minardi until the end of the millennium

PROST-MUGEN HONDA
Olivier Panis (left). Age: 31. F1 experience: Ligier 1994/96 (one win); Prost (ie Ligier under new name) 1997. Distinguishing marks: Won 1996 Monaco GP from 14th on the grid; set to miss part of 1997 when he broke his legs in Canada; thoroughly nice bloke
Shinji Nakano. Age: 26. F1 experience: Prost team made him practise on Microprose GP2 game pre-season. Distinguishing marks: Favoured candidate of engine supplier Mugen Honda
Jarno Trulli (see Minardi). Distinguishing marks: Transferred in wake of Panis's Canadian misfortune

TYRRELL-FORD
Mika Salo (left). Age: 31. F1 experience: Lotus 1994; joined Tyrrell in 1995. Distinguishing marks: Believed to be faster than any of the F1 equipment he has driven has ever let him demonstrate
Jos Verstappen. Age: 25. F1 experience: Benetton 1994; Simtek 1995; Arrows 1996; new to Tyrrell. Distinguishing marks: Followed around Europe by lots of Dutch people carrying Jos the Boss flags

ARROWS-YAMAHA
Damon Hill (left). Age: 37. F1 experience: Brabham 1992; Williams 1993/96 (21 wins, one world title); new to Arrows. Distinguishing marks: Reigning champion but released by Williams as he was on the cusp of his first world championship; strangely underrated despite his success; probably the driver with the finest musical taste in the whole paddock
Pedro Diniz. Age: 27. F1 experience: Forti 1995; Ligier 1996; new to Arrows. Distinguishing marks: Rich; level-headed; determined to prove that he's a serious racer

LOLA-FORD
Ricardo Rosset (left). Age: 29. F1 experience: Arrows 1996; switched to brand new Lola team. Distinguishing marks: But only for one race, and neither of the cars qualified for that; former champion triathlete in his native Brazil
Vincenzo Sospiri. Age: 31. F1 experience: Benetton test driver 1996. Distinguishing marks: Father breeds chickens

David Coulthard scored McLaren's first victory since November 1993 and admitted to having tears in his eyes on the cooling-down lap. Bereft of Optrex, he washed them away with Moët (above). Rookie team Stewart came well prepared, bringing enough noses to allow its drivers three accidents apiece before they ran out (below). By qualifying on pole, Jacques Villeneuve (far right) had less distance to travel to his first-corner shunt.

qantas
qust

first mclaren victory for three years ●
favourite villeneuve eliminated by irvine
fracas ● **schumacher's ferrari quic**

ampionship
first turn
om start

grand prix

11

cLaren had thought of everything. Its natty new silver-grey West uniforms even came with a matching pair of rather Germanic shades. Nice, if you like that sort of thing.

Tears were an optional extra as well.

David Coulthard freely admitted to crying on his slowing-down lap. Mika Hakkinen seemed about to join him in parc fermé. Even poker-faced boss Ron Dennis appeared to have sneaked off for a crafty blub before joining his drivers on the podium.

The reason for the snivel-fest? It had been McLaren's first Formula One victory since Senna. . . and Mercedes' first since Fangio. It was a sign that the Woking team was at last emerging from the spell cast by the late, great Brazilian. And it was a real team effort: Coulthard drove superbly, but McLaren handled a one-stop strategy to perfection too. Hakkinen's strong third was an added bonus.

Although it was churlish to mention as much at the time, McLaren did enjoy a slice of luck – in that the opposition didn't have any.

Runaway poleman Villeneuve threatened to exercise Stalinesque dominance, but lasted only a couple of hundred metres before being bundled off in a ménage à trois with Herbert and Irvine. Frentzen then led for Williams and was still in contention when overheating brakes deserted him with three laps to go, depositing him in the kitty litter. Few doubted, however, that Williams' time would come.

Michael Schumacher also came a cropper – due to either a faulty fuel rig or finger trouble in the Ferrari pit, depending on whom you believed. Either way, he was forced to make a flying visit home for forgotten fuel before the end, but still took second on compatriot Frentzen's demise.

While the party mood gripped the McLaren garage , the post-race atmosphere next door at Benetton was altogether more frosty. Alesi was the culprit, having chucked away a decent finish by attempting to run the only pit stop-free race strategy. Without bothering to tell anyone.

His team did everything they could to help, virtually throwing the contents of their pit – including 6ft 5in designer Nick Wirth – onto the main straight in a vain bid to draw his attention to his fuel warning light. But to no avail: after

Michael "We aren't ready to win the championship yet" Schumacher poked his Ferrari's nose into second place

"david **coulthard** freely admitted to **crying** on his **slowing**-down lap"

The first corner
shunt in full

At 14.00 Australian time, the 1997 grand prix season got underway. All of five seconds later we reached its first talking point, courtesy of Villeneuve, Irvine and Herbert. Or more precisely, their attempts to take the first corner on the same line, at the same time.

Villeneuve may have been on pole by a second and a half, but he lost it all and more when his fingers lingered on his FW19's hand-operated clutch for a split-second too long and left him tugging off the line. While Schumacher and Frentzen made good their escape, the fast-starting Herbert inched by the tardy French-Canadian down the outside.

But Irvine had also scorched off the line – enough to be shaping up for a gap that loomed tantalisingly inside the pole-winning Williams at Turn One. Sensing an opportunity he dived in with both feet. Unfortunately he shot himself in both of them.

Locked-up Ferrari leapt over kerb and hit Williams; Williams biffed Sauber and a can of worms opened. Exit Villeneuve

and Herbert into nearby gravel trap, Irvine into a parking space a little further up the road with cut front Goodyear and mangled suspension.

Ultimately, the words "racing" and "accident" sprang to mind. The stewards saw it that way, even if the three protagonists didn't.

Villeneuve on Irvine: "It was a stupid move from Eddie. He tried to overtake everyone at the first corner. He's been in that situation before and there's no point in talking to him about it. Wild moves are part of racing, but it is frustrating when you are the victim. I feel I could have won and this has taken 10 points away from me."

Herbert on Irvine: "Eddie can be a bit of a wild man. He ruins races. He needs to think a bit more seriously about what he's doing. On TV you can see him going far, far too quick on the inside, doing his normal, 'I was on the inside, it's my line, it's your problem' bit. He can be a bloody idiot sometimes."

Irvine on everybody else: "Three into one won't go. As I said to Villeneuve, I was ahead of him, I was on the inside, it was my corner. He said I wouldn't have made it, but he sliced the rear of my left-front tyre with his wing and I still got round. It was just a racing thing. I don't have to apologise to anyone."

Nor did he.

Gerhard Berger appreciates slick Benetton pit work (above). Had Jean Alesi bothered to do likewise, the mood in the team might have been better.

The cars of Villeneuve and Herbert form a symmetrically dissatisfied parking lot, left.

Blink and you'll miss it: this is a Formula One Lola, far left; failed to qualify, failed to do any more races.

13

fourth-placed Berger obediently stopped for gas, his team-mate pulled up too. On the grass, with an empty tank.

Agonising misfortune or gobsmacking stupidity? Jean protested that his radio was on the blink; insiders suggested that key faculties inside his helmet were too. Flavio Briatore's thunderous expression clearly indicated his opinion.

It looked like a few more tears would be shed before the afternoon was out.

damon's uphill struggle

You are the champion of the world, entering the year of your title defence. You have number one on your car, yet you have transferred from a team which won half of the previous season's races to one which has had scarcely a sniff of victory in nigh on 20 years.

You are also switching from a car which is the undisputed class of the field to one which appears to handle with all the precision of a Routemaster bus. How do you react?

In Damon Hill's case, you come out fighting. It seemed his Arrows A18-Yamaha was determined to make him redundant on race day.

With 20 minutes to go in qualifying it looked as though he would be able to drown his Saturday sorrows on the tiles. He had not set a time quick enough to get him onto the grid and, what's more, his nicely balanced race chassis had packed up, leaving him saddled with a spare that he admitted was scary to drive.

The world champion responded by driving it on doorhandles it didn't have, hitting the kerbs, dust and anything else he could in his bid to get into the race. It was all a bit rough and ragged. More the style of erstwhile partner Villeneuve than the smooth, unobtrusive habits for which himself had been known (and sometimes criticised) at Williams. But it worked. He even gained a further measure of respectability by bumping Verstappen's Tyrrell into the final grid slot before the session was over.

Damon's skill and tenacity could not disguise the fact that Tom Walkinshaw's team was in trouble. Its pre-season testing had been packed with lots of action and precious few miles; Hill's struggle, and the failure of team-mate Diniz to beat the 107 per cent grid cut-off time, underlined the need for urgent remedial work.

Ultimately the application of reason and Mr Walkinshaw's not inconsiderable weight saw Pedro allowed into the race, but they couldn't keep Hill in it beyond the formation lap. As the pack headed for their starting positions, a throttle sensor failure left Damon looking for a convenient spot to park. When he found one he bailed out, turned on his heel and walked briskly away.

It was to be the start of a troubled few months.

> "it seemed his **Arrows** A-18 Yamaha was **determined** to make him **redundant** on race day"

Williams drew a rare blank. Frentzen's FW19 is craned away (above left) after overheating brakes caused him to spin off when an easy second place was within reach.

How the other half lives: world champion Hill had to work harder just to qualify his Arrows than he ever had to do to put a Williams on pole. Then it conked out before the start.

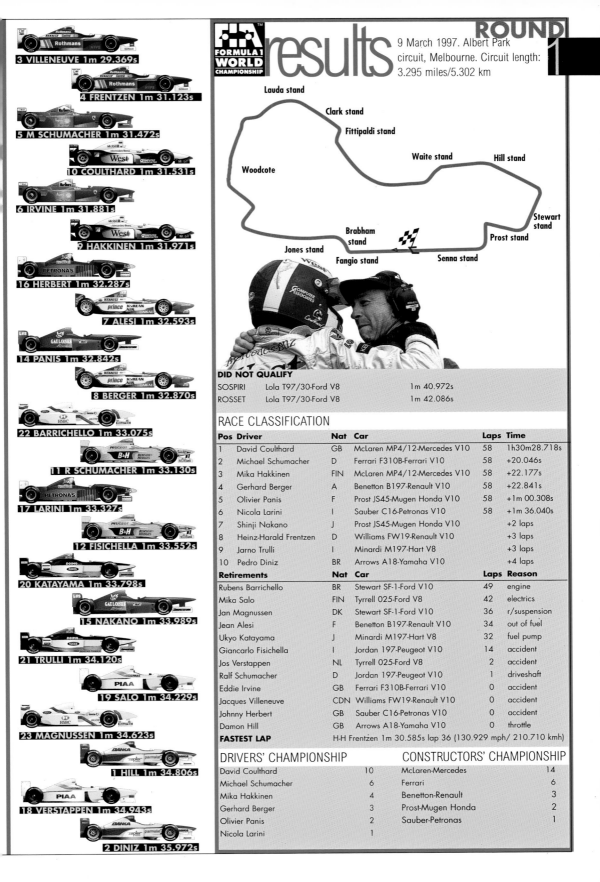

3 VILLENEUVE 1m 29.369s

4 FRENTZEN 1m 31.123s

5 M SCHUMACHER 1m 31.472s

10 COULTHARD 1m 31.531s

6 IRVINE 1m 31.881s

9 HAKKINEN 1m 31.971s

16 HERBERT 1m 32.287s

7 ALESI 1m 32.593s

14 PANIS 1m 32.842s

8 BERGER 1m 32.870s

22 BARRICHELLO 1m 33.075s

11 R SCHUMACHER 1m 33.130s

17 LARINI 1m 33.327s

12 FISICHELLA 1m 33.552s

20 KATAYAMA 1m 33.798s

15 NAKANO 1m 33.989s

21 TRULLI 1m 34.120s

19 SALO 1m 34.229s

23 MAGNUSSEN 1m 34.623s

1 HILL 1m 34.806s

18 VERSTAPPEN 1m 34.943s

2 DINIZ 1m 35.972s

FIA FORMULA 1 WORLD CHAMPIONSHIP

results

ROUND 1

9 March 1997. Albert Park circuit, Melbourne. Circuit length: 3.295 miles/5.302 km

Lauda stand
Clark stand
Fittipaldi stand
Waite stand
Hill stand
Woodcote
Stewart stand
Brabham stand
Prost stand
Jones stand
Fangio stand
Senna stand

DID NOT QUALIFY

SOSPIRI	Lola T97/30-Ford V8		1m 40.972s
ROSSET	Lola T97/30-Ford V8		1m 42.086s

RACE CLASSIFICATION

Pos	Driver	Nat	Car	Laps	Time
1	David Coulthard	GB	McLaren MP4/12-Mercedes V10	58	1h30m28.718s
2	Michael Schumacher	D	Ferrari F310B-Ferrari V10	58	+20.046s
3	Mika Hakkinen	FIN	McLaren MP4/12-Mercedes V10	58	+22.177s
4	Gerhard Berger	A	Benetton B197-Renault V10	58	+22.841s
5	Olivier Panis	F	Prost JS45-Mugen Honda V10	58	+1m 00.308s
6	Nicola Larini	I	Sauber C16-Petronas V10	58	+1m 36.040s
7	Shinji Nakano	J	Prost JS45-Mugen Honda V10		+2 laps
8	Heinz-Harald Frentzen	D	Williams FW19-Renault V10		+3 laps
9	Jarno Trulli	I	Minardi M197-Hart V8		+3 laps
10	Pedro Diniz	BR	Arrows A18-Yamaha V10		+4 laps

Retirements	Nat	Car	Laps	Reason
Rubens Barrichello	BR	Stewart SF-1-Ford V10	49	engine
Mika Salo	FIN	Tyrrell 025-Ford V8	42	electrics
Jan Magnussen	DK	Stewart SF-1-Ford V10	36	r/suspension
Jean Alesi	F	Benetton B197-Renault V10	34	out of fuel
Ukyo Katayama	J	Minardi M197-Hart V8	32	fuel pump
Giancarlo Fisichella	I	Jordan 197-Peugeot V10	14	accident
Jos Verstappen	NL	Tyrrell 025-Ford V8	2	accident
Ralf Schumacher	D	Jordan 197-Peugeot V10	1	driveshaft
Eddie Irvine	GB	Ferrari F310B-Ferrari V10	0	accident
Jacques Villeneuve	CDN	Williams FW19-Renault V10	0	accident
Johnny Herbert	GB	Sauber C16-Petronas V10	0	accident
Damon Hill	GB	Arrows A18-Yamaha V10	0	throttle

FASTEST LAP H-H Frentzen 1m 30.585s lap 36 (130.929 mph/ 210.710 kmh)

DRIVERS' CHAMPIONSHIP

David Coulthard	10
Michael Schumacher	6
Mika Hakkinen	4
Gerhard Berger	3
Olivier Panis	2
Nicola Larini	1

CONSTRUCTORS' CHAMPIONSHIP

McLaren-Mercedes	14
Ferrari	6
Benetton-Renault	3
Prost-Mugen Honda	2
Sauber-Petronas	1

Marlboro

grande premio do

If you get it wrong you get it right next time. So sang Gerry Rafferty; so proved Jacques Villeneuve when given a second chance to start. Berger (left) belied the fact he almost qualifies for a cheap bus pass. Talking of buses, Hill (right) got the Arrows up to fourth.

pile-up brings **relief** for **lucky villeneuve** ●

hoists **arrows** into **top six** for a while ● has

2

brasil

erger proves age is **no handicap • hill**
yone **noticed frentzen** anywhere?

grand prix year 1997

the sweet smell of success hung over the Williams pit. To visitors who'd been in Brazil for almost a week, it wasn't quite strong enough to overpower the whiff from the river-cum-sewage stream that runs through Sao Paulo's suburbs.

But it did suggest that anybody entertaining hopes of beating Jacques Villeneuve to the title had better make themselves known – and fast.

Villeneuve's first victory of the season wasn't without drama. He got away with tackling the first start without his brain engaged – the only rational explanation for a daft attempt to tough it out with Michael Schumacher at the first corner.

The Williams' resultant trip through the gravel would have ruined the Canadian's race had it not been stopped by Fisichella, who engineered a Keystone Cops-style calamity by spinning in the pack.

Second time round Jacques made good his escape after contemptuously sweeping Schuey aside. With the Ferrari doomed to lumber home fifth, hampered by this natural amphitheatre's high-speed curves, Villeneuve cleared off altogether. He was pegged back only by Berger's inspired Benetton in the closing stages, the veteran Austrian driving with the kind of speed and focus that reminds one of why his wallet is

Rubens Barrichello's shortbread tin on wheels (below right) failed to finish on his home soil.

Are friends electric? Not if your name is Ralf Schumacher: the Jordan driver (below) was stranded with

the second heaviest in F1, after Schumacher's.

Equally impressive was a man paid much less. Olivier Panis underlined both the durability of his new Bridgestone tyres and his own talent to give Alain Prost his first podium finish as a team owner. The chunky Frenchman also proved in the post-race press conference that his English is not as bad as he fears: just as well, because there were no Brits present to fly the flag.

That was not, in Damon Hill's case, for a lack of trying. A sensational leap in form saw him qualify in the top 10 and the world champion briefly resumed his former career on two wheels at the first start, with a momentary wall of death display after he was clobbered by Fisichella. He made the most of the restart and briefly held fourth place after a brilliant getaway.

True, he was a mobile chicane for a stream of faster but slower-starting cars before an engine fire intervened, but at least he caught the eye.

David Coulthard, stuck behind

> ## "villeneuve got away with tackling the first start **without** his **brain** engaged"

him for a chunk of the race, was a subdued 10th, one place behind the mysteriously off-form Heinz-Harald Frentzen and three adrift of Johnny Herbert, who was lucky to survive another tangle with Irvine at the first start.

This time the Ulsterman was wholly blameless, although he did not escape unpunished. He restarted in the spare Ferrari which was set up for Schumacher. Its seat belts crushed his unmentionables until the pain made him pit for vital adjustments. He took the flag 16th and the post-race jibes well, albeit between gritted teeth.

communication
breakdown

While one Williams romped home to victory, the other trailed home an also-ran, mired in a midfield train almost as long as its driver's sideburns.

Heinz-Harald Frentzen's transfer to Williams coincided with his adoption of a facial hair style that was more Slade than Sassoon. Unfortunately for Frank Williams, Frentzen's concurrent lack of form must have left him wondering – in Brazil at any rate – why he had given Damon Hill his marching orders to accommodate the hirsute German.

He may have led in Australia, but it wasn't long before Frentzen was feeling the heat that comes with a Williams contract. In Brazil Hill's Arrows qualified a mere tenth off Frentzen despite giving away a reputed 50bhp on a power track. After the restart, the world champion streaked clear of his replacement before his Yamaha went up in smoke.

Frentzen came in an embarrassed ninth and sullenly struggled to explain why this was so. Williams personnel were equally bemused, although as technical chief Patrick Head was cornered in the garage afterwards, his words

from the team's pre-season lunch lingered in the mind.

"Heinz-Harald comes from a culture where changing a roll-bar by one millimetre is regarded as major," he jested. The word was that the robust Patrick felt that Heinz-Harald failed to communicate adequately what he wanted done with the set-up of his FW19 and dithered over changes.

Frentzen responded by telling the TV microphones, as Keke Rosberg had before him, that his biggest problem as far as Williams was concerned was that he wasn't a reincarnation of Alan Jones, the team's first world champion back in 1980.

Back to Interlagos, though, where Frentzen was already making plans to cancel his vacation in favour of a busman's holiday in the form of a lengthy debrief at the factory with his engineers. It wasn't the best of starts, but things would improve.

fantasy F1 runs out of credit

Heard the one about the MasterCard Lola team? Its expiry date was stamped on the underside of its cars. Boom boom.

In Melbourne, Lola F1 had been the butt of paddock jokes. By Interlagos, however, the laughter had stopped as the Huntingdon team collapsed under the weight of mounting debts before the grand prix weekend.

It had been predicted that Lola's F1 return would be a short-lived disaster, yet not even the most cynical observers could foresee precisely just how brief and catastrophic it would be.

A public autopsy revealed that it was a miracle Lola got even this far.

Eric Broadley's company had been propelled through its hurried plans to enter grand prix racing on credit, courtesy of its high-profile MasterCard tie-up.

And there was the rub. Not only did the team have to rush through 18 months' work in six to be ready for Australia, its backing depended purely on how many customers MasterCard could persuade to donate to a money-spinning F1 club.

It didn't generate much dosh – and no wonder.

Lola's T97/30 chassis had never been near a wind tunnel and its ancient customer Cosworth V8s were hard pressed to pull teeth, let alone an F1 car. Drivers Vincenzo Sospiri and Ricardo Rosset were politely appalled by what they found after testing for about half an hour before Melbourne.

When they got there, neither could get within 10 seconds of the qualifying mark; another driver remarked that they would have been better off trying to get on the grid in a Lola F3000 car rather than its canine F1 creation. He was right.

The upshot was a messy MasterCard/Lola divorce and the winding-up of Lola F1 before its second GP. This would subsequently intro-

duce the liquidators to parent company Lola Cars, one of the world's most successful volume racing car constructors.

Spare a thought for Rosset and Sospiri, both of whom spent the Interlagos weekend banging fruitlessly on doors in the paddock.

The Italian felt particularly aggrieved, having not been informed of Lola's problems. Impressed by the sight of Rosset's face all over the Brazilian papers' sports pages, he rang his team-mate to congratulate him on getting so much publicity – only to be told the reason for the media's sudden interest by a less-than-cheerful Ricardo.

"Stopping here is the biggest mistake," reflected Rosset, "because when a Brazilian driver can't race in Brazil the publicity is really bad."

At least that was consistent with the car's performance.

20 laps to go. If anyone knows of a shorter F1 career, drop us a line: Lola's hardware made it to Brazil but the wherewithal to run it did not. It was game over for the grand prix dream of Eric Broadley (inset).

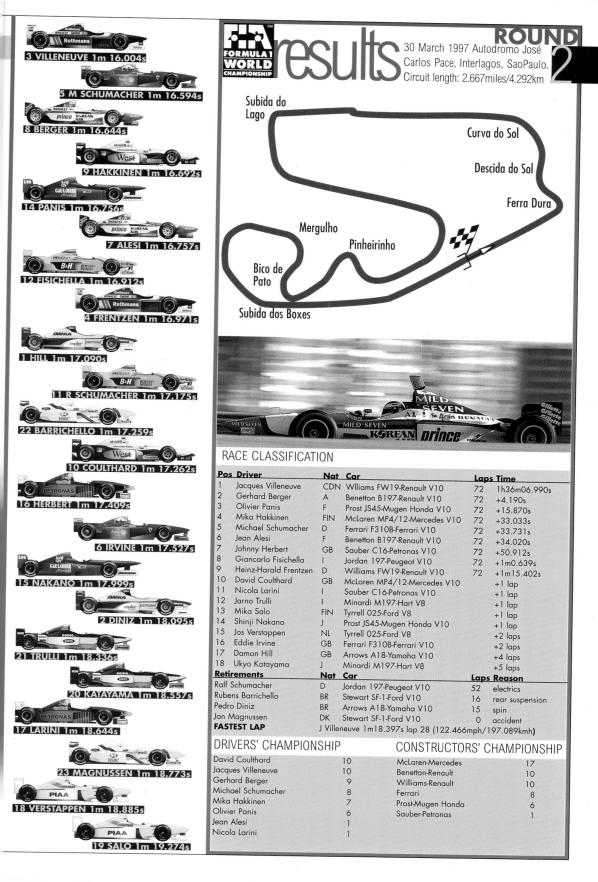

FIA FORMULA 1 WORLD CHAMPIONSHIP

results

30 March 1997 Autodromo José Carlos Pace, Interlagos, SaoPaulo.
Circuit length: 2.667miles/4.292km

ROUND 2

3 VILLENEUVE 1m 16.004s
5 M SCHUMACHER 1m 16.594s
8 BERGER 1m 16.644s
9 HAKKINEN 1m 16.692s
14 PANIS 1m 16.756s
7 ALESI 1m 16.757s
12 FISICHELLA 1m 16.912s
4 FRENTZEN 1m 16.971s
1 HILL 1m 17.090s
11 R SCHUMACHER 1m 17.175s
22 BARRICHELLO 1m 17.259s
10 COULTHARD 1m 17.262s
16 HERBERT 1m 17.409s
6 IRVINE 1m 17.527s
15 NAKANO 1m 17.999s
2 DINIZ 1m 18.095s
21 TRULLI 1m 18.336s
20 KATAYAMA 1m 18.557s
17 LARINI 1m 18.644s
23 MAGNUSSEN 1m 18.773s
18 VERSTAPPEN 1m 18.885s
19 SALO 1m 19.274s

Subida do Lago
Curva do Sol
Descida do Sol
Ferra Dura
Mergulho
Pinheirinho
Bico de Pato
Subida dos Boxes

RACE CLASSIFICATION

Pos	Driver	Nat	Car	Laps	Time
1	Jacques Villeneuve	CDN	Wlliams FW19-Renault V10	72	1h36m06.990s
2	Gerhard Berger	A	Benetton B197-Renault V10	72	+4.190s
3	Olivier Panis	F	Prost JS45-Mugen Honda V10	72	+15.870s
4	Mika Hakkinen	FIN	McLaren MP4/12-Mercedes V10	72	+33.033s
5	Michael Schumacher	D	Ferrari F310B-Ferrari V10	72	+33.731s
6	Jean Alesi	F	Benetton B197-Renault V10	72	+34.020s
7	Johnny Herbert	GB	Sauber C16-Petronas V10	72	+50.912s
8	Giancarlo Fisichella	I	Jordan 197-Peugeot V10	72	+1m0.639s
9	Heinz-Harald Frentzen	D	Williams FW19-Renault V10	72	+1m15.402s
10	David Coulthard	GB	McLaren MP4/12-Mercedes V10		+1 lap
11	Nicola Larini	I	Sauber C16-Petronas V10		+1 lap
12	Jarno Trulli	I	Minardi M197-Hart V8		+1 lap
13	Mika Salo	FIN	Tyrrell 025-Ford V8		+1 lap
14	Shinji Nakano	J	Prost JS45-Mugen Honda V10		+1 lap
15	Jos Verstappen	NL	Tyrrell 025-Ford V8		+2 laps
16	Eddie Irvine	GB	Ferrari F310B-Ferrari V10		+2 laps
17	Damon Hill	GB	Arrows A18-Yamaha V10		+4 laps
18	Ukyo Katayama	J	Minardi M197-Hart V8		+5 laps

Retirements	Nat	Car	Laps	Reason
Ralf Schumacher	D	Jordan 197-Peugeot V10	52	electrics
Rubens Barrichello	BR	Stewart SF-1-Ford V10	16	rear suspension
Pedro Diniz	BR	Arrows A18-Yamaha V10	15	spin
Jan Magnussen	DK	Stewart SF-1-Ford V10	0	accident

FASTEST LAP J Villeneuve 1m18.397s lap 28 (122.466mph/197.089kmh**)**

DRIVERS' CHAMPIONSHIP

David Coulthard	10
Jacques Villeneuve	10
Gerhard Berger	9
Michael Schumacher	8
Mika Hakkinen	7
Olivier Panis	6
Jean Alesi	1
Nicola Larini	1

CONSTRUCTORS' CHAMPIONSHIP

McLaren-Mercedes	17
Benetton-Renault	10
Williams-Renault	10
Ferrari	8
Prost-Mugen Honda	6
Sauber-Petronas	1

What is the most important element of F1 car design in the Nineties? Engine? Tyres? Aerodynamics? Heel depth? Shade of lipstick? Jordan scooped the award for the most magnetic paintwork of 1997.

On track Ralf Schumacher was persistently drawn into contact with solid objects; off track the car was more likely to be covered in Chanel than gravel.

girl
torque

Not that proof were needed, but Pedro Diniz demonstrates (right) that there's no more glamorous job in the world than being the son of someone who owns a chain of supermarkets.

gran premio marlboro de...

argenti

surge from **irvine** almost snatches win
expense ● brother **michael crashes** out

Jacques Villeneuve fought off a dose of Buenos Aires tummy and a nasty outbreak of Eddie Irvine yet still had enough strength left to spray champagne - which rostrum neighbour Schumacher was just about old enough to drink legally.

3
na2

Iet's not be coy: functioning toilets are in short supply in Buenos Aires. If you need one badly, you're in trouble. Yet Jacques Villeneuve appeared strangely unflustered.

A nasty bout of Buenos Aires tummy had left the French-Canadian, in his own words: "Spending too much time talking to the great white telephone." The lengthy conversations, however, didn't hamper his ability to drive an F1 car hard for a race distance. It was just as well, because he needed to drive his hardest for all 72 laps of the Argentine GP thanks to a rejuvenated Eddie Irvine.

Villeneuve was clearly quickest and then some, but at a price: he was making one pit stop

> **"schumacher** complained that his **vision** had been **impeded** off the line by a spurt of **engine oil** across his **visor** from the soon-to-retire **frentzen's williams"**

more than Irvine. This coincided with Eddie discovering that his Ferrari felt rather good when it had guzzled a chunk of its fuel load and enabled him to pick up his pace by the thick end of two seconds a lap.

Villeneuve drove flat out to stay ahead. He succeeded, but this was a sick man in a sick car. The Williams' gearshift had a mind of its own in the closing stages and he had to cope with Eddie's Ferrari looming ever larger in his mirrors during the final 10 laps – albeit driven by a man wary of the potential repercussions of a rash last-gasp lunge.

The irony was that Argentina showcased one of the best races of the year on a track which could well be South America's answer to the Brands Hatch Indy circuit minus the Kent venue's overtaking opportunities. Your average NCP offers more scope for passing than the Circuit Oscar A Galvez, but that didn't stop people trying.

Then again, Jordan might have been toasting its maiden grand prix win had Ralf Schumacher not bundled team-mate Fisichella aside in his haste to become

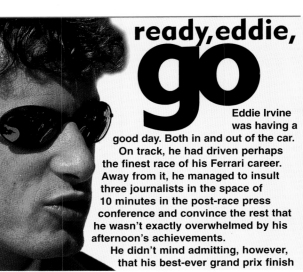

ready, eddie,
go

Eddie Irvine was having a good day. Both in and out of the car. On track, he had driven perhaps the finest race of his Ferrari career. Away from it, he managed to insult three journalists in the space of 10 minutes in the post-race press conference and convince the rest that he wasn't exactly overwhelmed by his afternoon's achievements.

He didn't mind admitting, however, that his best-ever grand prix finish the marque's first victor. Schu Jnr bounced back to third, his aggrieved team-mate flounced back to the pits and what should have been a festival afternoon for Eddie Jordan's men turned into a heated post-mortem.

Olivier Panis was another 'victim of Schumacher belligerence - this time from clumsy big brother Michael, who banged wheels with the Prost pilot on the run to the first corner and almost nerfed him through a pit lane advertising hoarding. Despite his subsequently wonky steering, Olivier was matching Villeneuve's speed lap-for-lap and had a pit stop in hand when his JS45 spilled its hydraulic guts and reduced Panis to a spectating role.

Schumacher Snr, meanwhile, watched all this from the pits. After his brush with Panis the German did not make it beyond the first corner. Rubens Barrichello, who had qualified his Stewart a remarkable fifth, found himself

Rubens Barrichello (left above) qualified his tartan missile a fabulous fifth fastest but was able to race no further than the first corner. Michael Schumacher had already used his Ferrari as a battering ram against Olivier Panis's Prost but found that the Italian machine wasn't robust enough (left) to elbow aside the Brazilian's Stewart. At least they both got to watch a reasonably exciting race.

had come at a mightily opportune time.

After failing to score points in the first two races, Irvine arrived in Argentina to find his future as a Prancing Horseman being called into question. It wasn't a first by any means – the Italian media, its hackles raised by Irvine's happy-go-lucky, couldn't-give-a-toss demeanour, regularly called for Irvine's head during 1996 – but this time its murmuring had substance.

They suggested that Ferrari's patience with its carefree charge had worn thin; that Mika Salo, a long-time favourite of Ferrari Sporting Director Jean Todt, would take his place in 1998; that Irvine would struggle to find a home anywhere else in the pit lane.

The rumourmongers were ultimately proved wrong, but Eddie did not underestimate the importance of his afternoon's work. Under different circumstances, indeed, it might even have produced his first F1 victory: there were those, Villeneuve included, who thought that Irvine might have been keeping a banzai move up his sleeve for those final few laps. If he had such as plan, however, he decided to keep it hidden.

"I got very close to Jacques, but on the straight he just disappeared," said Eddie. "I think I had more downforce than him and the Williams is very efficient anyway. I was on the rev limiter halfway down the straight, so there wasn't much chance of overtaking unless I did a do-or-die.

"And really," he added with a wry smile, "it probably wasn't the best time to do it..."

locked in an ungainly pirouette with the Ferrari team leader having been spun round by the German's left-front wheel.

Later, Schumacher complained that his vision had been impeded off the line by a spurt of engine oil across his visor from the soon-to-retire Frentzen's Williams. The normal picture, however, would soon be resumed as Villeneuve established himself at the front.

Despite Michael Schumacher's attempt to despatch him to Peru, Panis (left) could still have given Prost and Bridgestone their first win until he sprang a hydraulic leak.

young guns go for
each other

A strangely muted air hung over the Jordan camp after the race. Strange, because the Silverstone team is one of the more cheerful in the paddock. Odder still, it had just picked up its first podium of the season.

Third place for Ralf Schumacher in his third grand prix vindicated Eddie Jordan's decision to hire a pair of drivers whose combined age is well under half that of the Queen Mother and who have only slightly more F1 experience than her. But the 24th lap clash between the precocious 21-year-old Schumacher Junior and team-mate Giancarlo

"I made a little mistake in the corner before, then at the next one he sent me into the gravel," said Fisichella. "Ralf said he was sorry, but I'm really upset."

Schumacher, it seemed, was less than grief-stricken. Neither did he seem bothered about giving the pot a quick stir.

"He doesn't speak English properly," he shrugged. "My Italian is not that good – 'spaghetti', 'pasta'. We can't talk about food all the time!" Ultimately a shake of hands was agreed, although

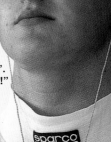

"schumacher, it seemed, was less than grief-stricken"

Fisichella cost the team what could have been an even greater reward.

Technical director Gary Anderson does not generally mince words and didn't now.

"The team threw away a win," he said. "We decided to change the strategy mid-race and bring Ralf in five laps early. That was it." Traffic did the rest, but the Fisichella incident hadn't helped.

Jordan himself said that he didn't know what to do with his charges. Their body language suggested that they had their own ideas about what they'd like to do to each other.

Fisichella and his management were aggrieved enough still to be mumbling about meetings and apologies as the paddock emptied.

Meanwhile, questions were being asked as to why Jordan mechanics didn't salute Schumacher's passing of the chequered flag from the pit wall. Answers were in short supply, but it appeared that a dispute over bonus payments was at the route of this incongruous gesture.

Things, it seemed, could only get better. Fortunately for EJ and his men they would. And fast.

Yellow rages: Fisichella surveys his creased cigarette packet, the result of an over-optimistic overtaking attempt which left team-mate Ralf Schumacher barely repentant and in a career-best third place.

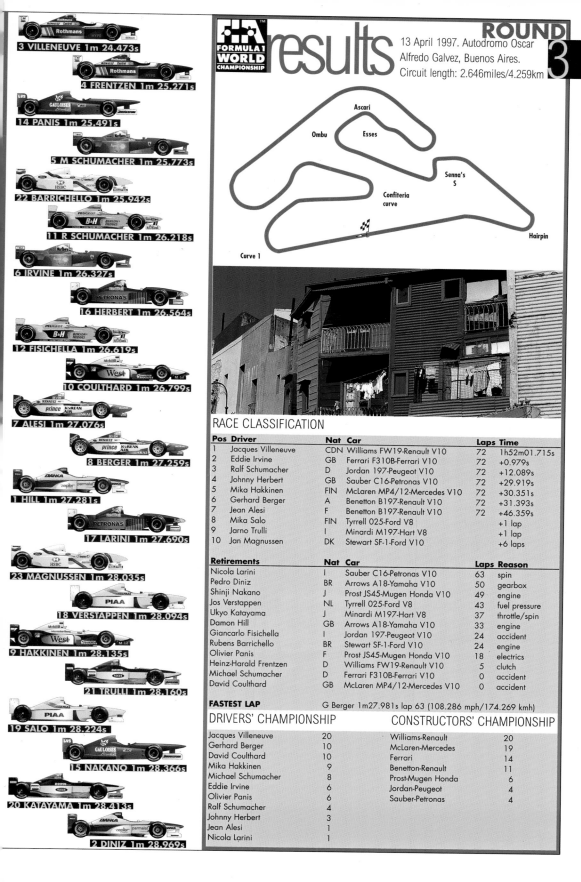

3 VILLENEUVE 1m 24.473s

4 FRENTZEN 1m 25.271s

14 PANIS 1m 25.491s

5 M SCHUMACHER 1m 25.773s

22 BARRICHELLO 1m 25.942s

11 R SCHUMACHER 1m 26.218s

6 IRVINE 1m 26.327s

16 HERBERT 1m 26.564s

12 FISICHELLA 1m 26.619s

10 COULTHARD 1m 26.799s

7 ALESI 1m 27.076s

8 BERGER 1m 27.259s

1 HILL 1m 27.281s

17 LARINI 1m 27.690s

23 MAGNUSSEN 1m 28.035s

18 VERSTAPPEN 1m 28.094s

9 HAKKINEN 1m 28.135s

21 TRULLI 1m 28.160s

19 SALO 1m 28.224s

15 NAKANO 1m 28.366s

20 KATAYAMA 1m 28.413s

2 DINIZ 1m 28.969s

FORMULA 1 WORLD CHAMPIONSHIP results

ROUND 3

13 April 1997. Autodromo Oscar Alfredo Galvez, Buenos Aires.
Circuit length: 2.646miles/4.259km

Ascari

Ombu   Esses

Senna's S

Confiteria curve

Hairpin

Curve 1

RACE CLASSIFICATION

Pos	Driver	Nat	Car	Laps	Time
1	Jacques Villeneuve	CDN	Williams FW19-Renault V10	72	1h52m01.715s
2	Eddie Irvine	GB	Ferrari F310B-Ferrari V10	72	+0.979s
3	Ralf Schumacher	D	Jordan 197-Peugeot V10	72	+12.089s
4	Johnny Herbert	GB	Sauber C16-Petronas V10	72	+29.919s
5	Mika Hakkinen	FIN	McLaren MP4/12-Mercedes V10	72	+30.351s
6	Gerhard Berger	A	Benetton B197-Renault V10	72	+31.393s
7	Jean Alesi	F	Benetton B197-Renault V10	72	+46.359s
8	Mika Salo	FIN	Tyrrell 025-Ford V8		+1 lap
9	Jarno Trulli	I	Minardi M197-Hart V8		+1 lap
10	Jan Magnussen	DK	Stewart SF-1-Ford V10		+6 laps

Retirements	Nat	Car	Laps	Reason
Nicola Larini	I	Sauber C16-Petronas V10	63	spin
Pedro Diniz	BR	Arrows A18-Yamaha V10	50	gearbox
Shinji Nakano	J	Prost JS45-Mugen Honda V10	49	engine
Jos Verstappen	NL	Tyrrell 025-Ford V8	43	fuel pressure
Ukyo Katayama	J	Minardi M197-Hart V8	37	throttle/spin
Damon Hill	GB	Arrows A18-Yamaha V10	33	engine
Giancarlo Fisichella	I	Jordan 197-Peugeot V10	24	accident
Rubens Barrichello	BR	Stewart SF-1-Ford V10	24	engine
Olivier Panis	F	Prost JS45-Mugen Honda V10	18	electrics
Heinz-Harald Frentzen	D	Williams FW19-Renault V10	5	clutch
Michael Schumacher	D	Ferrari F310B-Ferrari V10	0	accident
David Coulthard	GB	McLaren MP4/12-Mercedes V10	0	accident

FASTEST LAP G Berger 1m27.981s lap 63 (108.286 mph/174.269 kmh)

DRIVERS' CHAMPIONSHIP

Jacques Villeneuve	20
Gerhard Berger	10
David Coulthard	10
Mika Hakkinen	9
Michael Schumacher	8
Eddie Irvine	6
Olivier Panis	6
Ralf Schumacher	4
Johnny Herbert	3
Jean Alesi	1
Nicola Larini	1

CONSTRUCTORS' CHAMPIONSHIP

Williams-Renault	20
McLaren-Mercedes	19
Ferrari	14
Benetton-Renault	11
Prost-Mugen Honda	6
Jordan-Peugeot	4
Sauber-Petronas	4

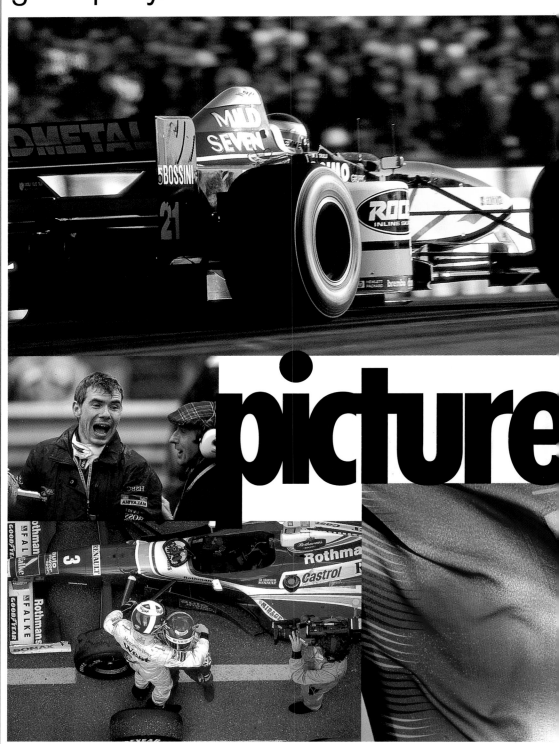

Photographers as artists in 1997, clockwise from far left: sun sets on Ukyo Katayama's F1 career; Barrichello is in there somewhere; Damon sideways in Monaco; Jan Magnussen and The Shadows; Fluttering Horse; best Brit cuddles best in the world, Jerez; Paul Stewart hears that Scotland have just turned over Latvia 2-0, or that his nascent team has just finished second in Monaco, or something. . .

17 GRAN PREMIO DI SAN MARINO IMOLA 1997

17 gran

san

frentzen breaks his **duck** • firs
irvine on song **again** • what ha

premio di
marino4

Smoke on the tarmac, champagne on his brow: Frentzen celebrates his first GP success with fellow Teuton Schumacher Mk1

...ver **one-two** for **germany** ●
...mon **hill** got in common with **barnsley?**

Villeneuve started as he would like to have carried on (above) and parried pressure from the usual Ferrari-driving suspect (inset below). Gearbox problems made him an unhappy Jacques, however. The Silver Arrows were a touch rusty in San Marino but Hakkinen (inset top) salvaged a point.

You can rely on Heinz-Harald Frentzen to enliven otherwise tedious press conferences with splendidly untranslatable German idioms. "The past is yesterday's snow," he declared roundly at one such gathering, to the obvious bewilderment of those present. In Imola, meanwhile, he hit upon a new überproverb: "Victory is like oil on my soul." Imperfect English, but it was easy to get the drift all the same.

Prior to Imola, however, the Williams team's problem had been that, unlike the media corps, it could not rely on Frentzen. While Villeneuve was steaming away and racking up points, his team-mate's first three races had resulted in a resounding haul of zero. Although Heinz-Harald's car had let him down twice – "I hope this is the valley of my luck graph," he had uttered sagely following clutch failure in Argentina – questions were being asked within the

ranks of the ultra-competitive Grove organisation as to whether Damon Hill's replacement was up to the job.

For Frentzen, Imola provided the perfect riposte. He drove with commitment and confidence, seized the initiative from former sparring partner Michael Schumacher (also the man who pinched Frentzen's former girlfriend) and Villeneuve in the pits and never slackened his grip – even when

> "for all it **gained** with frentzen, **williams** experienced **pain** with villeneuve"

Schumacher breathed noisily down his neck in the final laps.

For all it gained with Frentzen, Williams experienced pain with Villeneuve – who was up the creek with a faulty gearshift paddle.

Furthermore, Ferrari kept up the pressure in the constructors' title

trial and error

On the Friday before the grand prix, a quiet yet significant ceremony was taking place away from the hustle and bustle of the Imola paddock.

At the inside of Tamburello corner, the formerly flat-out left-hander where Ayrton Senna lost his life in 1994, the wraps came off a bronze statue fashioned in memory of the late, great Brazilian. Among those who attended was Frank Williams, Senna's last team boss.

As several onlookers remarked, it was a shame that this was not the only overt reminder that Williams and his team would have to endure of the terrible events of three years previously. The manslaughter trial arising from Ayrton's death was grinding along in a makeshift courtroom a few miles up the road from the track – and with it came the threat of possible manslaughter charges and suspended prison sentences hanging over the six accused: Frank Williams, his technical chief Patrick Head, McLaren-bound designer Adrian Newey, FIA safety officer Roland Bruynseraede and two circuit officials.

During a year in which the saga of whether or not F1 ringmaster Bernie Ecclestone would float the sport on the Stock Market constantly flitted in and out of the news, the Senna trial provided a macabre accompaniment. For the most part, however, it served only to muddy already opaque waters due to a fundamental lack of conclusive evidence – something about which the Italian authorities who sanctioned the trial had known from the start.

Amid claim and counter-claim were the revelations that Senna's Williams might have run over debris before the fateful impact, that fancy American-manufactured computer simulations don't actually reflect what happens to a racing car at speed and that Damon Hill was unable to recall enough about the weekend in question to be much help to either prosecution or defence.

It appeared to be a futile exercise which underlined no more than the fact that Italian law can be an ass. Three years on, we were no nearer knowing why the greatest driver of his generation had perished. The only conclusion to be drawn from the whole tawdry affair was that the memory of one of motor sport's true legends would best be served if he was permitted to rest in peace.

> "we were no nearer knowing why the **greatest** driver of his generation had **perished**"

courtesy of Eddie Irvine, who came barrelling through from mid-grid to third after a series of rivals obligingly ended their races as spectators.

These included two fellow Brits. Johnny Herbert, celebrating his 100th GP, moved up into fourth place when Ralf Schumacher's Jordan snapped a driveshaft only to have his Sauber's electrics come over all faulty. Then David Coulthard parked up with an accessory that would become increasingly fashionable alongside this year's McLaren-Mercedes – a trail of engine oil and smoke.

Cue Irvine. When Olivier Panis' Prost began to wobble with handling bothers, the Ulsterman swiftly dispatched the Frenchman and then held off Giancarlo Fisichella to take his second consecutive podium finish.

Further ahead, we had witnessed the first all-teutonic one-two in world championship history – and Schumacher was visibly dischuffed not to be the first element of the equation, having had his pit stop strategy dictated by a tyre he damaged while trying to lap Nicola Larini's wayward Sauber.

This helped cement the Italian's bid to clinch the unwanted goon of the afternoon award. He later got the Variante Bassa chicane completely wrong twice and ended up running through the pit lane on both occasions.

Collectors' item: rare shot of Larini caught not driving down the pit lane (above right). Nakano's fragmented Prost (below) was victim of the slings of misfortune which outraged an Arrows driver.

damon's frustration boils over

The Australian GP had hinted that Damon Hill's year as world champion would be harder than even the sternest sceptics had predicted.

At Imola it appeared that the full implications were finally dawning on Damon himself.

The most obvious signal came on the track, where the man Tom Walkinshaw had hired to be Arrows' Alan Shearer retired after a clumsy challenge worthy of a reserve match on Hackney Marshes.

His victim? Shinji Nakano. That's right, the man chosen by Mugen Honda to drive the second Prost, a rookie in

only his third grand prix – and the previous two had not been terribly inspiring, either.

Hence, undoubtedly, Hill's frustration. Having started from the pit lane when his A18 developed an oil leak on the grid, Damon admitted to "tugging round" at the tail of the field when he happened upon the Japanese novice.

It hadn't been the first time his car

had proved to be less than fully fluid retentive, nor would it be the last, but it would have the most costly net result: Hill was slapped with a one-race suspended ban by officialdom for causing an avoidable accident.

Damon's not-very-carefully-chosen words suggested that this wasn't far off how he regarded his decision to sign for Arrows.

"I had too much ground to make up," he complained, pronouncing himself "angry and cheesed off" with his weekend. "I don't feel I should be chugging along at the back."

Hill was at least in good company in having to visit the headmaster. Both Frentzen and Villeneuve left Italy with suspended bans under their belts. Unlike the Briton, however, they also had victories on their report form. At this stage you'd have put more money on Barnsley winning the Premiership than on Hill re-entering Formula One's winning circle.

There was more. Yamaha's latest-specification engine, which promised to put more horses in the V10's thinly populated stable, had been due to make its debut in Imola. It didn't: there'd be no sign of it for a couple more races. In the meantime niggling reliability problems, plus the odd stonking blow-up, thwarted the team at every turn.

Walkinshaw said he was glad not to be holding his breath. Neither was he going to bide his time and wait for things to pick up. The week after Imola Arrows' technical chief Frank Dernie was on his way out of the Leafield door as former McLaren and Ferrari guru John Barnard came in.

Tom is not one to mess about – and nor would his lead driver for much longer.

Tenner on Barnsley, anyone?

3 VILLENEUVE 1m 23.303s
4 FRENTZEN 1m 23.646s
5 M SCHUMACHER 1m 23.955s
14 PANIS 1m 24.075s
11 R SCHUMACHER 1m 24.081s
12 FISICHELLA 1m 24.596s
16 HERBERT 1m 24.723s
9 HAKKINEN 1m 24.812s
6 IRVINE 1m 24.861s
10 COULTHARD 1m 25.077s
8 BERGER 1m 25.371s
17 LARINI 1m 25.544s
22 BARRICHELLO 1m 25.579s
7 ALESI 1m 25.729s
1 HILL 1m 25.743s
23 MAGNUSSEN 1m 26.192s
2 DINIZ 1m 26.253s
15 NAKANO 1m 26.712s
19 SALO 1m 26.852s
21 TRULLI 1m 26.960s
18 VERSTAPPEN 1m 27.428s
20 KATAYAMA 1m 28.727s

FIA FORMULA 1 WORLD CHAMPIONSHIP

results

27 April 1997. Autodromo Enzo E Dino Ferrari, Imola. Circuit length: 3.063miles/4.930km

ROUND 4

Piratella · Tosa · Villeneuve · Variante Alfa · Acque Minerale · Traguardo · Tamburello · Rivazza · Variante Bassa

RACE CLASSIFICATION

Pos	Driver	Nat	Car	Laps	Time
1	Heinz-Harald Frentzen	D	Williams FW19-Renault V10	62	1h31m00.673s
2	Michael Schumacher	D	Ferrari F310B-Ferrari V10	62	+1.237s
3	Eddie Irvine	GB	Ferrari F310B-Ferrari V10	62	+1m18.343s
4	Giancarlo Fisichella	I	Jordan 197-Peugeot V10	62	+1m23.388s
5	Jean Alesi	F	Benetton B197-Renault V10		+1 lap
6	Mika Hakkinen	FIN	McLaren MP4/12-Mercedes V10		+1 lap
7	Nicola Larini	I	Sauber C16-Petronas V10		+1 lap
8	Olivier Panis	F	Prost JS45-Mugen Honda V10		+1 lap
9	Mika Salo	FIN	Tyrrell 025-Ford V8		+2 laps
10	Jos Verstappen	NL	Tyrrell 025-Ford V8		+2 laps
11	Ukyo Katayama	J	Minardi M197-Hart V8		+3 laps

Retirements	Nat	Car	Laps	Reason
Pedro Diniz	BR	Arrows A18-Yamaha V10	53	gearbox
Jacques Villeneuve	CDN	Williams FW19-Renault V10	40	gearbox
David Coulthard	GB	McLaren MP4/12-Mercedes V10	38	engine
Rubens Barrichello	BR	Stewart SF-1-Ford V10	32	oil pressure
Johnny Herbert	GB	Sauber C16-Petronas V10	18	electrics
Ralf Schumacher	D	Jordan 197-Peugeot V10	17	driveshaft
Shinji Nakano	J	Prost JS45-Mugen Honda V10	11	accident
Damon Hill	GB	Arrows A18-Yamaha V10	11	accident
Gerhard Berger	A	Benetton B197-Renault V10	4	spin
Jan Magnussen	DK	Stewart SF-1-Ford V10	2	spin
Jarno Trulli	I	Minardi M197-Hart V8	0	gearbox
FASTEST LAP		H-H Frentzen 1m25.531s lap 42 (128.937mph/207.504kmh)		

DRIVERS' CHAMPIONSHIP

Jacques Villeneuve	20
Michael Schumacher	14
Gerhard Berger	10
David Coulthard	10
Heinz-Harald Frentzen	10
Mika Hakkinen	10
Eddie Irvine	10
Olivier Panis	6
Ralf Schumacher	4
Jean Alesi	3
Giancarlo Fisichella	3
Johnny Herbert	3
Nicola Larini	1

CONSTRUCTORS' CHAMPIONSHIP

Williams-Renault	30
Ferrari	24
McLaren-Mercedes	20
Benetton-Renault	13
Jordan-Peugeot	7
Prost-Mugen Honda	6
Sauber-Petronas	4

Monza security dictates zoo-like conditions for Milanese autograph hunters (above). Unlike his Arrows-Yamaha, Damon's fans usually stood out (left and below).

fan

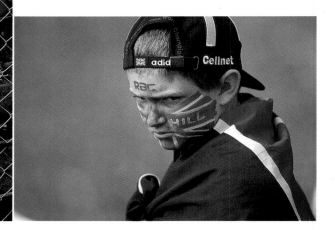

With a hairstyle like this (above), you could do with one of these (above right). Popular at Silverstone (right), such headgear was strangely inconspicuous at Hockenheim. Schumacher attracts a bigger crowd than Doncaster Rovers normally get (below right). This bloke looks as though he's been asleep for about 20 years (below) and his tee-shirt suggests as much – Wolf quit F1 in 1979!

tastic

schumacher **dominates** wet race ● Frentzen's first
williams ● **barrichello** an emotional **second**

Remember how Alfred Hitchcock used to pinch cameo roles in his own movies? Ferrari gangs up on Rubens Barrichello (far left) as team principal Jean Todt sneaks between Schumacher and third-placed Irvine after the German had once again proved no one could match him in the rain. Meanwhile, Barrichello wonders how much he can get for the Rolex he's just been promised by an ecstatic Jackie Stewart.

pole comes to nought as **rain** catches out or stewart

grand prix de
monaco
5

monte Carlo was raining the proverbial chats et chiens. It was the sort of day where staying in and watching the telly seemed more appealing than braving the elements – even if the Teletubbies were on all five channels.

Most of the Monaco Grand Prix field seemed to think that way. You couldn't blame them. The Principality, for all its billing as the most glorious anachronism in modern motor racing, is a godawful place to drive an F1 car at the best of

tartan army on the move

"Here, have a Rolex!"

Okay, so it wasn't quite like that, but Rubens Barrichello's show-stopping run to second place in the team's fifth GP left hardly a dry eye in the House of Stewart. Even Jackie – who can chat for Britain when the chips are down -– was speechless.

When an ITV camera was waved in front of him post-race the three-time world champion's voice quavered and he shambled away, choking back the tears, to join son and Stewart MD Paul in an emotional gathering at the Ford motorhome.

And why not? For a team which had not existed 18 months earlier second place

"**williams never** recovered from an **inexplicable** decision to **ignore** the pre-race **deluge** and start on **slicks** "

Enter Michael Schumacher, who dominated so completely that his rivals might have spent their time better watching him on the box and learning a few things.

Williams never recovered from an inexplicable decision to ignore the pre-race deluge and start on slicks even as Schumacher was swapping to a spare car set up for the wet.

Pole winner Heinz-Harald Frentzen and Jacques Villeneuve subsequently appeared to have started the race in reverse and both ended their races in the barriers – even after making a belated switch to wets.

In the meantime Schumacher performed a vanishing act of which David Copperfield would have been proud. A mid-race downpour strengthened his advantage, even though he highlighted how evil it was out there when he almost slipped up at Ste Devote corner within sight of the finish.

But he kept it on the island and Ferrari was amply rewarded. Schumacher's first win of the season gave him the

The Oxford boat crew would probably have exercised a greater degree of control in such conditions. As usual, Schumacher (left) appeared barely to notice the rain. A prize of a week in the Hotel de Paris for anyone who can satisfactorily explain why Williams started on slicks. . .

times, let alone when Casino Square is doing its best impression of the Swimming Pool complex. Seven hundred-odd horsepower and city streets with drainage problems don't mix. It takes a special kind of driver to make the combination work.

was an incredible achievement. No wonder Jackie was in such a hurry to deal out the Rolexes.

If Stewart was a horologist's dream, his team's lack of cold, hard results for the most part of its maiden F1 season was something of a nightmare. Poor reliability from its Ford V10 engine and niggling failures on an otherwise impressive chassis meant that Barrichello and Magnussen did not, by and large, grind round with the metronomic precision of Stewart's favoured Swiss timepieces.

Furthermore, it was evident that the lack of consistent running, not to mention a couple of scary suspension failures, had given the Dane's confidence a knock from which it took a large chunk of the season to recover.

Barrichello, by contrast, was a driver

reborn. Surefooted Bridgestones may have smoothed his passage at Monaco, but on a day when even Schumacher flirted with disaster the Brazilian's delicate touch in the damp was plain to see.

"It was so slippery out there that you could spin any time," he said later, wide-eyed at the recollection.

The gods let him off lightly, in the shape of a locked-up trip over the kerbs at the harbourside chicane. A similar incident cost Magnussen his nose; Rubens merely found his handling balance mildly rejigged and decided to settle for second.

"Never have I been more happy with any of my victories or championships," said JYS. "I didn't expect a result like that until our second or third year."

It would, however, be a while before another arrived.

championship lead and Eddie Irvine's strong run to third saw the team usurp Williams in the constructors' standings.

The Ulsterman started from way back, which meant that he couldn't do anything about Rubens Barrichello's remarkable second-placed Stewart – a fine effort by a team so new to F1 that its motorhome was bumped from the beautiful people's waterfront paddock to an unsightly location outside a car park.

Barrichello was helped by Bridgestone's excellent wet-weather tyres, which also carried 1996 winner victor Olivier Panis to fourth. But with three-quarters of the field crashing – Messrs Coulthard, Alesi, Hakkinen and Hill within the first two laps – any result at all was an achievement.

Ferrari was back, thanks to Schumacher.

taking the
mika

The rain was lashing down outside the Tyrrell motorhome, but underneath its awning the beers were flowing.

They weren't on Mika Salo – when did you last hear of a driver getting a round in? – but he had precipitated their arrival by bringing home two points.

He had used a unique tactic, too. Salo became the first man to run a non-stop race since refuelling was re-introduced in 1994 as his team took advantage of bizarre circumstances to work out its unusual strategy on the hoof.

The underpowered Ford V8 engine was Tyrrell's biggest handicap all season, but its drivability and economy were just the ticket for sodden Monaco. When Salo showed spectacularly low fuel consumption figures in the early laps, the men on the pit wall took the bold gamble of the rain holding out, the pace staying slow and Mika lasting two hours on his original fuel load.

There were, however, a few crossed fingers. And one or two problems, such as telling Salo about it.

The Finn's radio was on the blink and this really wasn't the sort of information that could be imparted on a pit board. So the crew kept quiet until it dawned on Mika that he had missed his intended pit stop window. . .

The team began to reduce engine revs and lean off its fuel mixture from the pits after the halfway mark – which made the Tyrrell harder to drive – while Salo went into petrol preservation mode. And that didn't mean trying to drive at a constant 56 mph.

"I was short-shifting, trying not to get wheelspin, rolling into corners," he said. "The biggest problem was the tyres: they were really worn out by the end."

He had also lost a front wing section in the first lap argy-bargy, which caused a few fluttering hearts in the Tyrrell camp. No radio meant that Salo could not tell the team and they only realised when the TV cameras finally picked him up late in the race.

Thinking he'd just been off, the mechanics leapt into the pit lane ready to for action. Their driver's cool head meant they weren't required and the strategy gave them two points instead of one.

"It needed the fuel management of a 747 captain flying into a headwind from Hong Kong," said technical director Harvey Postlethwaite. Not to mention plenty of bottle: the slightest of miscalculations and Salo would have stopped on the last lap.

Racing cars can't fly with broken wings (above left). Mika Salo (below) gave Tyrrell's pit crew its first afternoon off since 1994.

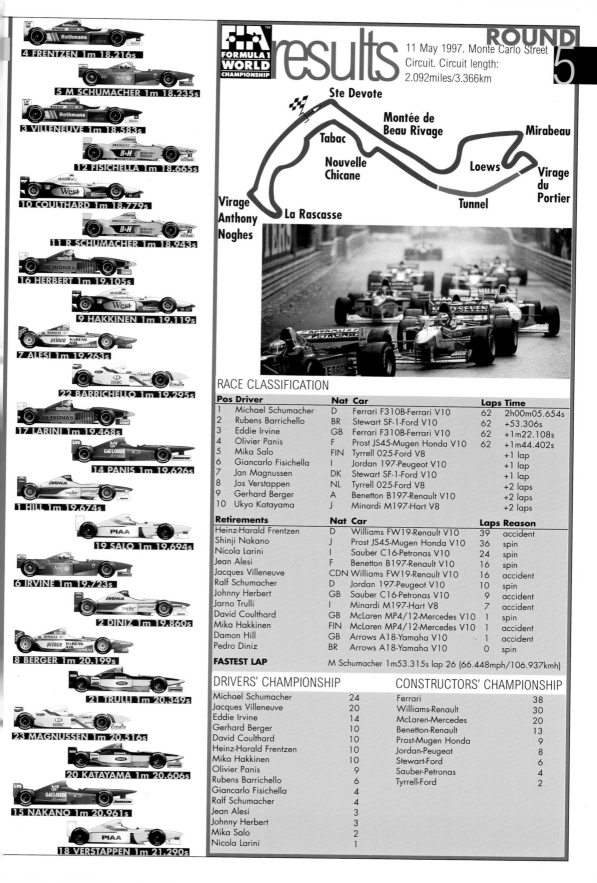

FORMULA 1 WORLD CHAMPIONSHIP

results

11 May 1997. Monte Carlo Street Circuit. Circuit length: 2.092miles/3.366km

Ste Devote
Montée de Beau Rivage
Mirabeau
Tabac
Nouvelle Chicane
Loews
Virage du Portier
Virage Anthony Noghes
La Rascasse
Tunnel

Starting grid (left column):

- 4 FRENTZEN 1m 18.216s
- 5 M SCHUMACHER 1m 18.235s
- 3 VILLENEUVE 1m 18.583s
- 12 FISICHELLA 1m 18.665s
- 10 COULTHARD 1m 18.779s
- 11 R SCHUMACHER 1m 18.943s
- 16 HERBERT 1m 19.105s
- 9 HAKKINEN 1m 19.119s
- 7 ALESI 1m 19.263s
- 22 BARRICHELLO 1m 19.295s
- 17 LARINI 1m 19.468s
- 14 PANIS 1m 19.626s
- 1 HILL 1m 19.674s
- 19 SALO 1m 19.694s
- 6 IRVINE 1m 19.723s
- 2 DINIZ 1m 19.860s
- 8 BERGER 20.199s
- 21 TRULLI 1m 20.349s
- 23 MAGNUSSEN 1m 20.516s
- 20 KATAYAMA 1m 20.606s
- 15 NAKANO 1m 20.961s
- 18 VERSTAPPEN 1m 21.290s

RACE CLASSIFICATION

Pos	Driver	Nat	Car	Laps	Time
1	Michael Schumacher	D	Ferrari F310B-Ferrari V10	62	2h00m05.654s
2	Rubens Barrichello	BR	Stewart SF-1-Ford V10	62	+53.306s
3	Eddie Irvine	GB	Ferrari F310B-Ferrari V10	62	+1m22.108s
4	Olivier Panis	F	Prost JS45-Mugen Honda V10	62	+1m44.402s
5	Mika Salo	FIN	Tyrrell 025-Ford V8		+1 lap
6	Giancarlo Fisichella	I	Jordan 197-Peugeot V10		+1 lap
7	Jan Magnussen	DK	Stewart SF-1-Ford V10		+1 lap
8	Jos Verstappen	NL	Tyrrell 025-Ford V8		+2 laps
9	Gerhard Berger	A	Benetton B197-Renault V10		+2 laps
10	Ukyo Katayama	J	Minardi M197-Hart V8		+2 laps

Retirements	Nat	Car	Laps	Reason
Heinz-Harald Frentzen	D	Williams FW19-Renault V10	39	accident
Shinji Nakano	J	Prost JS45-Mugen Honda V10	36	spin
Nicola Larini	I	Sauber C16-Petronas V10	24	spin
Jean Alesi	F	Benetton B197-Renault V10	16	spin
Jacques Villeneuve	CDN	Williams FW19-Renault V10	16	accident
Ralf Schumacher	D	Jordan 197-Peugeot V10	10	spin
Johnny Herbert	GB	Sauber C16-Petronas V10	9	accident
Jarno Trulli	I	Minardi M197-Hart V8	7	accident
David Coulthard	GB	McLaren MP4/12-Mercedes V10	1	spin
Mika Hakkinen	FIN	McLaren MP4/12-Mercedes V10	1	accident
Damon Hill	GB	Arrows A18-Yamaha V10	1	accident
Pedro Diniz	BR	Arrows A18-Yamaha V10	0	spin

FASTEST LAP M Schumacher 1m53.315s lap 26 (66.448mph/106.937kmh)

DRIVERS' CHAMPIONSHIP

Michael Schumacher	24
Jacques Villeneuve	20
Eddie Irvine	14
Gerhard Berger	10
David Coulthard	10
Heinz-Harald Frentzen	10
Mika Hakkinen	10
Olivier Panis	9
Rubens Barrichello	6
Giancarlo Fisichella	4
Ralf Schumacher	4
Jean Alesi	3
Johnny Herbert	3
Mika Salo	2
Nicola Larini	1

CONSTRUCTORS' CHAMPIONSHIP

Ferrari	38
Williams-Renault	30
McLaren-Mercedes	20
Benetton-Renault	13
Prost-Mugen Honda	9
Jordan-Peugeot	8
Stewart-Ford	6
Sauber-Petronas	4
Tyrrell-Ford	2

from behind the microphone

formula One may have switched TV channels but when it began broadcasting from its new home it was accompanied by an unmistakable sound – and we don't mean the Renault V10. We asked Murray Walker to comment on some of the key issues of the year

What do you feel about 1997 in general?

"It has been one of the best grand prix seasons I can remember for a long time. If you look at the way the season has swung, with Villeneuve and Schumacher alternating and going to the final race with just a point in it – it's been terrific."

What about the accident that settled it?

"I thought the last race was brilliant for the first 48 laps. Before the race I felt that Schumacher would have been a worthy champion but I think he tarnished his image with that manoeuvre. Villeneuve drove a great race and his deportment makes him a worthy champion. That said, I still think Schumacher is the best of his generation. Although he'd won fewer races than Villeneuve I think he'd had the better season up to that point."

Gerhard Berger is leaving Formula One after 14 seasons. Are you sad to see him go?

"I was delighted that Gerhard won a race. To come back as he did and win from pole with fastest lap was incredible. We never saw him at his best thereafter and I can only put that down to his physical problem. I am very sad to he him go because he's had a bloody good innings: he's won races, he's driven in great teams and he's given us all a gigantic amount of fun. I hope he continues to enjoy life out of Formula One as much as he did in it."

Would Williams have been better off if Damon Hill had been retained?

"I don't have a shadow of doubt about that. Villeneuve has won plenty of races and should have won more. But let's leave Villeneuve out of it. Would Damon have done better than Heinz-Harald Frentzen? It's hardly worth wasting breath giving an answer. I'm not trying to put the bloke down but he has been a gigantic disappointment. Heinz-Harald's weakness is that he appears to be a sensitive chap. Villeneuve couldn't give a stuff what anybody thinks about him but Frentzen does. That's no discredit, but if you are sensitive to what people think about you in F1 you're going to have a very hard time. It's tough enough if you've got armour-plated skin. I'd like to think that next season Frentzen will profit from a year's experience with the team and will go better. But there's no contest with Damon, who in my opinion is a better driver and a more rounded personality."

Have you been disappointed by

anyone else this year?

"I think the biggest disappointment of the year, against expectations, has been Ralf Schumacher. To be fair he's only young but we were blinded by the name. We all thought he was going to blow Fisichella away and he hasn't. My recurring image of the season is of Ralf flying into people or gravel traps."

Which of the newcomers have most impressed you?

"The three revelations of the season have been Wurz, Trulli and Fisichella. On a continuity basis you have to give it to Fisichella, simply because he's done all the races and he's achieved more. But I remember Trulli's drive in Austria as one of the best of the season. Had it not been for the engine in my opinion he would have won,

> ## "i **don't care** whether the drivers find them (1998 spec cars) more **difficult** or less **satisfying** to drive – they are paid a **gigantic** amount of **money** to do it"

which would have been incredible. Wurz looks to be an outstanding prospect for next season. He only did three races and in one of those he ended up on the podium."

Are you excited about prospects for 1998?

"I applaud the FIA for its new regulations, with narrower cars and grooved tyres. To reduce the speed of the cars and make them more entertaining to watch is a very good thing. I don't very much care whether the drivers find them more difficult or less satisfying to drive – it's something they want to do, they are paid a gigantic amount of money to do it and they should never forget that they are in show business. I would say the same to the teams, too. We all move around in this thing called Formula One and we get terribly in-bred but we should never lose sight of the fact that in order to thrive and survive the sport has to appeal to the man in he street. I would never call anything in motor racing dull, but even this year we've had some very processional races – Austria was a fabulous contest but it might not have looked like that to someone watching at home on TV. I want to see more overtaking and I want to see the cars sliding about. The FIA is trying to make it happen and if the teams and drivers don't like it, tough".

You've made your admiration for Damon Hill clear. How do you think your other compatriots have done this year? Let's start with David Coulthard.

"I think it's been a disappointing season for David, his two victories notwithstanding. I suppose if any driver other than Villeneuve or Schumacher

had won two races they'd be euphoric. It's been disappointing for David because he's been nearly there so many other times. He actually deserves more success than he's had. David is a super bloke but the jury is still out in terms of his potential greatness. I don't know if there is a missing element. If you compare Damon and David, the main difference is that Damon had longer with Williams. Would David have been as successful if he'd been allowed to carry on with Williams? The simple answer is that I don't know. I hope events prove my reservations are misplaced."

Given that Sauber was given a minus credit rating at the start of the year, Johnny Herbert hasn't done too badly, has he?

"No, but sadly I think he's missed the boat in terms of winning the world championship. He's never been in the right car at the right time. He was against Schumacher at Benetton and the Sauber isn't good enough. I can't

Unable to secure a seat in F1, Martin Brundle settled for one next to Murray Walker as grand prix racing entered a new era on British TV.

see him landing the Williams, Ferrari or McLaren seat he needs to win the title. That's a shame. He's one of the nicest blokes I've ever met, and I don't just mean in F1."

Eddie Irvine is a lot more content as Schumacher's team-mate than Johnny was. . .

"I have a gigantic admiration for the pragmatic way Eddie has accepted his situation as number two at Ferrari for as long as Michael Schumacher is there. The compensation is that he has had all the glamour, wealth and excitement that comes with being a Ferrari driver – and there can't be anyone who hasn't wanted to be one. He has put in some inspired drives – he was brilliant in Japan – and I wouldn't want to condemn some of his less brilliant drives because I suspect that the car has been as much to blame as him. I think he's very capable and you should never, ever underestimate him; he's as bright as a button and thinks every- thing through and as a result of that he's made the most of his situation. He has been the best team-mate Michael Schumacher has ever had. How would he get on in a Williams? I don't know."

All right then, what about you? Were you pleased with the way ITV performed in year one?

"I am not saying this for effect – it comes from the heart. When the BBC

lost the F1 contract I was flabbergasted, but I wasn't terribly worried. I was approaching the end of my career and if it had ended then, as I had expected it to, it would have been a natural stopping point.

"I was delighted to be offered the ITV job though I was apprehensive about going from the security of this cocoon which fitted like a glove to a bright, high-stepping outfit about which I knew nothing. To my delight it has worked like a charm. They are to a man extremely nice people and very professional. They care a great deal and in my opinion they have produced a superb product. I get irritated when I hear people say to me that it's not as good as the BBC. That's arrant rubbish. The footage comes from exactly the same source as the BBC's used to. There's no difference apart from the commercial breaks – I appreciate that no one who wants to watch continuous F1 is going to like that, but it's just part of the business. If it hadn't happened with ITV it would probably have happened with someone else, maybe satellite, and that would have been even less accessible.

"ITV gives it extra time, extra programming, extra interviews. I think it's sharp and pacy and I am more than impressed with what has been done."

Will you be back for more in 1998?
"Of course."

easy win as **villeneuve** retakes championship lea
● **panis** shows **promising** pace again ● **tyres**
a **major** factor for everyone else in **procession**

gran premio marlboro de

David Coulthard usually challenges
for the lead if he starts 33rd on
the grid so he was always going to
put Villeneuve under pressure after
qualifying on row two. However,
the French-Canadian (left) held off
the Scot – and everyone else – for
the rest of the afternoon.

españa

6

grand prix year 1997

The midfield was more tightly packed than Arsenal's defence used to be under George Graham (the authors fully accept, however, that there's some flair at Highbury nowadays). Fisichella heads Hill, Irvine and Panis – who eventually picked his way through the scrum to finish second.

If the 1997 Spanish Grand Prix was a football match it would have been a 0-0 draw where the offside trap reigned supreme. As a Formula One race it made for a drab, lifeless contest enlivened only by one issue: tyres.

And that says it all.

The fact was that Goodyear's rubber missed the target in the searing heat. Bridgestone was on the case but only a select few (one, actually) capitalised.

Knowing that his tyres would melt if overstretched, Jacques Villeneuve tempered his race-winning speed with some canny rubber preservation; he won. Olivier Panis, meanwhile, was the only man in Spain to have Bridgestone tyres and a reliable, competitive car. He came second.

The rest were not in it. And, quite frankly, who cared?

The splendid Villeneuve dominated proceedings from the first corner onwards, throttling back so much in the closing stages that he made Panis look more dangerous than was really the case. The Frenchman's hopes had already been snuffed out by a wayward – and lapped – Eddie Irvine, who dawdled along in front of the surging Prost for five laps despite of a multitude of blue warning flags.

This allowed Jean Alesi and Michael Schumacher, both of whom Panis had passed, to close up again and this prompted Alain Prost to cry foul. The four-time world champion was steaming

> "as a **formula one** race it made for a **drab**, lifeless contest enlivened **only** by one issue: **tyres**"

52

at what he saw as a dastardly Ferrari plan and he stormed off to let some of it off at the Scuderia's sporting director Jean Todt.

Panis settled for rolling his eyes and looking a bit cross: quite a contrast to Alesi, who fired a volley of abuse in Irvine's direction post-race. Maybe it was some kind of release after his own restrained performance, which preserved his Goodyears better than most and gave Benetton only its second

Prost talks to Panis (above) after his star driver was blocked by Irvine (but only for five laps, below right).

While Olivier Panis was providing Alain Prost with his best result as a team boss, off-track the quadruple world champion was not the paragon of cool he used to be at the wheel.

Now, as then, Prost – aka 'The Professor' – does not mince his words and he squarely blamed his former

block another to benefit my team," he said, somewhat pointedly.

This was perfectly true, felt paddock cynics, as Prost had hardly spoken to his team's number two, Shinji Nakano, since the start of the season. The Japanese novice had struggled to come to terms with F1, but in many observers' eyes had not been helped by his lack of test mileage, nor his team boss telling the French press that his car was "dead" as far as scoring points went.

Barcelona marked something of a turning point for Nakano (right), both on and off the track. Shinji did well to cling to Panis for the first 15 laps

professor **prost** learns **F1** lessons

employer Ferrari for an uncharacteristic display of ire during which he stomped down the pit lane to rail at the Italian team's top brass at half-distance.

The reason? Eddie Irvine, who delayed Panis enough to put the Frenchman's second position in greater doubt than it should have been. Prost was adamant that the Ulsterman was the pawn in a Ferrari master plan which allowed Michael Schumacher to close up to third-placed Alesi, who in turn was queuing up behind Panis.

Irvine pleaded innocence, saying that he thought the flags were for twice-lapped Jarno Trulli. Prost said that Eddie's team was the guilty party. "I would never ask one of my drivers to

before getting lost in traffic and then retiring with a gearbox problem. Meanwhile, a behind-the-scenes row looked to have secured his seat for the remainder of the season.

Prost had been toying with the idea of replacing Nakano with a Frenchman – Emmanuel Collard or Jean-Christophe Boullion – even though this would incur the wrath of engine supplier Mugen-Honda, who canvassed for Nakano originally.

The Japanese engineers were not amused by this – even less so when it was reported that Prost had shown their engine to personnel from Peugeot – long since confirmed as the team's engine supplier for 1998.

Nakano-san would be staying put.

recovered from knackering his first set) and David Coulthard. The Scot did everything right to establish himself in the first three, only to watch it all go wrong as his tyres fell apart. He even lost fifth on the last lap, when Johnny Herbert made the most of his extra grip to pull off a genuine overtaking manoeuvre, a rarity which earned him an extra point.

By then, the rest of the diminishing field seemed to have lost interest. After an afternoon like this, you really couldn't blame them.

The tyred and emotional Frentzen: eighth place is not a great result when you drive to work in a Williams.

merc gambles on F plan

From a journalist's point of view Mercedes is one of the more enlightened hosts at a grand prix. Every other weekend it invites scribblers to come for a cold beer and a biscuit or two while patient explanations are offered as to why a McLaren isn't on pole.

Usually these occasions are diverting if ultimately unproductive from a hard news point of view. Spain was different, however,

thanks to an innocuous aside sneaked in by Mercedes competitions boss Norbert Haug before proceedings were fully in swing.

Haug drew modest attention towards a fresh arrival in the back of the Silver Arrows: a new evolution engine. And this was no run-of-the-mill, mildly-tuned development.

Instead, it was the catalyst for a leap in form for the McLaren-Mercs which would make David Coulthard and Mika Hakkinen contenders at nearly every race for the rest of the season and establish the team as the likely combo to beat in 1998.

The new F-type V10 – sired, like all Merc F1 motors, from the Northants base of Ilmor Engineering – was only used for qualifying in Barcelona, but its longer-term significance could be gauged from the furrowed brows and occasional squawking issuing forth from other engine builders.

Haug remained impassive. "We believe it is fit to wear the Three-Pointed Star," he commented. Other teams were more fulsome in their praise. One even carried out provisional calculations based on the level of wing run by the practising McLarens to estimate a power output in the region of 775 bhp – about 25 more than the pace-setting Renaults. Coulthard said it had grunt all the way through the range and not just at the top end.

This was reflected in the team's grid positions – DC third and Hakkinen fifth at a track where the team has struggled to find a balance in recent years. However, it was clear that the new unit was not the panacea for all McLaren ills.

Both team and engine supplier stressed that the new motor had come on stream early and they were gambling performance against reliability.

There would be quite a few exploded Merc V10s in the months ahead, but the cars would at least be travelling at a fair old lick when their engines betrayed them.

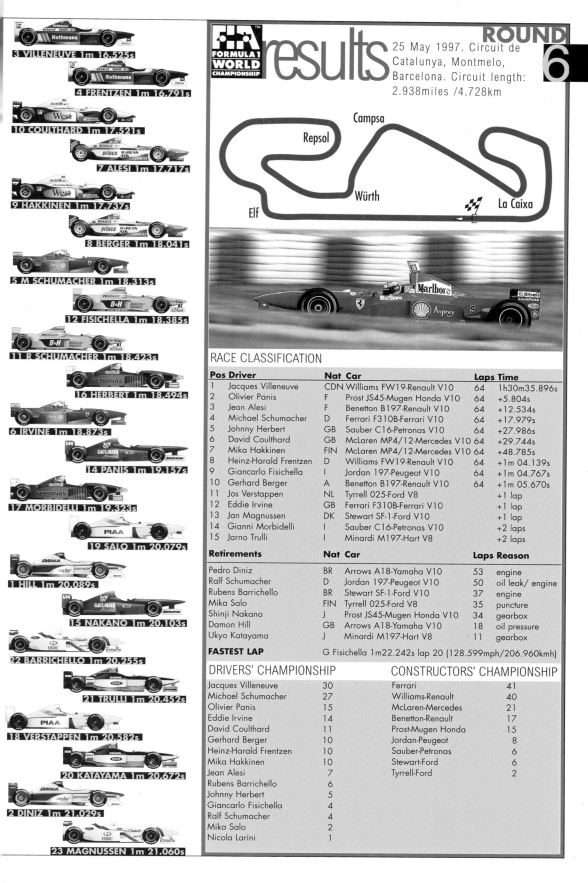

3 VILLENEUVE 1m 16.525s

4 FRENTZEN 1m 16.791s

10 COULTHARD 1m 17.521s

7 ALESI 1m 17.717s

9 HAKKINEN 1m 17.737s

8 BERGER 1m 18.041s

5 M SCHUMACHER 1m 18.313s

12 FISICHELLA 1m 18.385s

11 R SCHUMACHER 1m 18.423s

16 HERBERT 1m 18.494s

6 IRVINE 1m 18.873s

14 PANIS 1m 19.157s

17 MORBIDELLI 1m 19.323s

19 SALO 1m 20.079s

1 HILL 1m 20.089s

15 NAKANO 1m 20.103s

22 BARRICHELLO 1m 20.255s

21 TRULLI 1m 20.452s

18 VERSTAPPEN 1m 20.582s

20 KATAYAMA 1m 20.672s

2 DINIZ 1m 21.029s

23 MAGNUSSEN 1m 21.060s

FIA FORMULA 1 WORLD CHAMPIONSHIP results

25 May 1997. Circuit de Catalunya, Montmelo, Barcelona. Circuit length: 2.938miles /4.728km

ROUND 6

RACE CLASSIFICATION

Pos	Driver	Nat	Car	Laps	Time
1	Jacques Villeneuve	CDN	Williams FW19-Renault V10	64	1h30m35.896s
2	Olivier Panis	F	Prost JS45-Mugen Honda V10	64	+5.804s
3	Jean Alesi	F	Benetton B197-Renault V10	64	+12.534s
4	Michael Schumacher	D	Ferrari F310B-Ferrari V10	64	+17.979s
5	Johnny Herbert	GB	Sauber C16-Petronas V10	64	+27.986s
6	David Coulthard	GB	McLaren MP4/12-Mercedes V10	64	+29.744s
7	Mika Hakkinen	FIN	McLaren MP4/12-Mercedes V10	64	+48.785s
8	Heinz-Harald Frentzen	D	Williams FW19-Renault V10	64	+1m 04.139s
9	Giancarlo Fisichella	I	Jordan 197-Peugeot V10	64	+1m 04.767s
10	Gerhard Berger	A	Benetton B197-Renault V10	64	+1m 05.670s
11	Jos Verstappen	NL	Tyrrell 025-Ford V8		+1 lap
12	Eddie Irvine	GB	Ferrari F310B-Ferrari V10		+1 lap
13	Jan Magnussen	DK	Stewart SF-1-Ford V10		+1 lap
14	Gianni Morbidelli	I	Sauber C16-Petronas V10		+2 laps
15	Jarno Trulli	I	Minardi M197-Hart V8		+2 laps

Retirements	Nat	Car	Laps	Reason
Pedro Diniz	BR	Arrows A18-Yamaha V10	53	engine
Ralf Schumacher	D	Jordan 197-Peugeot V10	50	oil leak/ engine
Rubens Barrichello	BR	Stewart SF-1-Ford V10	37	engine
Mika Salo	FIN	Tyrrell 025-Ford V8	35	puncture
Shinji Nakano	J	Prost JS45-Mugen Honda V10	34	gearbox
Damon Hill	GB	Arrows A18-Yamaha V10	18	oil pressure
Ukyo Katayama	J	Minardi M197-Hart V8	11	gearbox

FASTEST LAP G Fisichella 1m22.242s lap 20 (128.599mph/206.960kmh)

DRIVERS' CHAMPIONSHIP

Jacques Villeneuve	30
Michael Schumacher	27
Olivier Panis	15
Eddie Irvine	14
David Coulthard	11
Gerhard Berger	10
Heinz-Harald Frentzen	10
Mika Hakkinen	10
Jean Alesi	7
Rubens Barrichello	6
Johnny Herbert	5
Giancarlo Fisichella	4
Ralf Schumacher	4
Mika Salo	2
Nicola Larini	1

CONSTRUCTORS' CHAMPIONSHIP

Ferrari	41
Williams-Renault	40
McLaren-Mercedes	21
Benetton-Renault	17
Prost-Mugen Honda	15
Jordan-Peugeot	8
Sauber-Petronas	6
Stewart-Ford	6
Tyrrell-Ford	2

grand prix player's du

canada

panis breaks **legs** horror **shunt**
misfortune ● villeneuve **throw**

Contrasting fortunes: while Michael Schumacher celebrates (left) what should unquestionably have been David Coulthard's victory, th

schumacher cashes in on coulthard's away in front of home crowd

with Olivier Panis . Third in the championship, the Frenchman (right) was going to be out of action for some time with leg injuries.

grand prix year 1997

Schumacher leads Villeneuve, Fisichella and Alesi at the start (above). Three of the four discussed Panis's accident when the race was abandoned (right). Villeneuve couldn't join them: he'd disappointed the home contingent by flying off the road on lap two.

david Coulthard should have won the Canadian Grand Prix. He knew it, Michael Schumacher knew it, but by the end of a manic Sunday in Montreal neither particularly seemed to care. Both were occupied by more sobering thoughts, prompted by a 150mph accident which left Olivier Panis in hospital with two broken legs and brought the race to a shuddering halt 13 laps early.

Almost up to that point the race was heading inexorably towards Coulthard and McLaren. The resurfaced Circuit Gilles Villeneuve had caught Goodyear on the hop and most of its drivers spent the race popping in and out of the pits, exchanging tyre after blistered tyre.

Not DC, though. With the sort of discipline normally reserved for men of the Gregorian persuasion, he managed to eke out over half of the race distance on his first set of rubber while still going quickly enough to nail down the race lead. With a pit stop in hand, he was cruising towards victory before disaster struck when he made a precautionary stop which delayed him for around a minute and handed victory to Schumacher.

For his rivals, it was one long hard struggle. Or a short one, if you were Jacques Villeneuve. The track which bears his family name gave him a swift kick in the groin as he deposited his Williams

> "david **coulthard should** have **won** the **canadian** grand prix. he **knew** it, michael **schumacher** knew it"

58

into the barriers while chasing early leader Schumacher on only the second lap. It was an embarrassing mistake in front of partisan crowd and a costly one for Williams, since within a handful of laps Heinz-Harald Frentzen had done enough damage to his tyres to force an early pit stop which confined him to fourth.

Schumacher was equally afflicted and had long since settled for second when the race fell into his lap. But with Panis

being airlifted to hospital, his condition then unclear, it made for hollow celebrations.

You had to feel for Giancarlo Fisichella, forced to contain his enthusiasm after an excellent drive during which his Jordan had harried Schumacher in the early stages. He was ultimately dislodged from second by Jean Alesi.

Not only had Alesi to overcome

panis gives cause for concern

Any serious shunt is thought-provoking and Olivier Panis's Canadian smash was no different.

It was bad enough having to look on haplessly as the Montreal marshals committed the major medical no-no of hauling Panis from the wreckage of his Prost before the emergency services arrived.

The drivers, circulating for three laps behind the Safety Car, could only draw their own conclusions from the sight of FIA Medical Delegate Sid Watkins and his team treating Panis at the trackside.

The accident was easy enough to explain. Olivier had become entangled in the first-lap fracas which removed Hakkinen from proceedings – a mêlée which had left the Frenchman at the tail of the field. While he stormed back up the order, still hoping for a points finish, he brushed a guardrail not far from the site of his accident on lap 43. Both incidents provided scope for incurring minor, yet potentially significant, damage.

Eight laps later, as Panis entered the Turn 4A-5 sequence – usually an easy fourth-gear, 150mph left-right jink – the rear end of his Prost snapped round sideways as if he'd put a wheel on a patch of invisible grass. The car smacked the wall on the inside of the corner nose-on, which sent it plunging towards the tyre barriers on the exit of the corner at what seemed like unabated pace.

The impact was massive and tyres

were sprayed like shrapnel all over the stricken Panis. Amazingly, he remained conscious throughout – hence his rather forceful suggestions to the marshals on the scene that he'd like to get out of the car, thank you very much. . .

Prost later stated that a broken left-rear suspension component was to blame – a diagnosis contradicted only by Panis himself, who reckoned he'd heard a noise from the back of the JS45-Mugen Honda.

"It was as if the transmission or gearbox had broken," he said. "The car free-wheeled and then it started to spin."

Hearteningly, two months later Panis was back in the paddock under his own steam, making excellent progress on his mending legs and gesturing provocatively to all and sundry from the pillion of a scooter. For a few moments back in June, the picture had looked very different.

Fisichella, he faced a new, youthful threat from within his own team: Benetton test driver Alexander Wurz, subbing for Gerhard Berger who produced a sick note on account of severe sinusitis. Wurz's first task was to give Alesi a wake-up call – by coming within a sniff of outqualifying him.

But it was nothing compared to the jolt administered by Panis's accident.

All that time it takes to screw together a Jordan. . . and Ralf Schumacher reverses the process in a matter of nanoseconds.

silver
arrows'
outrageous
fortune

While Panis' on-screen agony captivated attention, David Coulthard had minutes earlier been snared by a less physical form of sufferance.

At the conclusion of his second pit stop, a mere precaution which his copious lead allowed, the Scot's McLaren edged forward. All of two inches. Cue a wave of hands from Coulthard and frantic activity at the back of the car. A brief burst of distressed Mercedes engine, but no movement – unless you count the sinking of hearts among the Scot's fans, of whom there are many.

By the time Coulthard was able to fire the car up properly and pull away from his pit, ITV had long enough to schedule an ad break and comment from Simon and Tony. The race had just passed from McLaren's hands to Ferrari's: the beneficiary was Schumacher, whose tyre troubles made him a more likely candidate to receive Kwik-Fit vouchers for his next birthday than the 24th F1 win of his career.

Coulthard, meanwhile rejoined seventh, with no chance of the podium or, as it turned out, any points.

So what happened? "When I put it in gear it stalled straight away and when we started it back up again we had a problem resetting the electrics," he related. "That gave it 100 per cent throttle a few times. Then it stalled again. Finally, when it was cool enough, I got a gear and pulled away."

The incident's timing was cruel. Coulthard already had Schumacher well tucked up – the Ferrari had just pitted unexpectedly for a fourth set of rubber –and the race appeared to have doffed its cap and bowed to DC. So much so, in fact, that McLaren decided to call him in for tyres because Coulthard's Goodyears were starting to blister and the team figured it had time on its side.

To cap it all, within two laps the race was over anyway, thanks to Panis' explosive interface with the barriers.

Coulthard had the consolation of demonstrating that he and McLaren were still a force to be reckoned with and that Mercedes' latest F-type engine was smack on the pace.

Some consolation.

"That's that, basically," he concluded with a wry smile. "We led, we led handsomely and yet we ended up without a point."

At least he had proved one.

5 M SCHUMACHER 1m 18.095s

3 VILLENEUVE 1m 18.108s

22 BARRICHELLO 1m 18.388s

4 FRENTZEN 1m 18.464s

10 COULTHARD 1m 18.466s

12 FISICHELLA 1m 18.750s

11 R SCHUMACHER 1m 18.869s

7 ALESI 1m 18.899s

9 HAKKINEN 1m 18.916s

14 PANIS 1m 19.034s

8 WURZ 1m 19.286s

6 IRVINE 1m 19.503s

16 HERBERT 1m 19.622s

18 VERSTAPPEN 1m 20.102s

1 HILL 1m 20.129s

2 DINIZ 1m 20.175s

19 SALO 1m 20.336s

17 MORBIDELLI 1m 20.357s

15 NAKANO 1m 20.370s

21 TRULLI 1m 20.370s

23 MAGNUSSEN 1m 20.491s

20 KATAYAMA 1m 21.034s

results

15 June 1997. Circuit Gilles Villeneuve, Ile Notre Dame, Montreal. Circuit length: 2.747miles/4.421km

ROUND 7

Pits Hairpin

Island Hairpin

RACE CLASSIFICATION

Pos	Driver	Nat	Car	Laps	Time
1	Michael Schumacher	D	Ferrari F310B-Ferrari V10	54	1h17m40.646s
2	Jean Alesi	F	Benetton B197-Renault V10	54	+2.565s
3	Giancarlo Fisichella	I	Jordan 197-Peugeot V10	54	+3.219s
4	Heinz-Harald Frentzen	D	Williams FW19-Renault V10	54	+3.768s
5	Johnny Herbert	GB	Sauber C16-Petronas V10	54	+4.716s
6	Shinji Nakano	J	Prost JS45-Mugen Honda V10	54	+36.701s
7	David Coulthard	GB	McLaren MP4/12-Mercedes V10	54	+37.753s
8	Pedro Diniz	BR	Arrows A18-Yamaha V10		+1 lap
9	Damon Hill	GB	Arrows A18-Yamaha V10		+1 lap
10	Gianni Morbidelli	I	Sauber C16-Petronas V10		+1 lap
11	Olivier Panis	F	Prost JS45-Mugen Honda V10		+3 laps

Retirements	Nat	Car	Laps	Reason
Mika Salo	FIN	Tyrrell 025-Ford V8	46	engine
Jos Verstappen	NL	Tyrrell 025-Ford V8	42	gearbox
Alex Wurz	A	Benetton B197-Renault V10	35	transmission
Rubens Barrichello	BR	Stewart SF-1-Ford V10	33	gearbox
Jarno Trulli	I	Minardi M197-Hart V8	32	engine
Ralf Schumacher	D	Jordan 197-Peugeot V10	14	accident
Ukyo Katayama	J	Minardi M197-Hart V8	5	accident
Jacques Villeneuve	CDN	Williams FW19-Renault V10	1	accident
Eddie Irvine	GB	Ferrari F310B-Ferrari V10	0	spin
Mika Hakkinen	FIN	McLaren MP4/12-Mercedes V10	0	accident
Jan Magnussen	DK	Stewart SF-1-Ford V10	0	accident

FASTEST LAP   D Coulthard 1m19.635s lap 37 (124.185 mph/199.857kmh)

DRIVERS' CHAMPIONSHIP

Michael Schumacher	37
Jacques Villeneuve	30
Olivier Panis	15
Eddie Irvine	14
Jean Alesi	13
Heinz-Harald Frentzen	13
David Coulthard	11
Gerhard Berger	10
Mika Hakkinen	10
Giancarlo Fisichella	8
Johnny Herbert	7
Rubens Barrichello	6
Ralf Schumacher	4
Mika Salo	2
Nicola Larini	1
Shinji Nakano	1

CONSTRUCTORS' CHAMPIONSHIP

Ferrari	51
Williams-Renault	43
Benetton-Renault	23
McLaren-Mercedes	21
Prost-Mugen Honda	16
Jordan-Peugeot	12
Sauber-Petronas	8
Stewart-Ford	6
Tyrrell-Ford	2

grand prix de france 8

ferrari gives williams **surprise** trouncing
● rookie **wurz stuns** alesi ● **villeneuv**

OFFICIA[L]

te shower provides **thrills**
es his hair. . . yellow!

Let's prance: Schumacher
and the Ferrari team
celebrate another spot-on
piece of weather forecasting
by rival Williams.

michael Schumacher strode through parc fermé, chin jutting proudly, with a big, satisfied grin adorning his chops. He could afford to smile, because his French GP victory had just provided conclusive proof of what many suspected and quite a few feared

Ferrari was back.

And this time it wasn't purely personal.

While Schumacher's virtuoso triumph in Monaco was more down to his own brilliance than it was the F310B chassis' competitiveness, Magny-Cours under-lined that his team was increasingly a force to be reckoned with.

Not only did Schumacher take pole, victory and fastest lap, but team-mate Eddie Irvine split the Williams-Renaults of Frentzen and Villeneuve all race in third place. Eddie was troubled for the most part by nothing more than boredom. Not to put too fine a point on it, Ferrari had thrashed Williams at a track whose technical

> **"not only did schumacher take pole, victory and fastest lap, but team-mate eddie irvine split the williams-renaults"**

nature suggested that the FW19s would hand out a drubbing of their own.

All weekend Schumacher made rather unconvincing exclamations of surprise at his team's competitiveness. Come Sunday evening, several members of the Williams camp would no doubt have liked to tell him where to stick his

Double Deutsch: Schumacher and Frentzen set the pace as the Ferrari man tries in vain to justify his pre-race allegations that his car was more rocking horse than Prancing Horse.

Equity card. Frentzen and Villeneuve were both hampered by cars set up in anticipation of rain, but that didn't arrive until long after Williams' in-house barometer had forecast.

By then Schumacher had trotted off into the sunset on his Prancing Horse.

Perversely, the damp served to ignite a real yawn-a-minute contest on the very final lap. But Williams would have

not so mello

Villeneuve's arrival in France was her-alded by a startling new blonde hairdo. By Sunday, however, it appeared there was something even more yellow about his face. Like egg-yolk.

If Canada had been a bitter disappointment, events at Magny-Cours suggested that Jacques was digging himself deeper into the rut, not out of it. That he arrived looking like an extra from *Quadrophenia* could not disguise the fact that Ferrari's improving form had put Williams on its back foot. For the first time all season Villeneuve was not required to attend the post-qualifying press conference. He wound up a curiously subdued fourth, the direct result of a substantial accident during Saturday morning free practice which mangled his preferred race chassis and bruised his back.

He needed to prepare himself, more-over, for a possible battering to his ego. The previous Thursday, Villeneuve had been in fine form at Williams' pre-event media briefing, delivering a few tabloid nuggets from heaven by suggesting that fellow drivers hadn't really given a stuff about Olivier Panis's Canadian accident. And he couldn't see what all the fuss over a couple of broken legs was about anyway.

"I don't like how politically correct F1 has become, and how when someone

needed a hurricane, not a shower, to dislodge Schumacher from the lead.

The German had doubled an initial seven-second advantage over Frentzen when Heinz-Harald was (inadvertently) baulked by Irvine at the first round of pit stops. And the leader was content to tip-toe round on slicks during the final 15 laps, when it finally rained. Frentzen, knowing that a pit stop would ruin his chances of victory altogether, was damned if he came in and damned if he didn't. Staying out nearly paid off for him – the leading Ferrari briefly tripped the light fantastic across the gravel at Estoril corner – but no result other than a Schumacher victory would have been just.

The real excitement was behind, thanks to two men who did stop for tyres: Irvine and Villeneuve. Jacques managed to

Jacques Villeneuve's judgment failed him when he stuffed his preferred race car; some said the same was true when he last visited his barber.

yellow

has an accident everybody will act as if they were really sad when they really don't care," he frowned. If he were to be killed during a race, he added, he would want the show to go on.

It wasn't exactly Kevin Keegan on Alex Ferguson, but it provoked an outraged reaction. Some observers, such as Jackie Stewart, felt that if Villeneuve was right in some respects, his timing wasn't one of them. The word was that his employer was less than impressed and that he had been summoned for a carpeting on Saturday night. The fact that he had also hinted to the French press that he was being forced up a series of blind alley set-ups by Williams didn't curry much favour, either.

Ultimately the team did go the wrong way for the race, compromising Villeneuve's set-up in the hope of a rain shower which only materialised in the closing stages. Too late to give him a realistic chance of beating Irvine to the podium – and too late to stop an inevitable rash of 'Has Jacques lost it?' stories from making the news.

drop three places with a timid 'in' lap, made them up in the final two laps and then latched onto the third-placed Ferrari's tail. All of which made the BTCC-style final-corner lunge for a non-existent gap inside Eddie semi-understandable. It wasn't rewarded – Villeneuve spun into the pit lane and had to be content with fourth – but that was par for the course after a generally miserable weekend for the French-Canadian.

Coulthard also had cause to look glum after being nerfed into the gravel by Alesi on that thoroughly entertaining final tour. When Schumacher took pity on adventurous younger brother Ralf and allowed him to unlap himself within sight of the flag, it allowed Schmacher II to pass the stranded Scot and deprive DC of any points for the second race in succession. David's customary good humour also went missing for a while.

In the predominantly blue corner...his father was ace at rallycross, he himself was a past world champion on a mountain bike and now he'd mastered the art of forcing Franco-Sicilians to sulk. A good weekend's work for Alex Wurz, all in all.

wurz
case scenario

Compare and contrast the following words and actions, simultaneously made by two drivers from the same team.

Driver one walks through the paddock looking sulky, scowling at waiting journalists: "I have very little to say. I am sorry to have disappointed my public."

Driver two cheerfully answers a string of banal enquiries, pausing only to pull a few wheelies on a mountain bike for a team photo shoot: "I'm comfortable, but it could have been better."

The drivers are, respectively, Benetton's Jean Alesi and Alex Wurz, in the aftermath of a qualifying session in which the 23-year-old Austrian got the better of his mercurial team-mate by three-tenths. In only his second grand prix.

The reason for Alesi's discomfort was obvious. Since the Benetton reserve driver Wurz had been co-opted into the race team's ranks to sub for the sinus-stricken Gerhard Berger, he had qualified within a tenth of Jean in Canada, despite having zero prior experience

of the track. Now he had put one over him in his own backyard. The feeling in some quarters was that Alesi and Berger had been rumbled; that 18 months of going through the motions were being shown up by the efforts of an enthusiastic youngster with minimal F1 experience.

That wasn't quite true: Wurz could point to well over 1,500 test miles for the Enstone team, during which time he had impressed sufficiently with his speed, application and feedback to earn Berger's berth when his compatriot handed in a sick note. But for a driver who had last raced a single-seater (and that an F3 car) in 1995, he was performing outstandingly well.

It was enough to spur Alesi into raising his game.

While he had quickly faded from the picture in Canada, Wurz held on doggedly ahead of Jean in France until a botched pit stop and, finally, a spin left him on the sidelines. Jean, meanwhile, shot up to fifth, aided by a last-lap challenge on Coulthard that was ruder than it was optimistic.

Jean was repentant. Sort of. "I have apologised to him [Coulthard]," he admitted. "I know I am aggressive, but in that incident I was not doing anything out of order at all."

Whether you agreed with him or not, there was no doubting the fire in his belly. Nor who had ignited it.

66

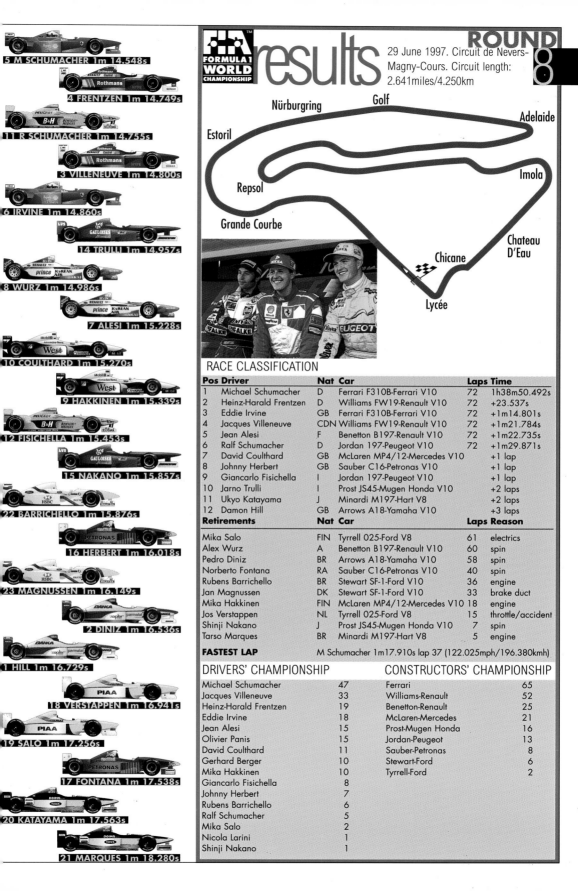

5 M SCHUMACHER 1m 14.548s

4 FRENTZEN 1m 14.749s

11 R SCHUMACHER 1m 14.755s

3 VILLENEUVE 1m 14.800s

6 IRVINE 1m 14.860s

14 TRULLI 1m 14.957s

8 WURZ 1m 14.986s

7 ALESI 1m 15.228s

10 COULTHARD 1m 15.270s

9 HAKKINEN 1m 15.339s

12 FISICHELLA 1m 15.453s

15 NAKANO 1m 15.857s

22 BARRICHELLO 1m 15.876s

16 HERBERT 1m 16.018s

23 MAGNUSSEN 1m 16.149s

2 DINIZ 1m 16.536s

1 HILL 1m 16.729s

18 VERSTAPPEN 1m 16.941s

19 SALO 1m 17.256s

17 FONTANA 1m 17.538s

20 KATAYAMA 1m 17.563s

21 MARQUES 1m 18.280s

FIA FORMULA 1 WORLD CHAMPIONSHIP results

ROUND 8

29 June 1997. Circuit de Nevers-Magny-Cours. Circuit length: 2.641miles/4.250km

Nürburgring · Golf · Adelaide · Estoril · Imola · Repsol · Grande Courbe · Chateau D'Eau · Chicane · Lycée

RACE CLASSIFICATION

Pos	Driver	Nat	Car	Laps	Time
1	Michael Schumacher	D	Ferrari F310B-Ferrari V10	72	1h38m50.492s
2	Heinz-Harald Frentzen	D	Williams FW19-Renault V10	72	+23.537s
3	Eddie Irvine	GB	Ferrari F310B-Ferrari V10	72	+1m14.801s
4	Jacques Villeneuve	CDN	Williams FW19-Renault V10	72	+1m21.784s
5	Jean Alesi	F	Benetton B197-Renault V10	72	+1m22.735s
6	Ralf Schumacher	D	Jordan 197-Peugeot V10	72	+1m29.871s
7	David Coulthard	GB	McLaren MP4/12-Mercedes V10		+1 lap
8	Johnny Herbert	GB	Sauber C16-Petronas V10		+1 lap
9	Giancarlo Fisichella	I	Jordan 197-Peugeot V10		+1 lap
10	Jarno Trulli	I	Prost JS45-Mugen Honda V10		+2 laps
11	Ukyo Katayama	J	Minardi M197-Hart V8		+2 laps
12	Damon Hill	GB	Arrows A18-Yamaha V10		+3 laps

Retirements	Nat	Car	Laps	Reason
Mika Salo	FIN	Tyrrell 025-Ford V8	61	electrics
Alex Wurz	A	Benetton B197-Renault V10	60	spin
Pedro Diniz	BR	Arrows A18-Yamaha V10	58	spin
Norberto Fontana	RA	Sauber C16-Petronas V10	40	spin
Rubens Barrichello	BR	Stewart SF-1-Ford V10	36	engine
Jan Magnussen	DK	Stewart SF-1-Ford V10	33	brake duct
Mika Hakkinen	FIN	McLaren MP4/12-Mercedes V10	18	engine
Jos Verstappen	NL	Tyrrell 025-Ford V8	15	throttle/accident
Shinji Nakano	J	Prost JS45-Mugen Honda V10	7	spin
Tarso Marques	BR	Minardi M197-Hart V8	5	engine

FASTEST LAP   M Schumacher 1m17.910s lap 37 (122.025mph/196.380kmh)

DRIVERS' CHAMPIONSHIP

Michael Schumacher	47
Jacques Villeneuve	33
Heinz-Harald Frentzen	19
Eddie Irvine	18
Jean Alesi	15
Olivier Panis	15
David Coulthard	11
Gerhard Berger	10
Mika Hakkinen	10
Giancarlo Fisichella	8
Johnny Herbert	7
Rubens Barrichello	6
Ralf Schumacher	5
Mika Salo	2
Nicola Larini	1
Shinji Nakano	1

CONSTRUCTORS' CHAMPIONSHIP

Ferrari	65
Williams-Renault	52
Benetton-Renault	25
McLaren-Mercedes	21
Prost-Mugen Honda	16
Jordan-Peugeot	13
Sauber-Petronas	8
Stewart-Ford	6
Tyrrell-Ford	2

villeneuve back on **top**, just ● schumacher and
to suffer **mechanical** failures ●**damon** sco

Running a natty line in fluorescent orange brake discs, the delayed Villeneuve hares after Hakkinen (left). The Finn's prayers went unanswered (above), his Mercedes V10 going pop when that first F1 win was once again in sight. While all that was going on, most of the crowd were cheering for a bloke whose victory prospects were no greater than those of a blown Mercedes.

race
british
9
kkinen lead only grand prix
arrows at last

grand prix year 1997

Jacques Villeneuve had plenty of time to think about his British Grand Prix pros-pects – about one-third of the way into the race, to be precise.

As is customary at Silverstone, Williams had taken pole position, Villeneuve beating team-mate Heinz-Harald Frentzen. Not since Nigel Mansell did the job for Ferrari in 1990 had any other team headed British GP qualifying, in fact.

In the race it was a different story. Villeneuve led the Ferrari of world championship leader Michael Schumacher, but not by much. In race trim the Ferrari was competitive and Schumacher assumed control at the first round of scheduled pit stops.

In had come Villeneuve, down the pit lane, on the speed limiter, into his pit and. . . still in his pit and. . . still in his pit. For 25 seconds the Williams crew wrestled with a front left wheel nut that was stuck fast. The nut had worked loose and ground itself away against the security device which prevents it becoming detached.

A similar problem had afflicted Damon Hill 12 months earlier, but that time the wheel had folded and Hill had been pitched off the road. On that occasion, Villeneuve won.

A repeat result looked out of the question by the time the problem was resolved.

It had already been a bad day for Williams, with Frentzen packed to the back of the class for causing the first start to be aborted by stalling. The German was then involved in a first-lap accident which put him out. Villeneuve rejoined the race a distant seventh but there would be two fallible factors to take into account: Ferrari and McLaren.

The McLaren of David Coulthard had held third from the start and was holding up most of the drivers behind him, the last of whom was the delayed Villeneuve, running at the back of a pack of cars all of whom had one stop to make – just as he now did. Coulthard's lethargy – his ill-handling car was eating its tyres – was an asset to the French-Canadian, although it may not have felt like it at the time, what with Schumacher racing away at the front.

However, the German was stopped by a failed left rear wheel bearing just as he appeared to be cruising to victory.

Villeneuve was back in the hunt. All of the serious contenders on a one-stop strategy – notably the Benettons of Jean Alesi and Alexander Wurz – had been stuck

> "what **goes** around **comes** around; we've **all** had bad **luck**, it's time **other** people had some"
>
> **jacques villeneuve**

behind Coulthard.

The one man who had – eventually – passed the struggling Scot was his team-mate Hakkinen. When all the fuel stops were done, and with Schumacher reduced to spectating, the Finn led by several seconds as Villeneuve returned to the circuit after his second scheduled stop (a routine affair).

On fresher tyres, the French-Canadian had caught the McLaren and was swarming all over it when the Finn's engine blew up with seven laps to go. Would he have got past otherwise?

"I don't think so," said Hakkinen. "I could control him."

Villeneuve wasn't so sure. "He was beginning to slide more and more," he said. "I could have made a move but it would have been difficult."

In the end, he didn't have to assess the potential difficulty

the gloves are off –and in about row six

Consider the reaction of most men who have just had a grand prix victory snatched from within their grasp. Remember Damon Hill at Silverstone in 1993, apparently on course for a maiden F1 success when his engine blew?

The chastened Englishman waved a kick in the direction of his Williams' rear end before stomping off – not unreasonably – for a pint in the British Racing Drivers Club suite, which happened to be on his way back to the pits.

Or Jean Alesi at Monza in 1994, stalking away from the circuit with body language so dark that nobody should have been surprised that he subsequently got from Milan to Avignon at a speed which would have made sound sweat. And he was using public roads.

Mika Hakkinen was even closer to a first F1 triumph than Hill or Alesi had been, his McLaren leading Jacques Villeneuve's Williams by just centimetres when his engine blew with seven laps to go.

The Finn parked at The Vale, hopped out and, rather than remonstrate with the failed piece of engineering alongside, he gave a gesture worthy of a winning FA Cup captain, turning to the crowd and waving both arms aloft in apparent triumph.

"I was happy that I'd driven well," he said. "It wasn't my fault I didn't win. It just happened, bang."

The adjacent crowd applauded warmly at his generosity in defeat and he rewarded them by pitching his racing gloves into the throng. He then blew his nose on his balaclava and, equally generously, kept that to himself.

His glorious failure had a side benefit. In the weeks leading up to the race the speculation was that McLaren would be ditching one of its drivers in 1998 and that Hakkinen was odds-on to get the chop. McLaren chief Ron Dennis had never lost faith with the Finn, but Mika's performance at Silverstone caught the attention of some of those who might just have been starting to do so.

factor. He cruised past the stranded Hakkinen to accept the gift of a second straight British GP victory, 10 seconds clear of the Benettons of Alesi and Wurz which had run in tandem all race. Did he have any sympathy for Hakkinen?

"You're not here to be nice to the other guys," he said. "What goes around comes around; we've all had bad luck, it's time other people had some. We are where we should have been at the beginning."

We'll take that as a 'No'.

The British press might have been interested mainly in those whose passports contained a juxtaposition of the words 'Damon' and 'Hill' but away from the headlines the best Brit was Coulthard, who came home fourth after struggling with his chassis for most of the afternoon.

David just held off Ralf Schumacher's Jordan, but it wasn't until about 40 seconds later that the crowd raised its loudest cheer of the day.

He used to get cheered for leading the British GP. Maybe that day will return; for now, Damon Hill had the novel experience of being cheered wildly for lumbering around in the lower reaches of the top 10 and scraping an unexpected point.

hill
responds to the
sound
of the crowd

team what the problem was and could only deduce from their stony lack of response that there had been some dreadful cataclysm. The fact that his radio was awash with high-grade energy drink and, therefore, only partly operative wasn't immediately apparent to him.

As the race wore on, the liquid dried up, communications improved a little and so did Hill's chances of a first world championship point.

Running 12th in the opening stages, Hill progressed eventually to seventh as others fell by the wayside. He was closing on sixth-placed Shinji Nakano when the Japanese driver's engine blew up just two laps from home.

"I didn't think I'd have caught him," said Damon. "I was pushing because there was a chance I might rattle him in the last few laps but he was just too far away."

Cheered to the rafters from the start, his right hand spent as much time waving to the crowd as it did on the steering wheel during the last couple of laps. Possibly for the first time in British GP history, the biggest roar from the spectators was reserved for the bloke in sixth place.

It was a sweet end to a weekend in which the national tabloid media had done everything from hinting that he was about to be sacked to suggesting he had turned sumo wrestler on the man from the *Mirror*.

"I was motivated more by the support I've had from the genuine fans than anything that might have gone on in the papers," pointed out Damon.

Actually, the sound of the crowd was one of the few things Damon Hill could respond to as he performed before his adoring public for the first time as reigning world champion.

Certainly, his pits-to-car radio was about as effective as a length of string and a couple of cocoa tins. On the warm-up lap a pipe leading to his drinks bottle had split and sprayed the radio's electric innards. As a result he could hear the team – intermittently – but they couldn't hear him. After the aborted first start – caused when Heinz-Harald Frentzen stalled his Williams – Hill sat on the grid asking the Arrows

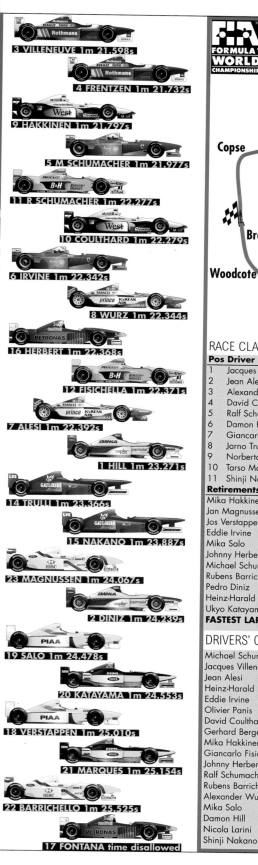

3 VILLENEUVE 1m 21.598s

4 FRENTZEN 1m 21.732s

9 HAKKINEN 1m 21.797s

5 M SCHUMACHER 1m 21.977s

11 R SCHUMACHER 1m 22.277s

10 COULTHARD 1m 22.279s

6 IRVINE 1m 22.342s

8 WURZ 1m 22.344s

16 HERBERT 1m 22.368s

12 FISICHELLA 1m 22.371s

7 ALESI 1m 22.392s

1 HILL 1m 23.271s

14 TRULLI 1m 23.466s

15 NAKANO 1m 23.887s

23 MAGNUSSEN 1m 24.067s

2 DINIZ 1m 24.239s

19 SALO 1m 24.478s

20 KATAYAMA 1m 24.553s

18 VERSTAPPEN 1m 25.010s

21 MARQUES 1m 25.154s

22 BARRICHELLO 1m 25.525s

17 FONTANA time disallowed

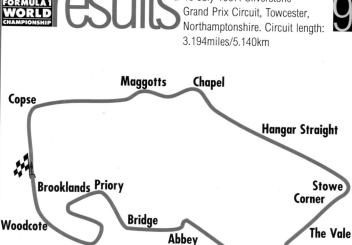

Copse
Maggotts   Chapel
Hangar Straight
Brooklands Priory
Stowe Corner
Woodcote
Bridge
The Vale
Luffield
Abbey Curve
Club Corner

RACE CLASSIFICATION

Pos	Driver	Nat	Car	Laps	Time
1	Jacques Villeneuve	CDN	Williams FW19-Renault V10	59	1h28m01.665s
2	Jean Alesi	F	Benetton B197-Renault V10	59	+10.205s
3	Alexander Wurz	A	Benetton B197-Renault V10	59	+11.296s
4	David Coulthard	GB	McLaren MP4/12-Mercedes V10	59	+31.229s
5	Ralf Schumacher	D	Jordan 197-Peugeot V10	59	+31.880s
6	Damon Hill	GB	Arrows A18-Yamaha V10	59	+1m13.552s
7	Giancarlo Fisichella	I	Jordan 197-Peugeot V10		+1 lap
8	Jarno Trulli	I	Prost JS45-Mugen Honda V10		+1 lap
9	Norberto Fontana	RA	Sauber C16-Petronas V10		+1 lap
10	Tarso Marques	BR	Minardi M197-Hart V8		+1 lap
11	Shinji Nakano	J	Prost JS45-Mugen Honda V10		+2 laps

Retirements	Nat	Car	Laps	Reason
Mika Hakkinen	FIN	McLaren MP4/12-Mercedes V10	52	engine
Jan Magnussen	DK	Stewart SF-1-Ford V10	50	engine
Jos Verstappen	NL	Tyrrell 025-Ford V8	45	engine
Eddie Irvine	GB	Ferrari F310B-Ferrari V10	44	transmission
Mika Salo	FIN	Tyrrell 025-Ford V8	44	engine
Johnny Herbert	GB	Sauber C16-Petronas V10	42	electronics
Michael Schumacher	D	Ferrari F310B-Ferrari V10	38	wheel bearing
Rubens Barrichello	BR	Stewart SF-1-Ford V10	37	engine
Pedro Diniz	BR	Arrows A18-Yamaha V10	29	engine
Heinz-Harald Frentzen	D	Williams FW19-Renault V10	0	accident
Ukyo Katayama	J	Minardi M197-Hart V8	0	accident
FASTEST LAP		M Schumacher 1m24.475s lap 34 (136.110 mph/219.047kmh)		

DRIVERS' CHAMPIONSHIP

Michael Schumacher	47
Jacques Villeneuve	43
Jean Alesi	21
Heinz-Harald Frentzen	19
Eddie Irvine	18
Olivier Panis	15
David Coulthard	14
Gerhard Berger	10
Mika Hakkinen	10
Giancarlo Fisichella	8
Johnny Herbert	7
Ralf Schumacher	7
Rubens Barrichello	6
Alexander Wurz	4
Mika Salo	2
Damon Hill	1
Nicola Larini	1
Shinji Nakano	1

CONSTRUCTORS' CHAMPIONSHIP

Ferrari	65
Williams-Renault	62
Benetton-Renault	35
McLaren-Mercedes	24
Prost-Mugen Honda	16
Jordan-Peugeot	15
Sauber-Petronas	8
Stewart-Ford	6
Tyrrell-Ford	2
Arrows-Yamaha	1

with two wins to his credit and fourth position in the championship, david coulthard was the most successful UK driver in 1997 – but there's more to F1 than merely beating your compatriots. so how did he view his season?

hink German music and the chances are that you'll arrive at one of two extremes: the brassy clamour of an oompah band or the subtler, occasionally melodic electro-automatism of Kraftwerk.

Unless, of course, you happen to be at the Mercedes-Benz motorhome – particularly if there's a whiff of Formula One success in the air. After Coulthard's victory at Monza in September it was Manfred Mann, *Davy's on the Road Again*, the most fitting anthem that could be found in Merc competition

best of... british

name-checking anyone called Mika.

While the champagne-soaked Hakkinen was still in his overalls, lapping up every moment in the wake of his first Formula One success, the showered and changed Coulthard was perched on the terrace of the adjacent McLaren motorhome, struggling to make himself heard over the cacophony of Norbert's would-be Nitespot.

The year started with his first victory for McLaren and the marque's first for 50 races, but progress was sometimes as rough as the music next door. . .

What are your impressions of the year as a whole?

"I'm satisfied with the fact I've won two grands prix but there should have been more, such as Canada. I finished fourth in the championship, which is reasonably okay, but I had a couple of bad races where I struggled a bit, particularly in Brazil and Japan.

chief Norbert Haug's extensive CD collection. Never mind Monza, the refrain could have been heard in Mombassa.

It had been the same in Melbourne, it would be the same again in Jerez – even if there are no Seventies rock songs

75

Generally I'd say I've every reason to be happy."

At the start of the year you were quoted at 16/1 to win the Australian Grand Prix – several drivers carried shorter odds to win the title, let alone one race. Did you think that was a bleak view?

"We always hoped there would be wins and the ones we got were pretty good – they weren't gifted to us. That makes me believe we've done a little

getting yourself in the best package and wringing its neck is concerned, no one could say that Jacques doesn't try. He gets stuck in, he's a racer and he qualifies well. He took a gamble in Jerez, he came down the inside of Michael, who calmly tried to squeeze him out. For it to end in that way I think swings it way back in Jacques' favour and I think he deserves to be champion."

Michael Schumacher is everyone's greatest adversary. What makes him so formidable?

"He's good in every department. There are no big weaknesses in his package. I don't think he's exceptional in one area that makes him head and shoulders

"in terms of **pure racing** i think i'm a **match** for him (michael **schumacher**). that's an area where i think i've traditionally been **strong**"

better than I had expected at the start of the year."

When you were at Williams, it was viewed as a disappointment if you didn't challenge for victory. Success in a McLaren appears to carry more kudos right now. Were these wins career highlights?

"Melbourne was a great start but I actually enjoyed Monza more. I know everyone said afterwards it was a boring race but I thought it was great. However, I admit that I was particularly pleased in Melbourne because I was under pressure from Michael Schumacher all the time and I didn't crack."

What do you make of this year's battle between Schumacher and Villeneuve?

"I think there are two ways of looking at it. When conditions are difficult, Michael once again showed that he's able to pull out something special and on that basis he perhaps deserved to win the championship. But as far as

above all the others. When you bring all the things together – qualifying, fitness, race strategy – he's 90 per cent in all of them rather than 95 in one and 75 in the others."

People say that he has been winning races in a car which is far from the best. How do you see it?

"Eddie Irvine has been quite close to him sometimes in qualifying, often only three or four tenths away. That's a reasonable benchmark that the car's obviously not bad. Michael has got a lot of experience to go with his confidence and all his natural strengths – and he's got the whole team behind him. It's a one-car team effectively and that's worth a lot."

When you are wheel to wheel with him, do you see him doing things that set him apart?

"In terms of pure racing I think I'm a match for him. That's an area where I think I've traditionally been strong. I don't think I have the same sort of qualifying consistency as he does and that's a weakness I've got to work on. When it comes to racing I don't fear taking on any of the guys out there. There are some who do back off – people I've passed around the outside in a wheel to wheel situation. They try hard to stop you but they aren't able to – I know it and they know it. Every time I'm in that situation I know I'll beat them."

Your dynamite starts have served you well again this year.

"That's just something I'm good at. There have been rumours that we've got some sort of tweak – and Jacques spread a few of them! I promise you, there was nothing on our car which helps it make good starts other than the driver. The difference between a good start and a bad start is me getting the revs right. That's all it is. I can't explain why I am good at them and someone else isn't – that's just the way it is."

You've finished this year as best Brit. Can you challenge for the championship in 1998?

"It's difficult to tell what's going to happen because the rules are changing radically. I think we can win the winter championship, if you like. We've got Adrian Newey, we've got Mercedes engines, we've got fantastic expertise and we've got funding to develop the car. On paper there's no one to beat us. It's just a shame that reality isn't like that but I certainly expect us to be competitive."

Go West, young man: after a difficult baptism with McLaren in 1996 David Coulthard became the team's first driver since the late, great Ayrton Senna to win a grand prix – and its first ever to wear a tea-towel.

"old man" berger makes sensation

offers serious challenge but is unfortunate

There were those who insisted that Gerhard Berger would be better off in a bath chair than a Benetton, but he gave the team it

mobil1 grösser preis vo

deu

meback to **win** ● **fisichella**

schuey **picks** up pieces again

of champagne since Michael Schumacher started wearing red overalls.

schland

if Gerhard Berger does ultimately look back upon 1997 as a disappointing farewell to Formula One racing, he will nevertheless allow himself a broad grin at the memory of the German Grand Prix.

In a year when the paddock fizzed with a new generation of youthful stars apparently showing the old guard the door, Berger – the establishment's

blue oval and out

For the first time since Monaco, a Ford-engined car played a decisive role in the outcome of a grand prix.

Problem was, it wasn't quite the kind of impact that either Stewart Grand Prix or the Blue Oval had in mind.

All season long engine tuner Cosworth had been pushing the envelope to boost the performance of its much-maligned V10. Judging by the straightline speeds recorded by Rubens Barrichello and Jan Magnussen, this was sometimes having the desired effect. However, this extra grunt carried a penalty: Stewart's motors were going

bang more often than John Wayne – but with rather more in the way of special effects.

Hockenheim showcased the most conspicuous Ford failure of the season, Magnussen's letting go on the straight with a smoke trail the Red Arrows would have struggled to match. The net result had a dramatic effect on the race result.

Berger, running behind the Dane, found himself plunged into a cloud of fog so thick that he needed a Shipping Forecast to navigate his way out.

"I honestly believed I had lost the race," he said. "I could not see the road ahead at all and had to stop the car, which cost me four or five seconds."

Actually, it was more like two – but it was still enough to drop him temporarily behind Fisichella after the pit stops.

spokesman-in-chief – showed the young guns a thing or two about hitting the target at Hockenheim.

That said, Giancarlo Fisichella was the only other driver in the field who looked capable of beating the Austrian. The 24-year-old Roman still had certain communication difficulties – by mid-season his command of English was still some way south of Joe Dolce's – but he sure as hell knows how to drive a racing car. So much so that he came within an ace of spoiling Berger's party piece.

The Benetton led until Fisichella managed to slip in front during their pit stops – aided by Jan Magnussen, whose spectacularly smoky retirement undoubtedly held Berger up. But the Jordan's lead lasted only as far as the first chicane when, under heavy pressure from Berger, he slipped up and let the wily Austrian back in front.

And that was that, because a lap later Fisichella's left rear Goodyear went up in smoke, taking with it Jordan's hopes of a maiden victory. When his engine imitated said tyre a few laps later, the Silverstone team's despair was complete.

Fisichella's disappearance let Michael Schumacher into second place after the kind of drive from which championships are hewn. Ferrari was never really on the pace all weekend, even less so after a botched refuelling effort forced the German to make a late splash-n-dash stop, yet Schumacher came away with six points in the bag and the title at his toes.

The Scuderia's salvation was that Williams made an even worse mess of Hockenheim. Both Heinz-Harald Frentzen and Jacques Villeneuve struggled in the thick of the pack: the German was Eddie Irvined at the first corner, though the lion's share of the

"the scuderia's **salvation** was that **williams** made an even **worse mess** of hockenheim"

However, Magnussen's retirement probably had a more serious effect on the Italian's afternoon, since Jordan suspected that he had punctured his tyre on debris from the exploded Ford.

"Something went into the tyre and cut the tread," speculated Jordan's technical director Gary Anderson. "Probably Magnussen's con rod. . ."

The deflating Goodyear left Fisichella fighting the 197 back to the pits with more haste than speed and as a result he spun in the stadium, ensuring that he would rejoin outside the top six. Not that it mattered: the flailing rubber had taken out an oil pipe and left his Peugeot on borrowed time.

"We told him about it and tried to stop him, but I don't think he wanted to hear it," said Anderson, "so he kept going until it stopped of its own accord. . ."

After a drive like that, who could blame him?

blame was apportioned to Frentzen; Villeneuve decamped to the gravel after trying to repass Jarno Trulli's fourth-placed Prost in a chicane. This was not the impression Williams wanted to create in front of future engine supplier BMW.

The latter's arch rival Mercedes had genuine hopes of a second win of the season on home soil. But the McLarens couldn't pull it off: Mika Hakkinen made the podium after an afternoon grafting rather than starring, while team-mate David Coulthard had his car's nose put out of joint by the Irvine/Frentzen interface at the first turn.

Sandwiched between the Arrows twins, Johnny Herbert amused himself by doing Ford V10 impressions (above) with his front left tyre.

no more mr has-been

Hockenheim, say the purists, is an emotionless, uninvolving place, a few miles of *autobahn* strewn with stop-start chicanes and held together by a Mickey Mouse stadium section.

Some put its coldness down to one thing alone: Hockenheim will forever be reviled as the circuit at which the great Jim Clark lost his life, while competing in a largely meaningless Formula Two race on April 7 1968.

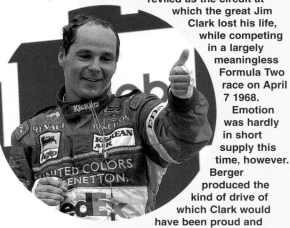

Emotion was hardly in short supply this time, however. Berger produced the kind of drive of which Clark would have been proud and his performance was given added poignancy by the off-track events which preceded it.

The veteran Austrian, who celebrated his 38th birthday in a hotel room bursting at the seams with his rivals later in the year, had been missing in action since the build-up to Canada thanks to a mystery sinus infection which required several painful operations. When he came back his knockabout mirth was kept beneath the sheets too.

For one thing, speculation suggested that the performances of stand-in Alexander Wurz had sealed Berger's F1 fate. Certainly it looked that way at Benetton, where boss Flavio Briatore was rumoured to have informed Gerhard that his services were surplus to requirements for 1998.

More pertinently, Berger's father Johann, to whom he was very close, had been killed in an air crash on the eve of the British Grand Prix, a fortnight before Hockenheim.

At a press conference before Germany, Berger was in sombre, philosophical mood, announcing that he was looking for "another motivation, another direction" to his career. This was interpreted both as an intent to retire and a signal to roll the dice for one last time. The race weekend suggested that the latter, given that Berger dragged his Benetton to the triple crown of pole, fastest lap and win: a first for the team since it was shorn of Schumacher.

"I was driving with special powers today," admitted the Austrian after his victory. "And no, I'm not going to tell you what they were."

He did, however, have a message for F1's kindergarten: "Maybe they need to practise a bit more. . ."

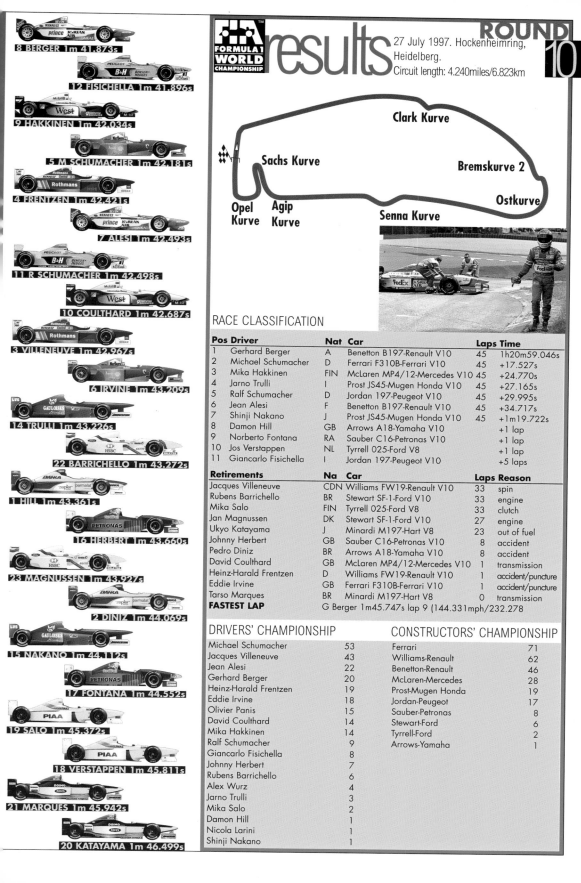

8 BERGER 1m 41.873s

12 FISICHELLA 1m 41.896s

9 HAKKINEN 1m 42.034s

5 M SCHUMACHER 1m 42.181s

4 FRENTZEN 1m 42.421s

7 ALESI 1m 42.493s

11 R SCHUMACHER 1m 42.498s

10 COULTHARD 1m 42.687s

3 VILLENEUVE 1m 42.967s

6 IRVINE 1m 43.209s

14 TRULLI 1m 43.226s

22 BARRICHELLO 1m 43.272s

1 HILL 1m 43.361s

16 HERBERT 1m 43.660s

23 MAGNUSSEN 1m 43.227s

2 DINIZ 1m 44.069s

15 NAKANO 1m 44.112s

17 FONTANA 1m 44.552s

19 SALO 1m 45.372s

18 VERSTAPPEN 1m 45.811s

21 MARQUES 1m 45.942s

20 KATAYAMA 1m 46.499s

FORMULA 1 WORLD CHAMPIONSHIP

results

27 July 1997. Hockenheimring, Heidelberg.
Circuit length: 4.240miles/6.823km

ROUND 10

Clark Kurve

Sachs Kurve

Bremskurve 2

Ostkurve

Opel Kurve   Agip Kurve

Senna Kurve

RACE CLASSIFICATION

Pos	Driver	Nat	Car	Laps	Time
1	Gerhard Berger	A	Benetton B197-Renault V10	45	1h20m59.046s
2	Michael Schumacher	D	Ferrari F310B-Ferrari V10	45	+17.527s
3	Mika Hakkinen	FIN	McLaren MP4/12-Mercedes V10	45	+24.770s
4	Jarno Trulli	I	Prost JS45-Mugen Honda V10	45	+27.165s
5	Ralf Schumacher	D	Jordan 197-Peugeot V10	45	+29.995s
6	Jean Alesi	F	Benetton B197-Renault V10	45	+34.717s
7	Shinji Nakano	J	Prost JS45-Mugen Honda V10	45	+1m19.722s
8	Damon Hill	GB	Arrows A18-Yamaha V10		+1 lap
9	Norberto Fontana	RA	Sauber C16-Petronas V10		+1 lap
10	Jos Verstappen	NL	Tyrrell 025-Ford V8		+1 lap
11	Giancarlo Fisichella	I	Jordan 197-Peugeot V10		+5 laps

Retirements	Na	Car	Laps	Reason
Jacques Villeneuve	CDN	Williams FW19-Renault V10	33	spin
Rubens Barrichello	BR	Stewart SF-1-Ford V10	33	engine
Mika Salo	FIN	Tyrrell 025-Ford V8	33	clutch
Jan Magnussen	DK	Stewart SF-1-Ford V10	27	engine
Ukyo Katayama	J	Minardi M197-Hart V8	23	out of fuel
Johnny Herbert	GB	Sauber C16-Petronas V10	8	accident
Pedro Diniz	BR	Arrows A18-Yamaha V10	8	accident
David Coulthard	GB	McLaren MP4/12-Mercedes V10	1	transmission
Heinz-Harald Frentzen	D	Williams FW19-Renault V10	1	accident/puncture
Eddie Irvine	GB	Ferrari F310B-Ferrari V10	1	accident/puncture
Tarso Marques	BR	Minardi M197-Hart V8	0	transmission
FASTEST LAP		G Berger 1m45.747s lap 9 (144.331mph/232.278		

DRIVERS' CHAMPIONSHIP

Michael Schumacher	53
Jacques Villeneuve	43
Jean Alesi	22
Gerhard Berger	20
Heinz-Harald Frentzen	19
Eddie Irvine	18
Olivier Panis	15
David Coulthard	14
Mika Hakkinen	14
Ralf Schumacher	9
Giancarlo Fisichella	8
Johnny Herbert	7
Rubens Barrichello	6
Alex Wurz	4
Jarno Trulli	3
Mika Salo	2
Damon Hill	1
Nicola Larini	1
Shinji Nakano	1

CONSTRUCTORS' CHAMPIONSHIP

Ferrari	71
Williams-Renault	62
Benetton-Renault	46
McLaren-Mercedes	28
Prost-Mugen Honda	19
Jordan-Peugeot	17
Sauber-Petronas	8
Stewart-Ford	6
Tyrrell-Ford	2
Arrows-Yamaha	1

magnificent damon robbed of victory as arr picks up pieces to tighten championship race
● herbert's gritty drive earns podium finish

Williams team-mates Damon Hill and Jacques Villeneuve. . . Hang on, that was last year. So this must be an optical illusion, or a clever piece of Apple Mac trickery. . . or did we really just see an Arrows at the front during the Hungarian GP?

lters on **last** lap ● lucky **jacques**

marlboro magyar

nagyi

j

11

85

Hill had a comfortable lead (above), but by the final lap his Arrows had been rendered even slower than usual (top). A warm feeling usually meant his engine has blown. In Hungary, it indicated he had qualified fourth – he was royally applauded (opposite below). A more common sight in 1997 was that of Ralf Schumacher spinning (opposite above).

amon Hill's 1997 season often had a touch of soap opera about it. What happened in the Hungarian GP, however, provided a plot twist to beat anything served up by East Enders or Coronation Street.

The sight of Hill grabbing the lead and dominating the race in a car previously dismissed as 110 per cent canine had hardened hacks pinching themselves. Yet there was nothing imagined about what was unfolding on the circuit.

From the 10th until the final lap at the Hungaroring, Hill's unloved Arrows A18-Yamaha held the Hungarian GP in an iron grasp. Neither would it have loosened had a gut-wrenching hydraulic failure not interrupted Arrows' reverie and handed victory to Jacques Villeneuve's Williams in the closing seconds.

It was neither fantasy nor fluke. Arrows' finest hour was down to smart team work, brilliant Bridgestone tyres

"hill's unloved arrow A18-yamaha held the hungarian GP in an iron grasp"

and a scintillating drive from the man himself. Hill blew a metaphorical raspberry in the general direction of the "Damon can't overtake" brigade with a wonderfully aggressive display during which he proved to be the only man capable of passing tyre-hobbled pole position winner Michael Schumacher's struggling Ferrari.

Winner Villeneuve led only one lap after a bad start. Fortunately for him it was the one which mattered most.

Unluckily for Williams, a fine drive from Heinz-Harald Frentzen went unrewarded. The German could be spied glaring at monitors left, right and centre, displaying the kind of ire which Arrows boss Tom Walkinshaw was struggling to conceal post-race.

Unlike most Goodyear runners, Frentzen had chosen harder-compound tyres which came into their own while their softer counterparts wilted in the heat. Heinz-Harald duly worked his way into the lead when Hill pitted for new tyres, only for a broken fuel filler to force his fire-breathing Williams into retirement.

Villeneuve, meanwhile, accepted the plaudits like a tennis player who'd seen a net-cord decide the match in his favour. He had spent more of the afternoon worrying about the close attention of David Coulthard's McLaren than he had about victory – until the Scot's habitual bad luck intervened and an engine failure put him out.

"Damon was worth a win today," said Jacques. "He drove an amazing race. But it's a better result for us because of the championship."

The lonely Johnny Herbert was rewarded with third ahead of the gripless Schumacher, left to ponder the ironies of nemesis Hill driving a car far

hydraulic wounds

After a race which explored opposite extremes of emotion, there were contrasting moods in the Arrows pit – which was perhaps to be expected.

If you were Damon Hill, you bounced around jauntily, spoke of how this was a second place won rather than a grand prix lost and looked as though you'd proved something to yourself as well as everybody else.

If you were everybody else, you looked as though a favourite pet's death had coincided with a visit from the VAT man.

Hill and team boss Tom Walkinshaw agreed publicly on one thing: that there was no mystery about Arrows' leap from also-ran to potential Derby winner.

The Hungaroring doesn't require an abundance of horsepower, so the allegedly underpowered Yamaha engine wasn't a handicap. The team had also improved its A18 chassis with each race since John Barnard arrived as technical chief. The changes affected everything down to the wheel nuts, which had been revised to allow quicker pit stops.

And then there was the Bridgestone factor, touted by Walkinshaw as the strongest card in Arrows' hand. Bridgestone came up trumps, sure – but while its other teams ran into trouble, Hill simply ran away and hid.

For months, Walkinshaw had insisted that his team could win a race this year – and he remained ominously deadpan as assorted media did their best not to guffaw in his face when considering the evidence to the contrary. Now, it seemed, he had the last laugh. Almost.

He saw no reason to smile about being second best, particularly when a split washer worth as much as an off-peak local phone call was to blame. Its failure caused the pressure in part of the hydraulic system to drop and the whole thing finally packed up with three laps remaining.

The upshot was a sticking throttle and gear shift. In the seconds it took to diagnose the failure the system gave up the ghost altogether and Hill only had enough pressure left to snatch third gear, rather than a higher ratio that might, just might, have helped him hold off Villeneuve.

Damon was adamant that it made no odds. "It was irrelevant because the throttle was broken anyway," he said. "The car stopped about three times and I thought, 'That's it, it's going to park'. I was truly amazed to finish."

Walkinshaw's face, and words, suggested that the pair were not singing from the same song sheet."I'm bitterly disappointed," murmured Tom. "We should have won and we lost. I don't see why I should be cheerful about that."

faster than its constituent parts should have permitted. While his former sparring partner carved ruthlessly through traffic out front, Schumacher was the traffic. In fact, his Ferrari become a mobile chicane behind which his brother Ralf, team-mate Eddie Irvine and – get this – the Prost of Shinji

Nakano were forced to sit and stew.

Until the last lap, that is, when Michael braked early. Ralf and Eddie saw him but Shinji didn't. The upshot was that Ferrari number two was deposited in the gravel trap by Prost number two and the Japanese rookie scooped the final point. Strange days indeed.

Johnny Herbert's Sauber didn't always perform with the quartz precision for which its country of origin is renowned, but in Hungary it allowed to him to remind everyone of his consummate racecraft.

herbert
rides
again

often, such as in Canada, his efforts went unrewarded.

Third place at the Hungaroring, however, was more than he had any right to expect given that qualifying had left him outside the top 10 at a track where overtaking is traditionally confined to the main road out of Budapest.

But Herbert's race performance was typically unobtrusive and uncharacter-

Amidst the scenes of unabashed Damon-mania you'd have been hard-pressed to notice that a second Brit was flanking Hill on the podium.

That mattered not a jot to Johnny Herbert. He was merely relieved to see Sauber back on track, following a string of races in which the Swiss team's school report had "could do better" pencilled in the performance column.

It was a frustrating scenario for Herbert, all the more so as the Sauber team hadn't seemed terribly interested in developing its basically sound package much beyond the basic.

"We've not made any progress," admitted Herbert before Silverstone. "What's happened is that everybody else has taken a step forward and we've stayed where we were. That's why we're going backwards."

As a result, Herbert often found himself trying to weave a silk purse on race day after having qualified a couple of rows shy of a sow's ear. Occasionally he pulled it off, as in Argentina. More

istically fruitful. After getting ahead of the tardy Benettons of Alesi and Berger off the line, Herbert channelled his aggression and concentrated on looking after his tyres while all around were destroying theirs. He subsequently moved up the track with every pit stop until, after his final visit, he was left with a handy-sized cushion over Michael Schumacher – whose Ferrari was doing a passable impersonation of the Thames Barrier on this occasion.

"I was saving the tyres because I knew they'd fall apart 10 laps before the end of my stint if I didn't," he said. "Once Michael was behind me, it was just a matter of pacing myself."

Dull? Perhaps. Overlooked? Almost certainly. Deserved? Undoubtedly.

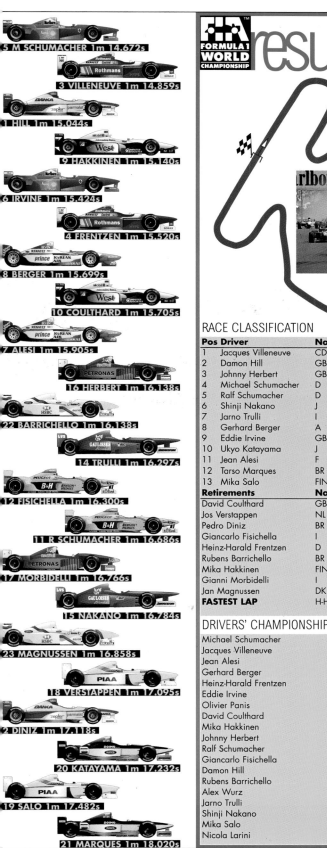

5 M SCHUMACHER 1m 14.672s
3 VILLENEUVE 1m 14.859s
1 HILL 1m 15.044s
9 HAKKINEN 1m 15.140s
6 IRVINE 1m 15.424s
4 FRENTZEN 1m 15.520s
8 BERGER 1m 15.699s
10 COULTHARD 1m 15.705s
7 ALESI 1m 15.905s
16 HERBERT 1m 16.138s
22 BARRICHELLO 1m 16.138s
14 TRULLI 1m 16.297s
12 FISICHELLA 1m 16.300s
11 R SCHUMACHER 1m 16.686s
17 MORBIDELLI 1m 16.766s
15 NAKANO 1m 16.784s
23 MAGNUSSEN 1m 16.858s
18 VERSTAPPEN 1m 17.095s
2 DINIZ 1m 17.118s
20 KATAYAMA 1m 17.232s
19 SALO 1m 17.482s
21 MARQUES 1m 18.020s

results

10 August 1997. Hungaroring, Mogyorod, near Budapest.
Circuit length: 2.466miles/3.968km

RACE CLASSIFICATION

Pos	Driver	Nat	Car	Laps	Time
1	Jacques Villeneuve	CDN	Williams FW19-Renault V10	77	1h45m47.149s
2	Damon Hill	GB	Arrows A18-Yamaha V10	77	+9.079s
3	Johnny Herbert	GB	Sauber C16-Petronas V10	77	+20.445s
4	Michael Schumacher	D	Ferrari F310B-Ferrari V10	77	+30.501s
5	Ralf Schumacher	D	Jordan 197-Peugeot V10	77	+30.715s
6	Shinji Nakano	J	Prost JS45-Mugen Honda V10	77	+41.512s
7	Jarno Trulli	I	Prost JS45-Mugen Honda V10	77	+1m15.552s
8	Gerhard Berger	A	Benetton B197-Renault V10	77	+1m16.409s
9	Eddie Irvine	GB	Ferrari F310B-Ferrari V10		+1 lap
10	Ukyo Katayama	J	Minardi M197-Hart V8		+1 lap
11	Jean Alesi	F	Benetton B197-Renault V10		+1 lap
12	Tarso Marques	BR	Minardi M197-Hart V8		+2 laps
13	Mika Salo	FIN	Tyrrell 025-Ford V8		+2 laps

Retirements	Nat	Car	Laps	Reason
David Coulthard	GB	McLaren MP4/12-Mercedes V10	65	hydraulic system
Jos Verstappen	NL	Tyrrell 025-Ford V8	61	air compressor
Pedro Diniz	BR	Arrows A18-Yamaha V10	53	alternator
Giancarlo Fisichella	I	Jordan 197-Peugeot V10	42	spin
Heinz-Harald Frentzen	D	Williams FW19-Renault V10	29	fuel nozzle
Rubens Barrichello	BR	Stewart SF-1-Ford V10	29	engine
Mika Hakkinen	FIN	McLaren MP4/12-Mercedes V10	12	gearbox
Gianni Morbidelli	I	Sauber C16-Petronas V10	7	engine
Jan Magnussen	DK	Stewart SF-1-Ford V10	5	accident

FASTEST LAP H-H Frentzen 1m18.372s lap 25 (113.257mph/182.269kmh)

DRIVERS' CHAMPIONSHIP

Michael Schumacher	56
Jacques Villeneuve	53
Jean Alesi	22
Gerhard Berger	20
Heinz-Harald Frentzen	19
Eddie Irvine	18
Olivier Panis	15
David Coulthard	14
Mika Hakkinen	14
Johnny Herbert	11
Ralf Schumacher	11
Giancarlo Fisichella	8
Damon Hill	7
Rubens Barrichello	6
Alex Wurz	4
Jarno Trulli	3
Shinji Nakano	2
Mika Salo	2
Nicola Larini	1

CONSTRUCTORS' CHAMPIONSHIP

Ferrari	74
Williams-Renault	72
Benetton-Renault	46
McLaren-Mercedes	28
Prost-Mugen Honda	20
Jordan-Peugeot	19
Sauber-Petronas	12
Arrows-Yamaha	7
Stewart-Ford	6
Tyrrell-Ford	2

formula gone

✝ he Arrows team led its second ever grand prix at South Africa in 1978 but had seldom looked like winning again until Damon Hill came within a lap of breaking the jinx during the team's 299th race in Hungary. For all its relative lack of success on the track, however, Arrows has accomplished one major feat: it has survived the past 20 seasons in Formula One. The list of those who haven't ranges from the famous to the facile. . .

Alfa Romeo

Lifespan: 1950-1951 & 1979-1985
Vital statistics: 110 GPs; 10 wins; two world champion drivers
Keynotes: No wins after Fangio took 1951 world title. MkII version of Alfa sometimes fast (particularly in 1980) but also fragile (particularly 1979-1985). Operation wound down after Fiat took control; it didn't need a second F1 team alongside Ferrari.

ALSO NO LONGER APPEARING AT A TR

f1's forgotten **teams**

Andrea Moda

Lifespan: 1992
Vital statistics: Qualified for a GP (Monaco, one of Roberto Moreno's greatest feats)
Keynotes: The result of Italian footwear magnate Andrea Sassetti's dream to be an F1 team owner. The car – a two-year old design study commissioned by BMW – was rush-produced after Sassetti's original plan to run cast-off Coloni chassis was quashed by the FIA. Vastly underfinanced team's trucks turned away from Italian GP paddock after Sassetti was subject to financial investigation by the authorities.

Beatrice

Lifespan: 1985-1986
Keynotes: Veteran US team owner Carl Haas commissioned Lola to build a customer F1 car with backing from conglomerate Beatrice, but management changes at sponsorship HQ led to F1 being declared an unsound investment. Gave out lots of pullovers and briefcases to the media during its short F1 stint.

BMS Lola

Lifespan: 1993
Keynotes: Another Lola customer project. Good news: Ferrari engines. Bad news: pretty much everything else.

Brabham

Lifespan: 1962-1987 & 1989-1992
Vital statistics: 394 GPs; 35 wins; four champion drivers; two constructors' titles
Keynotes: Hugely successful under guidance of company founder Sir Jack Brabham and, later, modern F1 power broker Bernie Ecclestone. Last win in 1985 and in gradual decline thereafter. Health deteriorated rapidly after the company was sold on. Last act of note was giving Damon Hill his F1 race debut, at Silverstone in 1992.

Coloni

Lifespan: 1987-1991
Keynotes: Italian F3 and F3000 entrant always struggled for cash. Brief flash of promise – on paper – with brief Subaru alliance in 1991 but flat-12 engine that came with the deal would have served better as a paperweight, or perhaps as a means of clubbing sponsors into submission. Coloni had last laugh: he sold the whole caboodle to Andrea Moda.

Eurobrun

Lifespan: 1988-1990
Keynotes: An amalgam of Swiss sports car racer Walter Brun's team and Euroracing, which ran the Alfa Romeo F1 project in the early 1980s: the most notable thing it did in F1 was paint its cars orange (1989).

Fondmetal

Lifespan: 1991-1992
Keynotes: Tidy car which emerged from ashes of Osella. Had the looks; had Gabriele Tarquini; had no money; folded.

Hesketh

Lifespan: 1974-1978
Vital statistics: Won 1975 Dutch GP
Keynotes: Darling of British sport when James Hunt challenged the world's best in an unsponsored F1 car built on a whim by Lord H. Eventually economic reality took over and team switched to

Nelson Piquet won the 1993 world championship for Brabham (far left). Less than a decade later the team had vanished. Above, a salvage crane remarkably fails to snap despite the weight of the Coloni-Subaru attached thereto.

running paying customers for a couple more years.

Kauhsen
Lifespan: 1979

Keynotes: Actually, that's overstating the lifespan quite a bit. Car failed to qualify a couple of times and project was sold to Arturo Merzario. Even today, there is no rational explanation for such a purchase.

Lambo
Lifespan: 1991
Keynotes: Lamborghini switched briefly from role of engine supplier to do the whole lot, spent a lot of money and swiftly went back to Plan A.

Larrousse
Lifespan: 1987-1994
Keynotes: Team ran Lola customer chassis with modest success for five years before doing its own thing, initially in partnership with low-volume specialist sports car manufacturer Venturi. Always struggling for money thereafter; posted an entry for the 1995 season but at the time of writing is approximately two years and eight months late for the Brazilian GP.

Life
Lifespan: 1990
Keynotes: Likely contender for fewest laps ever completed in a whole season. Original W12 engine didn't work; when the team switched to a more conventional V8 it was clear that the car didn't, either.

Lola
Lifespan: about five minutes, March 1997
Keynotes: Ambitious attempt to run an F1 programme of its own for the first time. Lola even had its own engines lined up. What it didn't have were the funds to push the project to fruition. Failed to qualify for Australian GP but the cars reached Brazil before notice of the team's demise was served. It almost took parent company Lola Racing Cars with it, but the famous constructor was saved by a takeover.

Lotus
Lifespan: 1958-1994
Vital statistics: 491 GPs; 79 wins; six champion drivers; seven constructors' titles
Keynotes: The most famous and most

ALSO NO LONGER APPEARING AT A TF

successful name to have disappeared from F1. Team Lotus lives on in name, with David Hunt – brother of late 1976 world champion James – trying to find the resources to bring it back into grand prix racing. Confusingly, a Dutch consortium is also trying to put together a Lotus F1 team. Although Ayrton Senna scored his first six F1 victories for Lotus in the mid '80s, the team was effectively in gradual decline after the sudden death of founder and inspiration Colin Chapman in December 1982.

factory team. Vittorio Brambilla scored one of funniest F1 victories at rain-soaked Austria in 1975, becoming so excited as he took the flag that he took both hands off the steering wheel and promptly crashed. Company taken over in 1989 by Japanese entrepreneur Leyton House. No one ever satisfactorily worked out what the plural of Leyton House should be. Reverted to March nomenclature in 1992 and was invisible entrant in 1993. Had just about everything it needed (apart from cars, engines and money).

March

Lifespan: 1970-1977, 1981-1982 & 1987-1992
Vital statistics: Three wins
Keynotes: Grew to become the world's largest racing car constructor and flirted with F1 as customer supplier and

Martini

Lifespan: 1978
Keynotes: Successful French F3 and F2 constructor tried but failed to compete at the top. Still building cars for junior formulae and in 1997 rediscovered the art of winning F3 races for the first time since 1988.

Merzario

Lifespan: 1978-1979
Keynotes: Ex-Ferrari driver attempts to extend F1 career by entering and driving his own cars. Made a guest appearance during 1997 Italian GP, performing as driver of FIA medical car – which he managed to get stuck in a gravel trap.

The Kauhsen (opposite above): it wasn't fast, it wasn't clever. Somehow, though, it was sold on. They have been waiting for Larrousse (opposite below) in Brazil since the spring of 1995. Is it a Leyton House? Is it a March (left)? Either way, it's extinct in F1.

Monteverdi

Lifespan: 1990
Keynotes: Took over struggling Onyx team, relocated it to Switzerland and then packed up after just two races. During this brief flirtation with F1 it managed to fit the differential backwards in JJ Lehto's car.

Osella

Lifespan: 1980-1990
Keynotes: Durable backmarker. Never obtrusive; even less so when the team transmuted into Fondmetal.

Pacific

Lifespan: 1994-1995
Keynotes: Kicked off with a car based on a 1992 design by Reynard and a budget fit for about 1982. Proof positive of how difficult grand prix racing is to crack: Pacific had won championships at every single-seater level south of Formula One.

Rebaque

Lifespan: 1979
Keynotes: Wealthy Mexican Hector Rebaque built his own car as alternative to being a Lotus customer. Did three races; qualified once; took his backing to Brabham instead and found he could do radical things such as finish in the top six.

Renault

Lifespan: 1977-1985
Vital statistics: 123 GPs; 15 wins
Keynotes: Pioneer of turbocharged revolution in F1. Politics always seemed to get in the way of the racing; key asset Alain Prost pipped to 1983 world title at the last gasp and promptly left. Team never won again. Continued briefly as engine supplier after its own withdrawal and returned in the same role in 1989. By far the most successful F1 engine builder of the 1990s.

ALSO NO LONGER APPEARING AT A TRACK NEA

Simtek

Lifespan: 1994-1995
Keynotes: Ambitious project always had to survive on shoestring budget. Jos Verstappen briefly elevated his car to sixth place in Argentina 1995, but writing was already on wall. When owner/designer Nick Wirth pulled the plug, his services were snapped up by Benetton.

Spirit

Lifespan: 1983-1985
Keynotes: Brought Honda back in to F1 but foundered after Japanese company dissolved partnership at end of 1983.

Three races into 1985, Spirit had evaporated.

Surtees

Lifespan: 1970-1978
Keynotes: 1964 world champion John Surtees enjoyed success as a manufacturer in F5000 and Formula Two but never matched it in F1. His team won the 1972 European F2 title with Mike Hailwood, who also achieved the company's best F1 result, finishing second in that year's Italian GP at Monza. Caused the BBC to threaten withdrawal of F1 TV coverage in 1976 by attracting Durex as a sponsor.

Theodore

Lifespan: 1978 & 1981-1983
Keynotes: Gave 1982 world champion Keke Rosberg his F1 break, winning rain-lashed 1978 International Trophy at Silverstone. Not so successful in championship events, however.

Toleman

Lifespan: 1981-1985
Keynotes: Recovered from comedic opening F1 gambit to become respected F1 player. Future looked perilous after Senna left at end of 1984; missed start of 1985 because it didn't have tyres to use. Arrival of Benetton sponsorship provided rescue package and by 1986 the team had become the Benetton Formula we know and love today.

Wolf

Lifespan: 1977-1979
Vital statistics: Three wins
Keynotes: Jody Scheckter gave the team a remarkable debut victory in Argentina and was leading championship until Lauda and Ferrari got fully into their stride; finished second to the Austrian in the end but life was never so good for Wolf again. Bits and bobs eventually sold off to Fittipaldi. Historical note: James Hunt drove his last grand prix in a Wolf (Monaco 1979).

The Onyx (far left) became a Monteverdi and – shortly afterwards – defunct. Renault (left) won races but has been more successful as an engine supplier than as an all-in constructor. Pacific chases Simtek (bottom): Simtek won the race to obsolescence – but not by much.

rain-master **schumacher** wins again ● fi
start with **safety car** ● another **poor**

Former British F3 champion Oliver Gavin led the field around for the opening few laps, unfairly assisted by air conditioning, windscreen wipers, headlights, a roof and other Merc ancillaries. Somewhere in the spray behind Villeneuve and Alesi lurks a Ferrari whose driver didn't find the conditions too much of a bother. Trying to escape from team boss Jean Todt's clutches, however, was an altogether more taxing challenge for Michael Schumacher.

belgian

.12

grand prix

grand prix
for **williams**

grand prix year 1997

michael Schumacher is paid as much as most of his rivals put together. The Belgian GP was yet another stark reminder that Ferrari's 25 million dollar man is worth every cent.

So bad was the weather that Belgium became the first GP ever started behind the Safety Car (driven by former British F3 champion Oliver Gavin). When Gavin's Mercedes coupé finally pulled over, Schumacher stamped his authority with a display of wet weather intelligence last demonstrated by the

Sunday afternoon rush hour, Francorchamps. One of these men didn't actually realise the race had started until informed by his team via radio. Clue: he's just behind Damon Hill. And his name's Johnny. And he drives a Sauber.

late Ayrton Senna at Donington Park in 1993.

Within a single racing lap the German – on intermediate tyres – had disposed of second-placed Jean Alesi and leader Jacques Villeneuve and had time to pull out five seconds on the French-Canadian. He then pulled away at the rate of 10 seconds per lap on the drying track – something he continued to do until he changed onto slick tyres on lap 15.

Such was his advantage that Schumacher simply cruised home thereafter. After all, he only had half a minute in hand at the flag. The rest had been in dazed submission long before that.

Giancarlo Fisichella wea-

thered the blows best with a mature drive to second that belied his tender years. His efforts looked all the more polished after Jordan team-mate Ralf Schumacher failed to follow his brother's example by crashing both before and after the start. Fisichella never once looked like dropping the ball, despite race-long pressure from Mika Hakkinen.

While Jordan jumped for joy, Williams was crestfallen. Both Villeneuve and Heinz-Harald Frentzen started on wet tyres and lost any benefit as Gavin's road car headed the field while the track was at its soggiest.

"fisichella **never** once looked like **dropping** the **ball,** despite race-long **pressure** from mika **hakkinen**"

warning:

genius at work

Watching Michael Schumacher master Spa in the rain brought to mind poetic imagery, memories of legendary drives of the past: Fangio at the Nürburgring in 1957; Clark at Monza 10 years later; Senna at Suzuka in 1988.

During the opening laps Schumacher demonstrated all too clearly the gap which exists between him and his rivals.

Hill had produced the drive of the season in Hungary but Schuey at Spa was something else. Eyeing the sky and knowing that Spa always dries quickly, Schumacher was brave enough to opt for halfway-house intermediate Goodyears for those sodden early laps. Yes, the Safety Car played into his

hands, but you'd have put money on Michael making the gamble work anyway given his knife/butter moves on Alesi and Villeneuve during that first racing lap.

Having the team working for you on a semi-exclusive basis helps too. As in Monaco Schumacher swapped his designated race chassis for the spare F310B, which featured a more compromised wet-weather set-up. This became steadily less competitive as the race wore on, but nobody was ever going to be able to make use of his mild disadvantage.

Rival team members were impressed and lined up along the pit wall to applaud the Ferrari as it crossed the line. The Scuderia was happy to give due credit. "It was Michael's call," admitted technical boss Ross Brawn. "He made such a gap in the wet that it didn't matter what happened in the dry."

Sporting director Jean Todt expressed the Prancing Horse's sentiments more overtly on the podium, handing his driver the winning constructor's trophy to go with his own silverware.

Undoubtedly Schumacher had earned it. A shining light on a miserable afternoon in Belgium, he not only underlined his credentials as the best driver of his generation but as the only man who really deserved to be world champion in 1997.

Second best: while his team-mate was driving into assorted solid objects, Giancarlo Fisichella (above) equalled Jordan's finest ever F1 result.

Disoriented colours of Benetton. Alesi leaves the slippery grey stuff for the even more slippery green stuff.

Soon after Olly relinquished the lead, Villeneuve passed up any claim he might have had for victory by slithering into the pit lane. He had no choice; he misjudged the entry to the Bus Stop chicane and ended up in the pits whether he liked it or not. While he was there the team gave him new tyres – but they were intermediates, not the slicks that the drying track demanded. Unsurprisingly he would be forced to make a further stop. Frentzen, meanwhile, slithered down the order as his wets lost their bite.

It wasn't only Williams who suffered Safety Car dramas. It took Johnny Herbert – without radio contact to his pits – a good half lap to realise that the race had actually started, but he recovered well to hold a sterling fourth ahead of the recovering Frentzen and Villeneuve.

Heinz-Harald eventually overhauled the Sauber and caught Hakkinen (he would finally get by 10 days later – see panel), but Villeneuve remained tucked up behind Herbert right to the end – a result that put an extra spring into Schumacher's Nike-assisted step towards the title.

Hakkinen's flying circus

Late on Saturday evening, when most drivers had made their post-debrief excuses and left, Mika Hakkinen was clustered in a corner of the paddock with Mercedes sport boss Norbert Haug.

Haug was in explanatory mode, making positive, decisive gestures. Hakkinen was nodding, yet appeared bemused.

Mika had a good cause to believe that someone up there just didn't like him. And we don't mean the FIA.

It all started in Saturday practice, when the Finn clattered the barriers heavily after losing control of his McLaren at the 150mph entry to Les Combes. Actually 'losing' control is a poor choice of verb: it was forcibly wrested from him by a rear suspension failure which was plain for all to see.

What wasn't quite so obvious was the precise cause. McLaren initially issued a statement blaming the carbon fibre elements at the rear of the car – only to discover later that a trusty steel lower link was responsible.

It wasn't the most confidence-inspiring way to enter qualifying, but Mika was unmoved and bounced back to take an excellent fifth on the grid in the spare MP4/12. Which brings us to problem number two.

At a random post-qualifying check, the fuel taken from Hakkinen's machine was found not to match the sample lodged with the FIA by McLaren pre-season. The upshot was that he was thrown to the back of the grid and his team was fined $25,000. Small change to the McLaren organisation, surely? That wasn't the point. McLaren appealed against the stewards' verdict, lost in a Paris courtroom a week later and thus rendered Mika's drive to the podium pointless. Quite literally. En route to his

temporary third place he'd had a go at getting himself excluded anyway – by sliding off while the field was running behind the Safety Car and then passing Frentzen to retake his original position.

This was a major no-no for the stewards, but after a hearing which dragged on late into the evening the Finn emerged with a suspended ban and a carpeting. Not an ideal way to end the weekend but in this context, getting off lightly.

One more thing. Two days later Hakkinen emerged with a sprain and a shaking from a 150mph shunt in Monza testing, proof positive that things don't only happen in threes.

3 VILLENEUVE 1m 49.450s

7 ALESI 1m 49.759s

5 M SCHUMACHER 1m 50.293s

12 FISICHELLA 1m 50.470s

9 HAKKINEN 1m 50.503s

11 R SCHUMACHER 1m 50.520s

4 FRENTZEN 1m 50.656s

2 DINIZ 1m 50.853s

1 HILL 1m 50.970s

10 COULTHARD 1m 51.410s

16 HERBERT 1m 51.725s

22 BARRICHELLO 1m 51.916s

17 MORBIDELLI 1m 52.094s

14 TRULLI 1m 52.274s

8 BERGER 1m 52.391s

15 NAKANO 1m 52.749s

6 IRVINE 1m 52.793s

23 MAGNUSSEN 1m 52.886s

19 SALO 1m 52.897s

20 KATAYAMA 1m 53.544s

18 VERSTAPPEN 1m 53.725s

21 MARQUES 1m 54.505s

FIA FORMULA 1 WORLD CHAMPIONSHIP results

24 August 1997. Circuit de Spa-Francorchamps.
Circuit length: 4.330 miles/6.968km

ROUND 12

Kemmel — Les Combes — Malmedy — Eau Rouge — Raidillon — Pouhon — Rivage — Fagnes — Rivage — Stavelot — Blanchimont — "Bus Stop" — La Source

RACE CLASSIFICATION

Pos	Driver	Nat	Car	Laps	Time
1	Michael Schumacher	D	Ferrari F310B-Ferrari V10	44	1h33m46.717s
2	Giancarlo Fisichella	I	Jordan 197-Peugeot V10	44	+26.753s
3	Heinz-Harald Frentzen	D	Williams FW19-Renault V10	44	+32.147s
4	Johnny Herbert	GB	Sauber C16-Petronas V10	44	+39.025s
5	Jacques Villeneuve	CDN	Williams FW19-Renault V10	44	+42.103s
6	Gerhard Berger	A	Benetton B197-Renault V10	44	+1m03.741s
7	Pedro Diniz	BR	Arrows A18-Yamaha V10	44	+1m25.931s
8	Jean Alesi	F	Benetton B197-Renault V10	44	+1m42.008s
9	Gianni Morbidelli	I	Sauber C16-Petronas V10	44	+1m42.582s
10	Eddie Irvine	GB	Ferrari F310B-Ferrari V10		+1 lap
11	Mika Salo	FIN	Tyrrell 025-Ford V8		+1 lap
12	Jan Magnussen	DK	Stewart SF-1-Ford V10		+1 lap
13	Damon Hill	GB	Arrows A18-Yamaha V10		+2 laps
14	Ukyo Katayama	J	Minardi M197-Hart V8		+2 laps
15	Jarno Trulli	I	Prost JS45-Mugen Honda V10		+2 laps

Retirements		Nat	Car	Laps	Reason
Jos Verstappen		NL	Tyrrell 025-Ford V8	25	spin
Ralf Schumacher		D	Jordan 197-Peugeot V10	21	accident
David Coulthard		GB	McLaren MP4/12-Mercedes V10	19	spin
Tarso Marques		BR	Minardi M197-Hart V8	18	spin
Rubens Barrichello		BR	Stewart SF-1-Ford V10	8	accident
Shinji Nakano		J	Prost JS45-Mugen Honda V10	5	gearbox

FASTEST LAP J Villeneuve 1m52.692s lap 43 (138.315mph/222.596kmh)

Mika Hakkinen FIN McLaren MP4/12-Mercedes V10 finished 3rd but was disqualified for using illegal fuel.

DRIVERS' CHAMPIONSHIP

Michael Schumacher	66
Jacques Villeneuve	55
Heinz-Harald Frentzen	23
Jean Alesi	22
Gerhard Berger	21
Eddie Irvine	18
Olivier Panis	15
David Coulthard	14
Giancarlo Fisichella	14
Mika Hakkinen	14
Johnny Herbert	14
Ralf Schumacher	11
Damon Hill	7
Rubens Barrichello	6
Alex Wurz	4
Jarno Trulli	3
Shinji Nakano	2
Mika Salo	2
Nicola Larini	1

CONSTRUCTORS' CHAMPIONSHIP

Ferrari	84
Williams-Renault	78
Benetton-Renault	47
McLaren-Mercedes	28
Jordan-Peugeot	25
Prost-Mugen Honda	20
Sauber-Petronas	15
Arrows-Yamaha	7
Stewart-Ford	6
Tyrrell-Ford	2

coulthard wins pit batt
surprise pole ● champions

Alesi (far right) and Frentzen scream towards the first chicane at the sta
however, is almost as popular as Ferrari – though he was powerless to

68 gran premio campa

r mclaren's second '97 **victory ● alesi** takes

ontenders schuey and jacques **off the pace**

to dictate that the absence of red paint at the front of the field caused fans to leave Monza faster than Thrust SSC. Alesi,
starting, quick-stopping Coulthard (far left and inset).

'italia 13

First in, last out. The pit stop competition, Williams traditional nemesis, dropped Frentzen to the tail of the leading group.

This should have been a cracking race and the final result – the top six cars covered by a dozen seconds – hint that it was.

In truth, it was little more than a controlled procession which was settled by smart thinking from David Coulthard and the pit lane professionalism of his McLaren crew.

Prior to the lone, crucial pit stop this was brewing up nicely. There was Jean Alesi leading, driving as we know he can after securing only the second pole position of his career. Heinz-Harald Frentzen's Williams was tucked in right behind, the German showing title-contending team-mate Jacques Villeneuve a clean pair of heels. And, just over a second behind Alesi, there was Coulthard, up from sixth on the grid after a characteristically breathtaking start.

Benetton; Williams; McLaren? Who would you put your money on in the pit lane?

Frentzen was first to stop and in his absence Alesi and Coulthard continued to lap faster and faster. David was biding his time and had fuel enough to keep going well past half-distance. "I had decided that I would stop when Jean came in. I was confident our guys would be able to turn me around faster."

As Alesi dived for the pits Coulthard followed; when they came out, as David had predicted, the order was reversed. Not by much, mind, but it was enough.

He had more fuel in and needed less; that made the difference and he was never seriously threatened again. "It felt quite comfortable, to be honest. You have to press on to keep your concentration up but I was driving just as fast as I had to."

Just how quickly a McLaren was able to go was

"just **how quickly** a mclaren was able to go was better **demonstrated** by mika **hakkinen**"

better demonstrated by Mika Hakkinen.

The Finn had spent the first part of the race in sixth place, boxed behind Giancarlo Fisichella's Jordan and Villeneuve. A late stop and a second dose of hyper-efficiency from McLaren elevated him to fourth, right on the tail of Frentzen, but a delaminated front tyre brought him quickly back into the pits. From there on, even your average Milanese cab driver would have struggled to keep up with him. Comfortably the fastest man on the track, he should have been on the podium and could even have menaced his team-mate; ninth place was poor reward.

But at least the locals were fairly happy. Alesi is still a cult figure among the rabid *tifosi*, not because he once won a race for Ferrari but more for the

heroic style in which he didn't used to win. And Italy's great hope Fisichella demonstrated once again why Benetton and Jordan were taking the trouble to go to court to squabble over his services for

let them e a t cake

The gateau confection contained rather more calories than Minardi has scored world championship points in its 12 seasons. Driver Tarso Marques handed it round. He wasn't having any himself, but a few corpulent guests dived in – including one who was on a £500 wager that he could outdiet a journalistic colleague by the end of the season.

Wiping the crumbs of soufflé from his mouth, he said it was worth the momentary aberration.

The food is always good at Minardi. So is the coffee. If the FIA launched an official catering championship, the small Italian team would be bang on the pace. Its cars may line up in the slowest half-dozen, but there is still impressive attention to detail when it comes to some of the more important things in life.

This time, the reason for largesse was to celebrate Gian Carlo Minardi's forthcoming 50th birthday. F1 power broker Bernie Ecclestone sent his own

personal greeting. "We need a few more Gian Carlos in F1," he wrote, "so that there is a bit more overtaking..."

Monza was the team's 201st grand prix. Since its debut in Brazil 1985 the team had scaled the heights of the front row of the grid – once, at Phoenix in 1990 – and had taken three fourth places. Apart from that, the team has been at the peak of its form in the kitchen.

So what motivates Minardi to keep going?

"It is enough just knowing that we are in Formula One," he said. "To me, that means we are one of the best 11 teams in the world. We are a small team and I don't think it is possible to repeat some of the results we used to get, the gap to the top teams is too big, but I am very proud of what Minardi has done and of some of the drivers we have brought in to Formula One, such as Jarno Trulli and Giancarlo Fisichella. I just enjoy taking part in F1; for me, that is motivation enough."

Alesi took only the second pole position of his career (above). The first one was at Monza, too.

Gian Carlo Minardi (below) is still waiting for his

team's maiden pole. He could be some time. . .

1998. His composed drive to fourth place eclipsed team-mate Ralf Schumacher, who pulled off one of the few passing manoeuvres on the circuit – albeit for 10th place – but then spoilt it by squeezing Johnny Herbert off the road at the best part of 200mph. On a weekend when the FIA was handing out suspended bans for everything from ignoring yellow flags to sneezing during the drivers' briefing, there were those at Jordan who were astonished that the young German escaped punishment.

And finally the world championship contenders. Villeneuve had reduced Schumacher's advantage by a point on Friday, when the FIA excluded Hakkinen from the results of the Belgian GP and promoted the French-Canadian one place. On Sunday he did so again. The difference was that he took a car

which was suited to Monza to fifth place; Schumacher took one which blatantly wasn't to sixth.

As the tifosi streamed on to the track – remembering, this time, to wait until the cars were off it – it was in the belief that Ferrari's first champion since 1979 was becoming more palpable by the race.

Transmission revamp: Jan Magnussen looks in vain for signs of something other than engine failure bringing his Stewart-Ford to a grinding halt.

balanced on a knife-edge

There was only one moment when it looked as though David Coulthard might not win the Italian Grand Prix. It came just a couple of laps before he stopped for fuel and tyres, as he chased Jean Alesi through the Ascari chicane.

In slow motion, it looked like a masterful piece of car control, the McLaren stepping sideways without losing much in the way of forward momentum – though in fact he dropped just over a second to Alesi on that particular lap.

How did it feel from where the Scot was sitting?

"That was a bit of a worry. I spun off in exactly the same place on the warm-up lap in 1995 and I just thought, 'Oh no, not again'. As far as I was concerned I was gone but somebody must have been looking after me today. It was a real case of. . . (at this point he runs out of words and does a passable impression of trying to control a MkII Escort with bald tyres on an ice rink).

"To be honest here's not much you can do to influence the car in that situation. It's not really about controlling it. They are on such a knife-edge that you've just got to hang on as best you can and wait for the car to sort itself out. Luckily for me it sorted itself out on the circuit, not in the gravel."

How much did the incident faze him? Next time around he set his fastest lap of the race to that point.

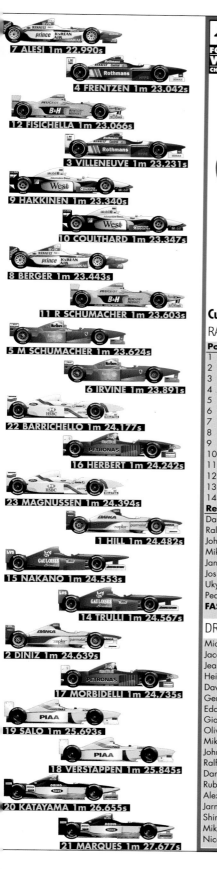

7 ALESI 1m 22.990s
4 FRENTZEN 1m 23.042s
12 FISICHELLA 1m 23.066s
3 VILLENEUVE 1m 23.231s
9 HAKKINEN 1m 23.340s
10 COULTHARD 1m 23.347s
8 BERGER 1m 23.443s
11 R SCHUMACHER 1m 23.603s
5 M SCHUMACHER 1m 23.624s
6 IRVINE 1m 23.891s
22 BARRICHELLO 1m 24.177s
16 HERBERT 1m 24.242s
23 MAGNUSSEN 1m 24.394s
1 HILL 1m 24.482s
15 NAKANO 1m 24.553s
14 TRULLI 1m 24.567s
2 DINIZ 1m 24.639s
17 MORBIDELLI 1m 24.735s
19 SALO 1m 25.693s
18 VERSTAPPEN 1m 25.845s
20 KATAYAMA 1m 26.655s
21 MARQUES 1m 27.677s

FIA FORMULA 1 WORLD CHAMPIONSHIP

results

7 September 1997. Autodromo Nazionale di Monza, near Milan. Circuit length:3.585miles/5.770km

ROUND 13

Curva di Lesmo
Curva del Serraglio
Seconda Variante
Variante Ascari
Parabolica
Curva Grande
Variante Goodyear

RACE CLASSIFICATION

Pos	Driver	Nat	Car	Laps	Time
1	David Coulthard	GB	McLaren MP4/12-Mercedes V10	53	1h17m04.609s
2	Jean Alesi	F	Benetton B197-Renault V10	53	+1.937s
3	Heinz-Harald Frentzen	D	Williams FW19-Renault V10	53	+4.343s
4	Giancarlo Fisichella	I	Jordan 197-Peugeot V10	53	+5.871s
5	Jacques Villeneuve	CDN	Williams FW19-Renault V10	53	+6.416s
6	Michael Schumacher	D	Ferrari F310B-Ferrari V10	53	+11.481s
7	Gerhard Berger	A	Benetton B197-Renault V10	53	+12.471s
8	Eddie Irvine	GB	Ferrari F310B-Ferrari V10	53	+17.639s
9	Mika Hakkinen	FIN	McLaren MP4/12-Mercedes V10	53	+49.373s
10	Jarno Trulli	I	Prost JS45-Mugen Honda V10	53	+1m02.706s
11	Shinji Nakano	J	Prost JS45-Mugen Honda V10	53	+1m03.327s
12	Gianni Morbidelli	I	Sauber C16-Petronas V10		+1 lap
13	Rubens Barrichello	BR	Stewart SF-1-Ford V10		+1 lap
14	Tarso Marques	BR	Minardi M197-Hart V8		+3 laps

Retirements	Nat	Car	Laps	Reason
Damon Hill	GB	Arrows A18-Yamaha V10	46	engine
Ralf Schumacher	D	Jordan 197-Peugeot V10	39	accident/susp
Johnny Herbert	GB	Sauber C16-Petronas V10	38	accident
Mika Salo	FIN	Tyrrell 025-Ford V8	33	engine
Jan Magnussen	DK	Stewart SF-1-Ford V10	31	transmission
Jos Verstappen	NL	Tyrrell 025-Ford V8	12	gearbox
Ukyo Katayama	J	Minardi M197-Hart V8	8	spin
Pedro Diniz	BR	Arrows A18-Yamaha V10	4	rear suspension

FASTEST LAP M Hakkinen 1m24.808s lap 49 (152.192mph/244.930kmh)

DRIVERS' CHAMPIONSHIP

Michael Schumacher	67
Jacques Villeneuve	57
Jean Alesi	28
Heinz-Harald Frentzen	27
David Coulthard	24
Gerhard Berger	21
Eddie Irvine	18
Giancarlo Fisichella	17
Olivier Panis	15
Mika Hakkinen	14
Johnny Herbert	14
Ralf Schumacher	11
Damon Hill	7
Rubens Barrichello	6
Alex Wurz	4
Jarno Trulli	3
Shinji Nakano	2
Mika Salo	2
Nicola Larini	1

CONSTRUCTORS' CHAMPIONSHIP

Ferrari	85
Williams-Renault	84
Benetton-Renault	53
McLaren-Mercedes	38
Jordan-Peugeot	28
Prost-Mugen Honda	20
Sauber-Petronas	15
Arrows-Yamaha	7
Stewart-Ford	6
Tyrrell-Ford	2

grand prix year 1997

5 YEARS AGO

JULY 12

Damon Hill started his first grand prix at Silverstone (below), taking his Brabham to 16th place. He was lapped four times by Nigel Mansell's Williams, for the development of which Hill was largely responsible.

AUGUST 30

Michael Schumacher scored the first grand prix victory of his career in Belgium (above right), in the formative stages of his Benetton career.

OCTOBER 4

1967 world champion Denny Hulme passed away while racing a BMW in Australia's most famous touring car race, the Bathurst 1000 km.

10 YEARS AGO

JUNE 21

The now absent Lotus team scored its final F1 success, courtesy of Ayrton Senna in Detroit (above).

AUGUST 16

Formula One paid its previous visit to Austria. The Osterreichring was a proper circuit in those days.

YEARS AGO

years ago. He took his Shadow-Cosworth to ninth place (left).

JANUARY 9

Wolf Racing did what few imagine a contemporary F1 team could do: it won its first grand prix, in Argentina (above right). Driver Jody Scheckter was back on track in 1997. The 1979 world champion, who walked away from the sport after retiring in 1980, reappeared to advise son Toby, a competitor in Britain's Formula Vauxhall Junior series.

MARCH 5

The BRM team started its final grand prix in South Africa. Larry Perkins was classified 15th, five laps down, his engine firing on only 10 of its 12 cylinders. Today, the BRM name is attached to a sports-prototype racer which registered the first retirement at the 1997 Le Mans 24 Hours.

MAY 22

Riccardo Patrese, the most experience man in Formula One history, started the first of his 256 grands prix in Monaco 20

JUNE 19

Jacques Laffite scored his and the Ligier team's first F1 victory in Sweden. As of 1997 the Ligier team changed its name to Prost; Laffite holds a commercial role within the organisation.

JULY 16

Jacques Villeneuve's late father Gilles began his F1 career at Silverstone, driving a McLaren M23 (below). The French-Canadian was a sensation. In his only drive for McLaren he was persuaded to pit by a faulty cockpit gauge, but for which he would probably have finished fourth.

JULY 16

In the same race which brought Gilles Villeneuve to the public's wider attention, Renault debuted the first turbocharged F1 car.

JULY 31

Hans Heyer failed to qualify for his home grand prix in Germany, but he decided to start the race anyway. His illicit F1 career lasted nine laps before the gear linkage of his ATS Penske broke.

OCTOBER 23

Late 1976 world champion James Hunt scored the final F1 win of his career at Fuji. Hunt would also have been 50 in 1997.

30 YEARS AGO

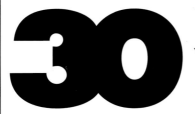

JUNE 4

This year the most famous Formula One engine in history, the Cosworth DFV, celebrated the 30th anniversary of its winning debut in the back of Jim Clark's Lotus in the Dutch GP at Zandvoort (above).

JULY 2

Le Mans, more famous for its round-the-clock sports car race, staged the French GP for the only time. Jack Brabham was the winner.

40 YEARS AGO

JULY 20

Vanwall became the first British constructor to win a world championship grand prix, Stirling Moss and Tony Brooks sharing the driving at Aintree.

AUGUST 4

Juan Manuel Fangio scored his final grand prix victory (below), wearing down and beating the Ferraris of Peter Collins and Mike Hawthorn at the Nürburgring. It was also to be Maserati's last F1 victory. That year, Fangio took his fifth world championship, a feat which remains unequalled.

50

YEARS AGO

JUNE 1

In 1997 McLaren chief (below on the right) Ron Dennis's birthday cake contained 50 candles.

SEPTEMBER 18

Team patron Gian Carlo Minardi also celebrated his 50th birthday. At that point, his cars had started 201 grands prix without winning any of them. "I love being part of the sport, I need no further motivation that that," he said.

60 YEARS AGO

NOVEMBER 11

Vittorio Brambilla was 60 in 1997. Affectionately known as the Monza Gorilla, Brambilla celebrated so enthusiastically at the conclusion of his only F1 win, at Austria in 1975 (above), that he crashed on his slowing-down (supposedly) lap.

70

YEARS AGO

APRIL 20

Phil Hill (at Monaco in 1961, right), the first of three men called Hill to win the world championship and the first American to do so, celebrated his 70th birthday in '97. Hill is still an occasional visitor to modern F1 events.

=14 grösse

oste

If only everything in life was as reliable as, erm, a Williams-Renault. Once again, Villeneuve picked up the pieces as his rivals fell apart. In Austria, his slow start went unpunished.

hakkinen **dominates** for one lap. . . **bang!** ● tr
chances killed by 10 second **penalty** ● villeneuve is

reis von

reich

ads a race for first time. . . **bang!** ● schumacher's
teful **recipient** of another **10** title points

The tartan army was on fine form, Barrichello and Magnussen qualifying and running in the top six – at least to begin with. Given that his Ferrari handled like a kite in a gale, Michael Schumacher was surprised to be able to challenge compatriot Frentzen for third (below). A stop-go penalty eventually overwhelmed one German – and the following Coulthard overwhelmed both of them.

jacques Villeneuve had every reason to look like the cat that had stashed away the cream. He may have dismissed the new A1-Ring's qualities as a racing circuit but he won the Austrian Grand Prix in a fashion as convincing as any of his previous victories.

But that wasn't the only reason for the beaming smile which this habit-ually undemonstrative young man was doing his best to restrain afterwards.

Going into the race, the paddock was awash with rumour about Villeneuve's relationship with Williams – or more specifically with its technical director, Patrick Head. The pair were said to have quarrelled before qualifying over the arcane details of car set-up.

Head, stiff upper lip typically intact, dismissed this as nonsense – then in the next breath bemoaned the disappear-ance of the scruff-of-the-neck driving

Michael rows the bo

Monza suggested it; the A1-Ring con-firmed it. Ferrari, so often smelling of roses this season, was now altogether less fragrant.

In practice Schumacher's F310B looked truculent, even truck-like, in its dislike of corners. Neither was it particu-larly scintillating on the straights. While Villeneuve and Williams were moving and shaking the Scuderia was simply shaken. The team gave Schuey and Irvine such a brief splash of gas for their qualifying runs that neither could complete a slowing-down lap.

Schumacher's car even began to cough on his flyer, helping Irvine to become the first team-mate ever to outqualify Michael more than once. In truth, it was the Ulsterman's decision to run softer

style which had characterised the French-Canadian's performances earlier in the year. Villeneuve's response was an aggressive, focused drive on a track he disdainfully described as "very safe, if that's what you want".

But his post-race Cheshire Cat grin also told of a championship battle that was shaping up to go down the wire.

Michael Schumacher could have finished on Villeneuve's tail had he not been stung by a 10-second stop-go penalty for nipping by Heinz-Harald Frentzen's Williams under yellow flags – something for which Ferrari team-mate Eddie Irvine was at least partly responsible.

Not even Michael at his most aggressive could salvage more than a point – but it was a vital point, because it was just enough to keep Villeneuve off the top of the championship table for the first time

"the **first** time all year that the **williams duo** had celebrated **together**. it **couldn't** have come at a **better** time"

one

Goodyear tyres which really made the difference. But this same choice also knackered his race and played a part in his team-mate's, too.

Schumacher's car was much better in race trim – though even Michael was mystified that he was able to threaten Frentzen's third spot by half-distance. But Eddie was rather more steady, his tyres fading in and out like a prog rock anthem as he fought to keep the Ferrari on the same lap chart.

Having been passed by Jean Alesi, who had already found time to make a pit stop, Irvine attempted to respond round the outside at the Remus Kurve right-hander. The pair touched, Jean rode up over his rear wheel, took off Harrier-like over the top of the Ferrari and briefly helicoptered round before crashing down in the gravel trap.

Alesi was miffed and unsurprisingly failed to concur with Irvine's accusations that the Frenchman had simply lost control of the Benetton.

"If it didn't cost me a $10,000 fine, I would punch him in the face," promised Jean between gritted teeth.

He wasn't the only one gnashing his chops.

Schumacher arrived at the corner on the next lap, shaping up to pass Frentzen while the Williams was baulked by the tardy Gerhard Berger. Unaware of the waved yellow flags, Schumacher slotted inside Heinz-Harald and put some daylight between them as the uncooperative Berger stitched up the Williams for two more laps.

The move earned Michael a 10-second stop-go penalty (he felt that insufficient flags had been waved) and a one-way ticket to the lower reaches of the top 10.

Schumacher finally fought back into the points as Barrichello crashed his Stewart and Damon Hill left the door ajar at the Remus Kurve – but it wasn't enough to dispel the impression that Ferrari had dropped the ball.

With the Nürburgring only a week away, it could hardly afford not to pick it up – and pronto.

Above: If your engine blows up on lap one, there's not much for it but to check out the tractor-pulling on Austrian TV.

trulli, madly, deeply

"How much will it cost if I punch Eddie Irvine?"

"Jarno Trulli is an Italian world champion of the future," claimed out-going Benetton boss Flavio Briatore at the start of the season. Austria provided evidence that he might have a point.

Briatore had a vested interest. He was Trulli's manager on a long-term basis and had been responsible for putting the 23-year-old Italian in a Minardi after only 18 months in single-seater racing. He also engineered Trulli's subsequent promotion to Prost as substitute for the injured Olivier Panis.

But while Briatore was confident in his charge's abilities, the paddock jury was still out. Trulli looked a little like Ayrton Senna and had been likened to him by those who'd seen him in karting or German Formula Three, yet he never showed the sort of gifts in a Minardi as the late Brazilian had during his first year at Toleman. Six drives for Prost showed flashes of promise – fourth at Hockenheim, for example – but were blended with mysterious slumps in form which would sometimes allow unrated team-mate Shinji Nakano to outpace him.

Prost was generally impressed, however, and at the A1-Ring Trulli proved why. He was assisted by his Bridgestone tyres, which had a significant edge over Goodyear in qualifying, but his race day performance also bore all the hallmarks of a driver with a future at the top.

Upon Hakkinen's smoky demise at the end of lap one, Trulli led as he pleased, pulling away with nine consecutive fastest laps while driving, he insisted, well within himself. Yes, the tyre-troubled Barrichello helped him by holding up Villeneuve. And yes, Jacques caught him hand over fist when he finally got by the Stewart. But Trulli was suffering what would become terminal engine problems by this stage and had already decided to concentrate on a podium finish.

However, the single most impressive thing was his detachment. Not only was Trulli truly in the spotlight, he knew that a recovered Panis was about to take back his drive at the following race and that Austria could be his final chance to secure a seat with the team in 1998.

Yet he appeared totally unflustered, even when pounding round at the front of a grand prix field for the first time.

"Why shouldn't I be?" he said. "I've spent 14 years of my life racing and most of the time I've been at the front. Formula One is no different, just another kind of racing."

Young shoulders, old head.

since Barcelona.

Furthermore, Heinz-Harald Frentzen's third place allowed the British team to put clear daylight between itself and the Scuderia in the constructors' contest.

For once, however, the German was lucky. Career bridesmaid Mika Hakkinen led for about a mile before his McLaren-Mercedes went bang; team-mate David Coulthard's silky run to second merely added a pinch of salt to the unfortunate Finn's wounds.

Jarno Trulli suffered a similar fate, having taken advantage of a Bridgestone benefit – which allowed his Prost and the Stewarts of Rubens Barrichello and Jan Magnussen to qualify brilliantly – to lead the first half of the race. But his engine, which had already proffered its sick note while Villeneuve chased him down before his pit stop, popped its clogs in the closing stages and allowed Frentzen onto the podium – the first time all year that the Williams duo had celebrated together.

It couldn't have come at a better time.

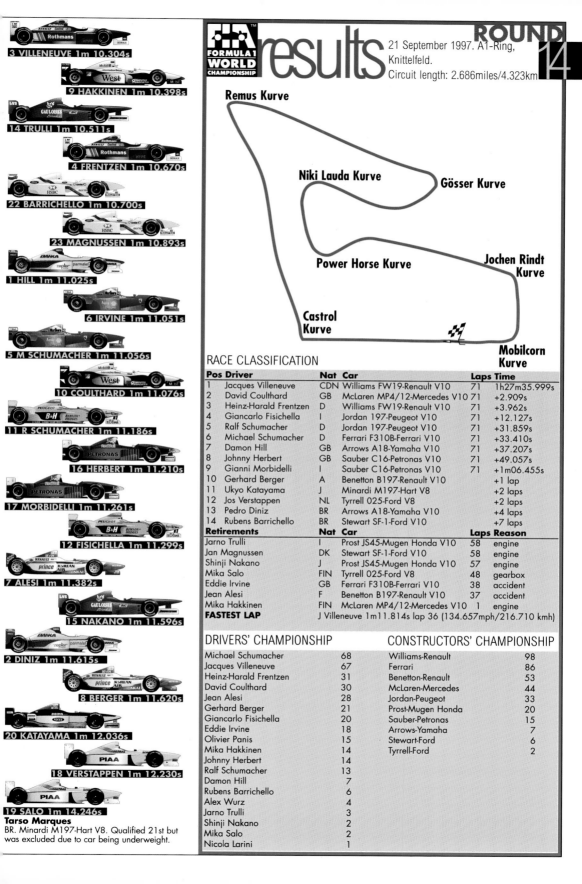

3 VILLENEUVE 1m 10.304s

9 HAKKINEN 1m 10.398s

14 TRULLI 1m 10.511s

4 FRENTZEN 1m 10.670s

22 BARRICHELLO 1m 10.700s

23 MAGNUSSEN 1m 10.893s

1 HILL 1m 11.025s

6 IRVINE 1m 11.051s

5 M SCHUMACHER 1m 11.056s

10 COULTHARD 1m 11.076s

11 R SCHUMACHER 1m 11.186s

16 HERBERT 1m 11.210s

17 MORBIDELLI 1m 11.261s

12 FISICHELLA 1m 11.299s

7 ALESI 1m 11.382s

15 NAKANO 1m 11.596s

2 DINIZ 1m 11.615s

8 BERGER 1m 11.620s

20 KATAYAMA 1m 12.036s

18 VERSTAPPEN 1m 12.230s

19 SALO 1m 14.246s

Tarso Marques
BR. Minardi M197-Hart V8. Qualified 21st but
was excluded due to car being underweight.

FIA FORMULA 1 WORLD CHAMPIONSHIP results

21 September 1997. A1-Ring, Knittelfeld.
Circuit length: 2.686miles/4.323km

ROUND 14

Remus Kurve

Niki Lauda Kurve

Gösser Kurve

Power Horse Kurve

Jochen Rindt Kurve

Castrol Kurve

Mobilcorn Kurve

RACE CLASSIFICATION

Pos	Driver	Nat	Car	Laps	Time
1	Jacques Villeneuve	CDN	Williams FW19-Renault V10	71	1h27m35.999s
2	David Coulthard	GB	McLaren MP4/12-Mercedes V10	71	+2.909s
3	Heinz-Harald Frentzen	D	Williams FW19-Renault V10	71	+3.962s
4	Giancarlo Fisichella	I	Jordan 197-Peugeot V10	71	+12.127s
5	Ralf Schumacher	D	Jordan 197-Peugeot V10	71	+31.859s
6	Michael Schumacher	D	Ferrari F310B-Ferrari V10	71	+33.410s
7	Damon Hill	GB	Arrows A18-Yamaha V10	71	+37.207s
8	Johnny Herbert	GB	Sauber C16-Petronas V10	71	+49.057s
9	Gianni Morbidelli	I	Sauber C16-Petronas V10	71	+1m06.455s
10	Gerhard Berger	A	Benetton B197-Renault V10		+1 lap
11	Ukyo Katayama	J	Minardi M197-Hart V8		+2 laps
12	Jos Verstappen	NL	Tyrrell 025-Ford V8		+2 laps
13	Pedro Diniz	BR	Arrows A18-Yamaha V10		+4 laps
14	Rubens Barrichello	BR	Stewart SF-1-Ford V10		+7 laps

Retirements	Nat	Car	Laps	Reason
Jarno Trulli	I	Prost JS45-Mugen Honda V10	58	engine
Jan Magnussen	DK	Stewart SF-1-Ford V10	58	engine
Shinji Nakano	J	Prost JS45-Mugen Honda V10	57	engine
Mika Salo	FIN	Tyrrell 025-Ford V8	48	gearbox
Eddie Irvine	GB	Ferrari F310B-Ferrari V10	38	accident
Jean Alesi	F	Benetton B197-Renault V10	37	accident
Mika Hakkinen	FIN	McLaren MP4/12-Mercedes V10	1	engine

FASTEST LAP J Villeneuve 1m11.814s lap 36 (134.657mph/216.710 kmh)

DRIVERS' CHAMPIONSHIP

Michael Schumacher	68
Jacques Villeneuve	67
Heinz-Harald Frentzen	31
David Coulthard	30
Jean Alesi	28
Gerhard Berger	21
Giancarlo Fisichella	20
Eddie Irvine	18
Olivier Panis	15
Mika Hakkinen	14
Johnny Herbert	14
Ralf Schumacher	13
Damon Hill	7
Rubens Barrichello	6
Alex Wurz	4
Jarno Trulli	3
Shinji Nakano	2
Mika Salo	2
Nicola Larini	1

CONSTRUCTORS' CHAMPIONSHIP

Williams-Renault	98
Ferrari	86
Benetton-Renault	53
McLaren-Mercedes	44
Jordan-Peugeot	33
Prost-Mugen Honda	20
Sauber-Petronas	15
Arrows-Yamaha	7
Stewart-Ford	6
Tyrrell-Ford	2

mclarens dominate until big bang
villeneuve wins to take control of title

Mika Hakkinen presses on towards another comprehensive engine failure. A promising day turned sour for Mercedes on home turf.

strife in the schumacher family • lucky
ce • point for returning panis

reis von
emburg 15

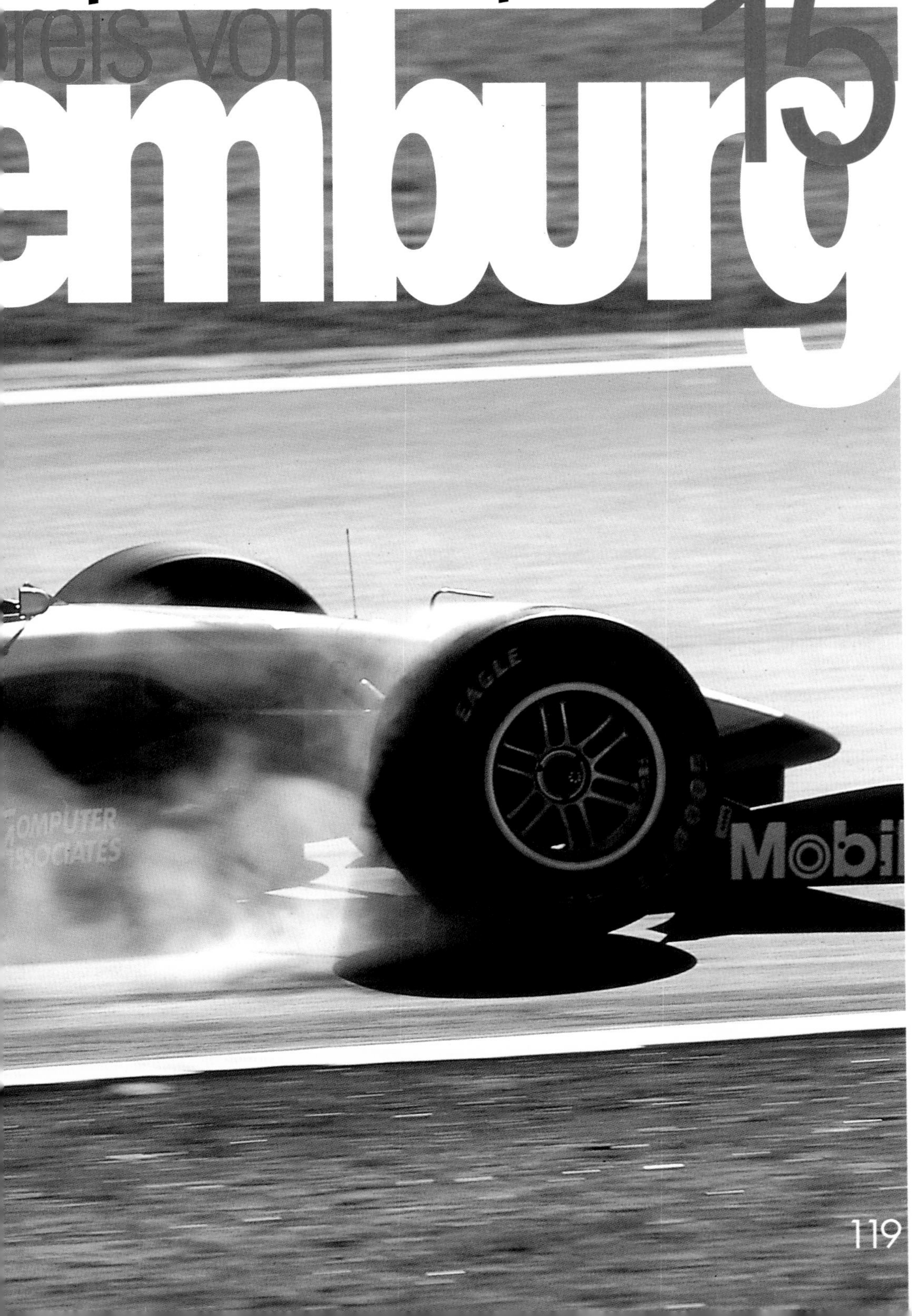

before the Luxembourg Grand Prix the title battle between Michael Schumacher and Jacques Villeneuve was poised on a knife edge. Afterwards, it appeared all over bar the shouting.

If that was the case it had ended with a bang, not a whimper. Problem was, the bang arrived two races too soon to the sound of crunching carbon, as Ralf Schumacher's Jordan interlocked violently with his brother's Ferrari at the first corner.

The accident seriously damaged Michael's front suspension – and with it his championship aspirations. He could only watch from the pits as Villeneuve romped home to a victory that, on pace alone, he didn't deserve.

Such is the fortune on which championships can be decided. Jacques' luck had held in Hungary and it held doubly in Luxembourg – or rather Germany, since this race was named by somebody with a failed CSE in West European Geography. Not only did the French-Canadian survive a wheel-banging match with Heinz-Harald Frentzen at the same bend which claimed Schumacher – he also profited when the Patron Saint of Mechanical Mayhem visited the Nürburgring mid-race, sidelining four of the top six but leaving Villeneuve well alone.

Chiefly – and most cruelly – affected were McLaren duo Mika Hakkinen and David Coulthard, who had been vanishing into the distance before their Mercedes motors

> ## "chiefly – and most cruelly – affected were the mclaren duo, who had been vanishing into the distance"

both let go within the space of one acutely embarrassing lap.

The feisty Stewarts of Rubens Barrichello and Jan Magnussen, potential points-scorers both, also came unstuck, leaving Villeneuve struggling to stay awake out front.

Frentzen's race was more interesting, because he'd inadvertently knocked off his ignition switch off when he rubbed wheels with his team-mate. He was down among the Tyrrells before his Williams fired up, but he took it back towards the front at an impressive rate of knots.

By the end, he'd split the Benettons of Jean Alesi and Gerhard Berger to join Jacques on the podium – and leave the

Jacques Villeneuve (far left) was patently not the fastest man in Germany (aka Luxembourg if it's commercially convenient), but he went away with 10 points nonetheless. The problems affecting so many leading runners allowed Jean Alesi (opposite below) to finish second for approximately the 2744th time in his career.

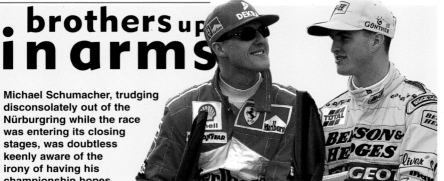

brothers up
in arms

Michael Schumacher, trudging disconsolately out of the Nürburgring while the race was entering its closing stages, was doubtless keenly aware of the irony of having his championship hopes reduced by brother Ralf's flying Jordan, which in turn had been hit by Giancarlo Fisichella's sister car.

Whether he found it quite so amusing as certain sections of the paddock is rather less likely.

Before Ralf became the airborne catalyst which gave Jacques Villeneuve a critical advantage, the brothers Schumacher had fought shy of one another on-track all season.

Indeed, their raceday skirmishes bore an air of fraternal back-slapping. Michael had allowed Ralf to recover a lost lap and thus score a point in France, while Ralf returned the favour by not attempting to unseat his tyre-troubled sibling from fourth in Hungary – and then cheerily admitted it afterwards! Bet that went down well at Jordan. . .

The first-corner fracas obviously went down badly all round – not that you could get anybody by the name of Schumacher to admit it. Such incidents are usually accompanied the bile and recrimination of a House of Commons debate. This one brought forth the kind of PR-friendly blather usually reserved for daytime TV – even from the visibly hacked-off Schu Snr.

"It's a shame the incident happened with my brother," he said, "but you can't blame anybody for that sort of accident."

So far, so bland, but neither Jordan driver added anything of interest – beyond a bit of mutual finger-pointing.

Schumacher Jnr: "Everybody braked a bit late and there wasn't enough room. Obviously the consequences were very bad for my team and my brother."

Fisichella: "I hit Ralf because there was nowhere else to go. He closed the door a little, but he was just taking the same line as everybody else."

Reactions elsewhere were altogether more extreme, with a hail of criticism being directed at Ralf in particular by thrice former world champion Niki Lauda. In truth, that seemed a bit unfair: Ralf was launched into Michael by a nudge from his team-mate, the Castrol S is stupidly tight for a first corner and they weren't the only pair to touch.

But given Ralf's apparent eagerness not to make himself too many mates up and down the pit lane in the course of his debut F1 season, perhaps he shouldn't have been too surprised.

121

rubber stamp hovering just above a record ninth constructors' title for Williams.

Pre-race, Villeneuve underlined the absence of any psychological enmity between the title protagonists, claiming they were too focused to indulge in the "silly games" that had marked – and sometimes enlivened – previous down-to-the-wire battles.

But come Sunday afternoon, Jacques couldn't resist a quick tweak of the knife.

"We've just put one over Michael and Ferrari," he bubbled. "I'm sure they'll remember that, because now it's two in a row."

There was no clearer indication of how Ferrari's cookie had just apparently crumbled.

diniz ready

The leading Arrows driver drove a solid race at the Nürburgring. But it was a little overlooked.

For almost half the distance he kept Olivier Panis tucked up behind, even though the Frenchman's Prost was clearly faster than the ill-handling Yamaha-powered machine. But the two points scored reinforced Arrows' eighth place in the constructors' standings; hardly earth-shattering, but indicative of progress nonetheless.

Before the season began, you could have got juicily long odds on the above being written about any Arrows driver bar one D Hill. But they are written about Pedro Paulo Diniz – the man whose sponsorship effectively paid the world champion's wages.

To several seasoned observers it was Diniz rather than Hill who emerged from 1997 with the most credit chez Arrows.

Although the 27-year-old heir to a

Brazilian supermarket fortune could never compete with Damon's show-stopping Hungary drive, his seasonal highlights were, in context, no less noteworthy. They included outqualifying and outperforming Hill at Spa, the ultimate driver's track, and finally laying to rest the ghost of his first F1 season with Forti in 1995 – during which he earned several unprintable sobriquets alluding to his stash of cash but lack of pace.

Hill was more charitable, rating Pedro "a good little pedaller", but he was more than that: Diniz was faster than his exalted team-mate on several occasions, though a combination of bad luck and, sometimes, bad judgment let him down.

Bad judgment was the last thing Arrows boss Tom Walkinshaw had been accused of upon pairing Hill with Diniz. This, said the cynics, was an astute move which secured Tom's team a $12m pay-day and a clear-cut number one on whom to focus.

Wrong. Diniz proved himself wholly worthy of Arrows' interest, justified Walkinshaw's assertion that he could be "unbelievably fast" on occasion and served up a family-sized portion of humble pie for his critics, most of whom were by now queuing up to label him the year's most improved driver.

Others quietly felt that Diniz had been flattered by a disinterested and demotivated Hill for much of the year. It didn't look that way in Germany, where Hill was tigering along ahead of Diniz until he stalled and lost 30 seconds in the pits.

It was, said Damon, pathetic: the kind of adjective formerly used in close association with his team-mate. But that was all in the past. You'll have a job getting any juicily long odds on Diniz next year.

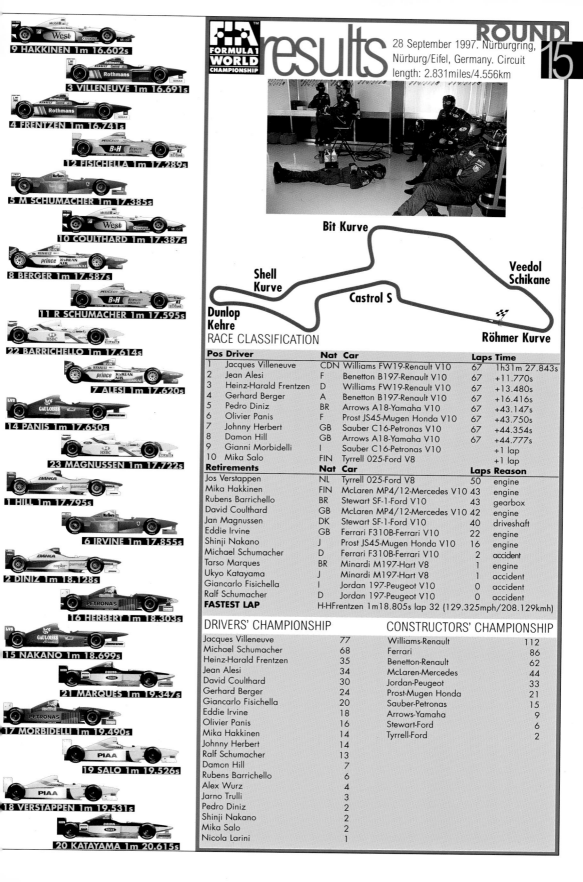

9 HAKKINEN 1m 16.602s

3 VILLENEUVE 1m 16.691s

4 FRENTZEN 1m 16.741s

12 FISICHELLA 1m 17.289s

5 M SCHUMACHER 1m 17.385s

10 COULTHARD 1m 17.387s

8 BERGER 1m 17.587s

11 R SCHUMACHER 1m 17.595s

22 BARRICHELLO 1m 17.614s

7 ALESI 1m 17.620s

14 PANIS 1m 17.650s

23 MAGNUSSEN 1m 17.722s

1 HILL 1m 17.795s

6 IRVINE 1m 17.855s

2 DINIZ 1m 18.128s

16 HERBERT 1m 18.303s

15 NAKANO 1m 18.699s

21 MARQUES 1m 19.347s

17 MORBIDELLI 1m 19.490s

19 SALO 1m 19.526s

18 VERSTAPPEN 1m 19.531s

20 KATAYAMA 1m 20.615s

Bit Kurve

Shell Kurve

Veedol Schikane

Castrol S

Dunlop Kehre

Röhmer Kurve

RACE CLASSIFICATION

Pos	Driver	Nat	Car	Laps	Time
1	Jacques Villeneuve	CDN	Williams FW19-Renault V10	67	1h31m 27.843s
2	Jean Alesi	F	Benetton B197-Renault V10	67	+11.770s
3	Heinz-Harald Frentzen	D	Williams FW19-Renault V10	67	+13.480s
4	Gerhard Berger	A	Benetton B197-Renault V10	67	+16.416s
5	Pedro Diniz	BR	Arrows A18-Yamaha V10	67	+43.147s
6	Olivier Panis	F	Prost JS45-Mugen Honda V10	67	+43.750s
7	Johnny Herbert	GB	Sauber C16-Petronas V10	67	+44.354s
8	Damon Hill	GB	Arrows A18-Yamaha V10	67	+44.777s
9	Gianni Morbidelli	I	Sauber C16-Petronas V10		+1 lap
10	Mika Salo	FIN	Tyrrell 025-Ford V8		+1 lap

Retirements		Nat	Car	Laps	Reason
Jos Verstappen		NL	Tyrrell 025-Ford V8	50	engine
Mika Hakkinen		FIN	McLaren MP4/12-Mercedes V10	43	engine
Rubens Barrichello		BR	Stewart SF-1-Ford V10	43	gearbox
David Coulthard		GB	McLaren MP4/12-Mercedes V10	42	engine
Jan Magnussen		DK	Stewart SF-1-Ford V10	40	driveshaft
Eddie Irvine		GB	Ferrari F310B-Ferrari V10	22	engine
Shinji Nakano		J	Prost JS45-Mugen Honda V10	16	engine
Michael Schumacher		D	Ferrari F310B-Ferrari V10	2	accident
Tarso Marques		BR	Minardi M197-Hart V8	1	engine
Ukyo Katayama		J	Minardi M197-Hart V8	1	accident
Giancarlo Fisichella		I	Jordan 197-Peugeot V10	0	accident
Ralf Schumacher		D	Jordan 197-Peugeot V10	0	accident
FASTEST LAP			H-HFrentzen 1m18.805s lap 32 (129.325mph/208.129kmh)		

DRIVERS' CHAMPIONSHIP

Jacques Villeneuve	77
Michael Schumacher	68
Heinz-Harald Frentzen	35
Jean Alesi	34
David Coulthard	30
Gerhard Berger	24
Giancarlo Fisichella	20
Eddie Irvine	18
Olivier Panis	16
Mika Hakkinen	14
Johnny Herbert	14
Ralf Schumacher	13
Damon Hill	7
Rubens Barrichello	6
Alex Wurz	4
Jarno Trulli	3
Pedro Diniz	2
Shinji Nakano	2
Mika Salo	2
Nicola Larini	1

CONSTRUCTORS' CHAMPIONSHIP

Williams-Renault	112
Ferrari	86
Benetton-Renault	62
McLaren-Mercedes	44
Jordan-Peugeot	33
Prost-Mugen Honda	21
Sauber-Petronas	15
Arrows-Yamaha	9
Stewart-Ford	6
Tyrrell-Ford	2

Pool cue: in-between improving his lap times on a Sony Playstation Olivier Panis embarked on a taxing fitness programme.

fighting
back to
fitness

by autumn canada was a distant memory for olivier panis

When Olivier Panis's Prost plunged violently into the guard-rail during the Canadian Grand Prix, it was perhaps not surprising that he initially attempted to get out of the car unaided. Quite simply, the Frenchman wasn't used to hurting himself.

"Breaking my legs did come as a bit of a shock to my system," he said. "I've always been in good physical shape – I don't even usually pick up colds. It was new experience for me to have a serious injury."

Three months later he stepped back into a racing car for the first time, albeit a Formula Three chassis.

And he flew.

"I suppose it was a bit of a step back," said Olivier, "but it was important to start off in something less physically demanding, even if I had to readjust to using a conventional gear lever. But it was a good exercise for me to rediscover the sensations of a racing car – and I even did a decent F3 lap time."

It was actually a bit more than decent. The following week he was back in his Prost at Magny-Cours, where he astounded the team with his pace.

"He was amazing," said engineer Humphrey Corbett. "We decided to put the tyre pressures up because we thought it would take him time to build up heat – but he did a competitive time on his first flying lap. It was incredible. It wasn't just as though he had never been away – it was almost as if he'd been at driving school for the last couple of months. He was much calmer, more reflective. It was an absolutely phenomenal performance."

And now here he was, on the eve of the Luxembourg Grand Prix, raring to race again.

What was the worst moment for you after the accident?

"The hardest thing was understanding what was going on around me and knowing what had really happened. I think I realised quickly enough and the doctors were swiftly on hand to reassure me."

Have you ever had any doubts that your career might be in jeopardy?

"No. It might have looked very dramatic but at the end of it all I only had two broken legs and they were clean fractures. There were some muscular complications afterwards but there was never any doubt that I would make a recovery. The doctors always made me aware of that so I knew it was only a question of time.

"Obviously it hasn't all been easy because I've had a couple of very serious operations. But the surgeons have looked after me well and I would say that I am absolutely back to 100 per cent fitness. During the past couple of months there have been times when I have felt the pain but my family and friends have been there when I needed them. Right now I feel in very good shape."

What did you think when you saw the accident on video?

"It was a big one! But I'm not looking backwards. Accidents are part and parcel of Formula One. It's over and done with and I'm looking forward, thinking about my future – and aiming to drive even better than before."

How did you feel when you got back in the F1 car at Magny-Cours?

"It all came back very quickly. It was just like being in the car I had before the accident – with the notable exception that the engine was more powerful and the tyres were better. I did a pretty good time so I was happy."

How rigorous a training programme did you need to get you ready?

"In terms of hours, I don't know. After the shunt I had two and a half full months at the rehabilitation centre and after that I resumed physical training. I've been doing about four hours a day for the last fortnight."

People say you are calmer since the accident. Did you have time to think about things while you were away?

"Yes. I realised that we all have problems in everyday life and something I've come to appreciate in the last couple of months is that you should ignore the minor irritations and focus on the good things. That's a positive outcome. I realise how lucky I am to be able to race a Formula One car. It's not something everyone can do and now I'm keen to get started."

During your absence there has been talk of Jacques Villeneuve or Damon Hill joining you in 1998. How would you feel about a top driver like that being your team-mate?

"Why should it be a problem? Having two quick drivers in the team enables you to develop the car faster and that is what we need. I don't believe in all this number one and two stuff; you should work together to improve the car and then it's every man for himself in the race."

And with that he's away, off to score a point on his comeback. The last three months have opened Olivier Panis's eyes to one or two things but they have not hindered his racing prospects – real or virtual. "If he challenges you to a race on a Sony Playstation, don't accept, "advises a team spokesman. " He's had a bit of time to practise recently."

ferrari plays **tactical** game to **perfection**
villeneuve in **trouble** ● title in the **balance**

fuji television

japanese grand prix •16

grand prix

There is no truth in the rumour that Ferrari is planning an assault on the world chess championship: Schumacher and the boys from Maranello celebrate their major tactical triumph.

ichael Schumacher received the chequered flag with the kind of celebration more usually found on a football terrace than in a racing car.

The string of Mansellesque punches he let rip on winning in Japan told you everything you needed to know about the significance of his success – and they were also the last thing Williams needed to see on a weekend when the constructors' championship battle was

"frentzen secured a record ninth constructors' title for williams: not that this dispelled the communal sulking"

secured but crippling losses were sustained in the drivers' war.

What's more, there had been fully 24 hours to contemplate the prospect after Jacques Villeneuve, a one-race suspended ban hanging over his head for yellow-flag violations earlier in the season, failed again to slow for a warning flag in Saturday morning practice.

By that evening the team had been told the news it feared: that the championship leader's weekend was over. Williams appealed, thus allowing the Canadian to start from pole, but nobody held out much hope of him being able to keep whatever result he obtained.

And on Sunday Ferrari ensured he wouldn't have much to hold on to on anyway, giving Villeneuve the run-around with a display of superbly successful gamesmanship.

Eddie Irvine – shooting star one minute, chicane the next – gifted his team-mate a win which gave Schumacher the momentum in the title chase. Villeneuve trailed home fifth to collect two points he was not destined to keep. While Schuey pranced onto the podium, Jacques skulked home wearing the expression of a man given chopsticks to eat yoghurt.

Williams could have been forgiven for wishing to apply a different sort of stick to Heinz-Harald Frentzen's tardy posterior early on. But as the race wore on H-H came on strong, displacing Mika Hakkinen at his first pit stop and Irvine with an up-yours block into the first corner after his last.

Chasing Schumacher seemed futile, since his old enemy was 10 seconds ahead with a dwindling number of laps left. Yet he had trimmed the gap by half even before Damon Hill came to his aid, holding off Schumacher for a lap and allowing Frentzen to close. What irked Schumacher was that the world champion was being lapped at the time.

Frentzen ran out of time to capitalise,

Villeneuve demonstrates the art of leading a grand prix as slowly as possible (far left). Meanwhile Frentzen's lethargy (left) appeared to be less deliberate – though the German finally perked up and did enough to secure the constructors' title for Williams.

villeneuve's
flagging spirit

Jacques Villeneuve's hopes of clinching the title with one race to go were cut short in one moment of madness.

What made it all the dafter was that it happened on Saturday morning, when the burning issue is set-up, not speed.

The Williams pilot's crime was to squirt his FW19 past

Jos Verstappen's Tyrrell, parked beside a back straight with fuel-feed problems, while yellow flags were being waved beside it. Normally, this is a slap-on-the-wrist infringement; problem was, Jacques' wrist was already stinging after two similar previous offences, the second of which had left him sitting on long-term probation.

Yet despite his familiarity with North America, Villeneuve appeared to have some difficulty grasping the concept of three strikes and out, cheerfully admitting to anyone who would listen that he'd not only seen the flag but had chosen to ignore it.

"When you are flat down the straight and you see the incident, I don't think you should just step on the brakes," he said. Schumacher, sitting beside him at the time, nodded in agreement; he, along with Frentzen and three other drivers, were all punished for ignoring the flag. But then they didn't have suspended bans hovering over them.

Rumour and counter-rumour rumbled around the paddock afterwards: that Villeneuve would quit F1 if he was excluded; that he would be kicked out of the final race as well; that F1 power-brokers Max Mosley and Bernie Ecclestone were weighing up his fate on the phone. As the sun sank into the ground, the reality was that the son of the late Gilles Villeneuve would not be allowed to start the Japanese Grand Prix..

Williams, feeling it had nothing to lose, allowed its driver to keep his pole position by appealing. A fat lot of good it did them – something tacitly acknowledged when the appeal was withdrawn the following Thursday, five days before a Parisian court was due to decide Villeneuve's fate.

On a day when the international news agenda was set by the crucial England-Italy World Cup tie, Villeneuve had made a bold bid to maintain the F1 title race's place in the spotlight. It also earned him the dubious honour of having media crews sticking microphones in his every orifice for the rest of the event.

"I haven't really enjoyed this weekend," he grumbled upon leaving the track. Ultimately, however, he owed his discomfort to just one person.

Himself.

grand prix year 1997

but second place secured a record ninth constructors' title for Williams: not that this dispelled the communal sulking which pervaded its pit garage.

Schumacher, meanwhile, sought an audience with Hill, who'd disappeared after cheerfully justifying his defensiveness.

If only, remarked someone afterwards, Damon had been that hard to pass in Austria.

Suzuka marked Ukyo Katayama's final F1 race on home soil. He is retiring to concentrate on mountaineering; apparently, tackling K2 with a pick-axe is easier than challenging MichaelSchumacher with a Minardi.

prancing horseplay
wins the day

Schumacher's words were more closing-time-down-the-pub than post-race press conference.

Irvine, he bubbled, was "the best team-mate I've ever had": a man who'd sacrificed his race for the greater good of Maranello, who helped shuffle his Ferrari partner to the front of the pack and covered his backside once he was in situ.

Schumacher may have been uncharacteristically sentimental, but he was spot on with his praise. Irvine's Suzuka expertise, honed during three years of driving in the lucrative Japanese Formula 3000 Championship, ensured that Ferrari was able to run rings around Villeneuve's attempts to influence the outcome of a race in whose results he was never likely to be classified.

Jacques never stooped so low as to consider taking Schumacher off, but his actions off the line – delaying the whole field to the tune of up to five seconds per lap – suggested he rather hoped somebody else might. Hakkinen, swarming all over the Ferrari, was the biggest threat.

Irvine's intervention ensured the Finn remained only that. With Schumacher calmly holding the McLaren up under braking, Eddie swept by the pair of them at the chicane two laps in. He then breezily dispatched Villeneuve – one of the manoeuvres of the season, that – and set about proving exactly how much Jacques was holding back, pulling out a 12-second lead in a few laps.

Villeneuve, sensing the futility of his efforts to get Schumacher arrested, sped up before his first pit stop. But he wasn't going quickly enough to stop Schumacher nipping past as the Williams exited the pits afterwards, despite Jacques' rather clumsy attempted block.

To the French-Canadian's disbelief, things only got worse. Irvine, lying in wait a few seconds up the road, loitered long enough to let his team-mate into a lead he never relinquished before blatantly – but fairly – holding Villeneuve up long enough to persuade Williams to call him in for an early second stop.

A stuck fuel nozzle cost Villeneuve a further five seconds and put the tin lid on a bad day at the office. "I find it difficult to accept that somebody can give up their first win like that," he sighed.

Predictably, Irvine didn't give a monkey's. "Once I got in front, I was just waiting for the phone call," he shrugged.

It may not have been what Bob Hoskins had in mind, and it sure wasn't sporting, but when has that ever counted for anything in latter-day F1?

In short, it had been a master plan brilliantly executed.

130

3 VILLENEUVE 1m 36.071s

5 SCHUMACHER 1m 36.133s

6 IRVINE 1m 36.466s

9 HAKKINEN 1m 36.469s

8 BERGER 1m 36.561s

4 FRENTZEN 1m 36.628s

7 ALESI 1m 36.682s

16 HERBERT 1m 36.906s

12 FISICHELLA 1m 36.917s

14 PANIS 1m 37.073s

10 COULTHARD 1m 37.095s

22 BARRICHELLO 1m 37.343s

11 R SCHUMACHER 1m 37.443s

23 MAGNUSSEN 1m 37.480s

15 NAKANO 1m 37.588s

2 DINIZ 1m 37.853s

1 HILL 1m 38.022s

20 KATAYAMA 1m 38.983s

21 MARQUES 1m 39.678s

18 VERSTAPPEN 1m 40.259s

19 SALO 1m 40.529s

17 MORBIDELLI qualified 18th in 1m38.556s but did not start due to being injured in qualifying

FIA FORMULA 1 WORLD CHAMPIONSHIP results

ROUND 16

12 October 1997. Suzuka Circuit International Racing Course, Ino-Cho, Suzuka-City. Circuit length: 3.644 miles/5.864km

First Curve
S Curve
Degner Curve
Underpass
Chicane
Hairpin
Spoon Curve

RACE CLASSIFICATION

Pos	Driver	Nat	Car	Laps	Time
1	Michael Schumacher	D	Ferrari F310B-Ferrari V10	53	1h29m48.446s
2	Heinz-Harald Frentzen	D	Williams FW19-Renault V10	53	+1.378s
3	Eddie Irvine	GB	Ferrari F310B-Ferrari V10	53	+26.384s
4	Mika Hakkinen	FIN	McLaren MP4/12-Mercedes V10	53	+27.129s
5	Jean Alesi	F	Benetton B197-Renault V10	53	+40.403s
6	Johnny Herbert	GB	Sauber C16-Petronas V10	53	+41.630s
7	Giancarlo Fisichella	I	Jordan 197-Peugeot V10	53	+56.825s
8	Gerhard Berger	A	Benetton B197-Renault V10	53	+1m00.429s
9	Ralf Schumacher	D	Jordan 197-Peugeot V10	53	+1m22.036s
10	David Coulthard	GB	McLaren MP4/12-Mercedes V10		+1 lap
11	Damon Hill	GB	Arrows A18-Yamaha V10		+1 lap
12	Pedro Diniz	BR	Arrows A18-Yamaha V10		+1 lap
13	Jos Verstappen	NL	Tyrrell 025-Ford V8		+1 lap

Retirements	Nat	Car	Laps	Reason
Tarso Marques	BR	Minardi M197-Hart V8	46	gearbox
Mika Salo	FIN	Tyrrell 025-Ford V8	46	engine
Olivier Panis	F	Prost JS45-Mugen Honda V10	36	engine
Shinji Nakano	J	Prost JS45-Mugen Honda V10	22	wheel bearing
Ukyo Katayama	J	Minardi M197-Hart V8	8	engine/spin
Rubens Barrichello	BR	Stewart SF-1-Ford V10	6	spin
Jan Magnussen	DK	Stewart SF-1-Ford V10	3	spin

did not start: Gianni Morbidelli I Sauber C16-Petronas V10 (injured during qualifying)

FASTEST LAP H-H Frentzen 1m38.942 lap 48 (132.577mph/213.361kmh)

Jacques Villeneuve CDN Williams FW19-Renault V10 was allowed to race under williams appeal against disqualification for failing to reduce speed under the yellow flags during a practice session. Finished fifth but appeal was subsequently withdrawn and points deducted

DRIVERS' CHAMPIONSHIP

Michael Schumacher	78
Jacques Villeneuve	77
Heinz-Harald Frentzen	41
Jean Alesi	36
David Coulthard	30
Gerhard Berger	24
Eddie Irvine	22
Giancarlo Fisichella	20
Olivier Panis	16
Mika Hakkinen	17
Johnny Herbert	15
Ralf Schumacher	13
Damon Hill	7
Rubens Barrichello	6
Alex Wurz	4
Jarno Trulli	3
Pedro Diniz	2
Shinji Nakano	2
Mika Salo	2
Nicola Larini	1

CONSTRUCTORS' CHAMPIONSHIP

Williams-Renault	118
Ferrari	100
Benetton-Renault	64
McLaren-Mercedes	47
Jordan-Peugeot	33
Prost-Mugen Honda	21
Sauber-Petronas	16
Arrows-Yamaha	9
Stewart-Ford	6
Tyrrell-Ford	2

Several young drivers created a strong impression in F1 during 1997 – but nowadays it appears to be harder actually to get in to F1 than it is to forge a reputation once you're there. Vacancies are few and far between, candidates are plentiful. Here are 10 of the best of those currently bubbling under.

Ricardo Zonta (Brazil), above right
1997 record: FIA Formula 3000 champion
Worth noting: Won the opening race of the season but was then disqualified for an unproved gearbox irregularity. Crashed in his next two races but bounced back from trough of depression to win three times and take title with a race to spare. Smiles a lot (except when he hasn't scored a point after three races).

1998 prospects: F1 testing role is probably the best he can hope for but he's set his sights high. He was talking to Ferrari by October. As others have found to their cost in recent years, there is no automatic conduit to lead drivers from F1's approved training ground to the principal stadia.

the men mo

Jason Watt (Denmark), far left
1997 record: Third in FIA F3000 Championship
Worth noting: Not quite the best F3000 rookie – that was Montoya – but arguably the find of the season. Disastrous time with Alfa Romeo in the 1996 International Touring Car Championship but put career back on track with a string of storming drives, most notably resisting fierce pressure to win at Spa. Rivals Zonta for the broadest smile in motor racing, a feature which is seldom extinguished in Watt's case.
1998 prospects: A wanted man with backing from an unlikely source – a Danish classified advertising paper.

Nick Heidfeld (Germany), above
1997 record: McLaren F1 test driver;
German F3 champion
Worth noting: Odds-on favourite for his national F3 crown – but he only

scraped home at the final meeting of the year. Future progress assured by support of McLaren and Mercedes.
1998 prospects: More mileage in a McLaren – and he'll race for a new F3000 team being set up on his behalf by his F1 patrons.

Juan Pablo Montoya (Colombia), above
1997 record: Second in FIA F3000 Championship
Worth noting: Seeks to be his country's first F1 driver since Roberto Guerrero in 1983. Incredible self-confidence and car control. Scored three wins – but it could have been more if he had been as consistent as he was fast. His refusal to give up is admirable – though it occasionally gets him into trouble,

likely

usually when he's trying to hang on to a place in the top three with a car that's falling to pieces. Could make it as a circus entertainer if his racing career falters: shows uncanny sense of balance on a quad bike.

1998 prospects: Wanted by just about every F3000 team and touted as a possible F1 tester for everyone from Williams down.

Nicholas Minassian (France), above right
1997 record: Won just about everything in the British F3 series – apart from the title
Worth noting: Scuppered his own chances when he threw gravel at a backmarker whom he alleged had held him up in a race at Thruxton. That incident cost him a few seconds and race victory; the subsequent ban cost him a month out of the car and several chances to score – yet he was still in with an outside chance of the title to the last. So he's quite fast.
1998 prospects: Lots of F3000 teams are interested in him – but would be more interested still if his dad owned a chain of Brazilian supermarkets. Cash could be a problem.

Jonny Kane (Northern Ireland), above left
1997 record: British F3 Championship winner
Worth noting: A dynamic blend of

speed and common sense in a wiry frame. Kane was favourite to win the F3 crown with the crack Paul Stewart Racing squad – and once arch-rival Minassian had been suspended he concentrated on making sure he scored points at every opportunity. His occasional conservatism may not have been spectacular, but it proved effective.
1998 prospects: Would like to do F3000, but he's no different to most young British drivers – and certainly no richer. Money's too tight to mention.

Jörg Müller (Germany), above
1997 record: Arrows F1 test driver; raced for Nissan at Le Mans; broke leg in Nissan when testing in Spain

Worth noting: F3000 champion in 1996 found that there were few career opportunities for an underfinanced German with a sense of humour. Brilliant racer whom most compatriots rate way above Ralf Schumacher. "The trouble is that no one is interested in someone called Müller," says Jörg. "Every second bloke in Germany is called Müller."

1998 prospects: Nothing that's likely to be worthy of him – but he'll get on and do it without complaining.

Jamie Davies (England), below
1997 record: Fourth in FIA F3000 Championship

Worth noting: Probably the most prolific Yeovil native in international motor racing right now. Led points table at mid-season but failed to score in last four races. Progress hampered by the fact that he was forced to change engineers almost as often as an F1 driver changes tyres. Excellent, no-nonsense racer who is missing only one thing.

1998 prospects: Unfortunately, that one thing is money. One of the favourites for the F3000 title if he can get a deal together.

Max Wilson (Brazil), top right
1997 record: Fifth in FIA F3000 Championship

Worth noting: With a little more qualifying consistency he would be the complete package. The fact he is such a good racer helps him overcome occasionally lousy grid positions. Hard but fair: could have tipped Watt out of the race lead at Spa on several occasions, but always found a way of avoiding collisions, most of which involved using large tracts of grass. Very small; very intense; very quick.

1998 prospects: Currently appearing on an F3000 shopping-list near you.

Soheil Ayari (France), below

1997 record: Seventh in FIA F3000 Championship

Worth noting: All right, that doesn't sound like a brilliant statistic – but he did win in Helsinki after pulling off one of the overtaking manoeuvres of the season. And he was French F3 champion in 1996. And he's a jolly nice bloke.

1998 prospects: Prost is looking to create a feeder stream for its grand prix outfit by combining a Formula 3000 programme with F1 testing. Soheil is one candidate – but not the only one.

urvives schuey's **lunge**
rmer champ **slammed**
ving ● hakkinen **wins** at last

Crunch moment: Villeneuve turns into Dry Sack curve and Schumacher turns into Villeneuve. The incident left the Canadian to celebrate with Hakkinen and Coulthard (top), while the German practised for a rumoured part in next year's Littlewoods catalogue.

137

grand prix year 1997

Frentzen heads Villeneuve, Hakkinen and Hill – who is about to be passed around the outside by the kerb-mauling Coulthard. Schumacher is already clear and on his way to a third world championship title. Probably.

It's hardly as popular an aerial destination as, say, Frankfurt or Paris, but Jerez has its own international airport, a long way removed from the glorified potting shed which used to stand on the site, unannounced by any form of signpost.

On the Thursday before the European Grand Prix a small crowd of German enthusiasts stood outside, playing spot the celebrity. There was Rubens Barrichello, well worth an autograph. And Jan Magnussen, happy to chat for five minutes.

But then there was a buzz. One of Michael Schumacher's fleet of pet dogs has been spied in the baggage collecting area. Could he? Will he?

For the knot of fans there is mild disappointment. When the Schumacher posse arrives it contains Corinna, Michael's wife, their daughter Gina-Maria and no fewer than three canine accomplices. (Michael is already at the circuit, exchanging lightweight pre-race chat in a press conference with arch-rival Jacques Villeneuve.)

But the mood around the arrivals hall is bright. Schumacher's manager Willi Weber exudes confidence and has already had celebratory tee-shirts and caps printed, proclaiming Ferrari's first world champion for 18 years.

By Sunday evening, however, it wouldn't only be the Schumacher hounds who were returning to their Lausanne home with tails between their legs.

The climax to the F1 season started brightly enough, Villeneuve, Schumacher and Heinz-Harald Frentzen setting qualifying times identical to within a thousandth of a second. There was no finer way to set the stage.

At the pre-race drivers' briefing it was made clear that anyone who in any way interfered with the outcome of this global showpiece would face the severest possible sanctions. There was even talk

"villeneuve, schumacher and heinz-harald frentzen set **qualifying** times **identical** to within a **thousandth** of a second"

of a ban for the whole of 1998 if anyone should attempt to influence the outcome of this two-horse race.

There was no doubt that this warning had absolutely the desired effect.

Witness Ralf Schumacher's reaction as his brother came up to lap him. He moved over double-quick to let Michael through – as was customary – but seconds later darted out of the way even more smartly to make room for Villeneuve.

Schumacher Mk1 had been in control of the race from the first turn, making the most of a poor start from Villeneuve. Jacques even yielded ground to Frentzen and was happy to sit and watch lest his team-mate should be able to do anything to unsettle the leader. He wasn't and so it came down to a straight fight between the two, a contest which appeared to be going Michael's way for much of the afternoon.

It was on the 48th of 69 laps, just after the second and final pit stops, that the title was settled in the fashion of so many last-ditch title contests. Going into the Dry Sack curve, a piece of tarmac evocatively named after a local sherry

schumacher
under
pressure

The atmosphere in the Jerez media centre was electric. It was more like a soccer terrace than a working area as Schumacher's every move was greeted by raucous cheers from the Italian and German media corps. Until halfway around lap 48.

Then they fell silent – though their printed message the following day spoke volumes. Here are just a few of the things that were said. . .

"We call on Schumacher to apologise, not only to Villeneuve but to all Ferrari people. This is no way to behave and we are not interested in victory at all costs. What happened was a dirty trick, an unworthy gesture which in normal life would have criminal consequences."
Corriere dello Sport

"Gone is his [Schumacher's] nice boy next door image."
Frankfurter Allgemeine Zeitung

"Michael, why on earth did you do it?"
Bild (Germany's top-selling paper)

"His image as a champion has been shattered."
La Stampa

"Michael showed his true colours. It looked to me as if he was out to take Jacques off. At least he's consistent. . ."
Damon Hill

"Michael made a mistake, just like any man can make a mistake."
Luca di Montezemolo, Ferrari President

"Michael Schumacher has been summoned to appear before an extraordinary meeting of the World Motor Sport Council."
The FIA

brand, Villeneuve suddenly pitched for the inside. The manoeuvre caught the German unawares. The corner was Villeneuve's. . . and then Schumacher turned right.

Initially Schumacher insisted he was more sinned against. Villeneuve, he said, had effectively used him as a brake and would not have made the corner had he not been there.

"I knew he was capable of deciding to take me off," countered Villeneuve, "but he didn't do it well enough."

Indeed not. Schumacher bobbled to the outside of the corner and bogged down in the gravel. After spinning his wheels uselessly for 20 seconds he climbed out and went to stand on the wall, to see whether Jacques would reappear. It was reminiscent of Adelaide in 1994, when he and Damon Hill ended the season on a destructive note. Except this time the Williams kept going. . . and kept going.

Jacques had to slow down and said that his car behaved mighty strangely after the clash. Not so strangely, however, that he was unable to make it to the end. He moved across on the last lap and the McLarens of Hakkinen and Coulthard swept through triumphantly to finish the season as the Silver Arrows had started it.

But third place was enough for Villeneuve. Before the race, almost everybody you spoke to had agreed that Schumacher would be a worthy champion; by the time the race was run everyone concurred that the right man now wore the crown.

By the following Tuesday, even Schumacher – by then facing an appearance before an FIA hearing – was admitting that he might have made an error of judgment.

For the sake of a tug on his steering wheel the reputation of a genius had been tarnished – perhaps forever.

Hi-Ho Silver Arrows: McLaren celebrates its first 1-2 since Japan 1991.

plot thickens as finn wins

There was a certain irony in Mika Hakkinen's first grand prix victory. A man who had deserved to win at on merit at Silverstone, the Nürburgring, the A1-Ring and – arguably – in Hungary finally broke his duck because of what many – notably Ferrari – believed was a tacit agreement.

Villeneuve denied he had been told to move over on the last lap. "To fight would have been too much of a risk," he said.

Williams technical director Patrick Head was likewise adamant that he had not been cooking up schemes when he visited McLaren during the race; that, he said, was a courtesy visit after Frentzen got lost during a routine stop and ploughed through the McLaren and Benetton pits *en route* to Williams.

Hakkinen passed team-mate Coulthard a couple of laps from home after the Scot let him through, a move for which little rational explanation was forthcoming.

The Finn saw no reason not to celebrate his success. "I lost a lot of time behind Jacques at the start," he reasoned. "I could have gone faster but it would have been risky to pass him. I didn't want to interfere with his title chances."

No one questioned that Hakkinen deserved a win, it was just that the manner of it seemed somehow inappropriate. McLaren chief Ron Dennis added further fuel to the collaboration theory by commenting, simply, "The good guys won."

And this on a day when F1 bid *adieu* to a couple of its reputed good guys. If Hakkinen's success was dwarfed by Villeneuve's, the performances of Gerhard Berger and Ukyo Katayama barely merited mention.

In their final races they finished fourth and 17th respectively. Berger, you are sure, will be back in the paddock before long; the friendly Japanese is going off to climb K2 – alongside which the notion of trying to win a grand prix in a Minardi doesn't look so daunting.

3 VILLENEUVE 1m 21.072s

5 M SCHUMACHER 1m 21.072s

4 FRENTZEN 1m 21.072s

1 HILL 1m 21.130s

2 HAKKINEN 1m 21.369s

10 COULTHARD 1m 21.476s

6 IRVINE 1m 21.610s

8 BERGER 1m 21.656s

4 PANIS 1m 21.735s

7 ALESI 1m 22.011s

3 MAGNUSSEN 1m 22.167s

22 BARRICHELLO 1m 22.222s

DINIZ 1m 22.234s

16 HERBERT 1m 22.263s

5 NAKANO 1m 22.351s

11 R SCHUMACHER 1m 22.740s

2 FISICHELLA 1m 22.804s

17 FONTANA 1m 23.281s

20 KATAYAMA 1m 23.409s

21 MARQUES 1m 23.854s

9 SALO 1m 24.222s

18 VERSTAPPEN 1m 24.301s

results

26 October 1997. Circuito Permanente de Jerez, Jerez de la Frontera. Circuit length: 2.751miles/4.428km

Peliqui

Ayrton Senna chicane

Expo 92

Michelin

Ducados

Dry Sack

RACE CLASSIFICATION

Pos	Driver	Nat	Car	Laps	Time
1	Mika Hakkinen	FIN	McLaren MP4/12-Mercedes V10	69	1h38m57.772s
2	David Coulthard	GB	McLaren MP4/12-Mercedes V10	69	+1.654s
3	Jacques Villeneuve	CDN	Williams FW19-Renault V10	69	+1.802s
4	Gerhard Berger	A	Benetton B197-Renault V10	69	+1.919s
5	Eddie Irvine	GB	Ferrari F310B-Ferrari V10	69	+3.789s
6	Heinz-Harald Frentzen	D	Williams FW19-Renault V10	69	+4.537s
7	Olivier Panis	F	Prost JS45-Mugen Honda V10	69	+1m7.145s
8	Johnny Herbert	GB	Sauber C16-Petronas V10	69	+1m12.960s
9	Jan Magnussen	DK	Stewart SF-1-Ford V10	69	+1m17.487s
10	Shinji Nakano	J	Prost JS45-Mugen Honda V10	69	+1m18.215s
11	Giancarlo Fisichella	I	Jordan 197-Peugeot V10	68	
12	Mika Salo	FIN	Tyrrell 025-Ford V8	68	
13	Jean Alesi	F	Benetton B197-Renault V10	68	
14	Norberto Fontana	RA	Sauber C16-Petronas V10	68	
15	Tarso Marques	BR	Minardi M197-Hart V8	68	
16	Jos Verstappen	NL	Tyrrell 025-Ford V8	68	
17	Ukyo Katayama	J	Minardi M197-Hart V8	68	

Retirements	Nat	Car	Laps	Reason
Damon Hill	GB	Arrows A18-Yamaha V10	47	hydraulics
Michael Schumacher	D	Ferrari F310B-Ferrari V10	47	accident
Ralf Schumacher	D	Jordan 197-Peugeot V10	44	alternator
Rubens Barrichello	BR	Stewart SF-1-Ford V10	30	gearbox
Pedro Diniz	BR	Arrows A18-Yamaha V10	11	spin

FASTEST LAP Heinz-Harald Frentzen 1m23.135s lap 30 (119.145mph/191.745kmh)

DRIVERS' CHAMPIONSHIP

Jacques Villeneuve	81
Michael Schumacher	78
Heinz-Harald Frentzen	42
Jean Alesi	36
David Coulthard	36
Gerhard Berger	27
Mika Hakkinen	27
Eddie Irvine	24
Giancarlo Fisichella	20
Olivier Panis	16
Johnny Herbert	15
Ralf Schumacher	13
Damon Hill	7
Rubens Barrichello	6
Alex Wurz	4
Jarno Trulli	3
Pedro Diniz	2
Shinji Nakano	2
Mika Salo	2
Nicola Larini	1

CONSTRUCTORS' CHAMPIONSHIP

Williams-Renault	123
Ferrari	102
Benetton-Renault	67
McLaren-Mercedes	63
Jordan-Peugeot	33
Prost-Mugen Honda	21
Sauber-Petronas	16
Arrows-Yamaha	9
Stewart-Ford	6
Tyrrell-Ford	2

formula One cars are not cheap. Multi-million pound works of art, they are the product of months of drawing office labour, weeks in wind tunnels, days of testing and hours of hard toil aimed at gaining vital tenths of a second.

This makes it all the more surprising that drivers should attempt to use them as battering rams.

At least, that's how the 1997 Formula One World Championship was decided. As the final race drew to its conclusion, Michael Schumacher aimed his Ferrari at Jacques Villeneuve's Williams and attempted to nerf him off the road and out of the contest. Against the odds, it didn't work: Villeneuve bounced away almost scot-free and raced away to the crown as his rival disappeared in a cloud of dust.

When it cleared, he found himself facing an enquiry into his driving standards from motor sport's governing body, the FIA. More importantly, he was rebuked by Italy as a whole. You don't get away with doing something like that in a Ferrari – all the moreso when you don't succeed.

It was a suitably controversial end to a storming season in which the initiative swung back and forth. Yet another brilliant chassis was the basis for the Williams team's record-breaking ninth constructors' title, although former

Jacques
Villeneuve
FIA
Formula 1
World
Champion

jacques' pot

Indycar champ Villeneuve wobbled occasionally on his way to the drivers' crown. And Heinz-Harald Frentzen, for the acquisition of whose services Frank Williams had decided world champion Damon Hill was dispensable, appeared to have left his talent down the back of a sofa for much of the year.

Ferrari was inspired by Schumacher's genius but didn't produce a car which was always capable of doing him justice. They could have given the German a

"villeneuve wobbled occasionally on his way to the drivers' crown"

ground, although McLaren re-entered the frame. Wins for David Coulthard and Mika Hakkinen book-ended the season, even if they tussled with an unwieldy chassis between times. The Mercedes engine was an absolute grenade – extremely powerful, but likely to blow at any second.

By the campaign's end the package was sorted, leaving Coulthard as top Brit with the promise of even more to come for next season.

The home fires didn't burn as brightly as usual this year. Eddie Irvine blew hot and cold at Ferrari – even though "hot" was warm enough to give him five podiums. Johnny Herbert drove better than ever but wasn't so well-rewarded, primarily because his Sauber team was stalled in neutral on the development front.

And then there was the world champion, Damon Hill. The Williams refugee went from hero to zero at first. His new Arrows team began with a car that was positively canine, notwithstanding the fact that a greyhound would have given it more than a run for its money.

But the team progressed. Hill came within a lap of the F1 upset of the decade in Hungary – and that was a timely reminder of Damon's class during a year when team-mate Pedro Diniz occasionally gave him food for thought.

pram and he would still have qualified in the top six. As it was, he proved himself the best driver of his generation with superb performances at Monaco and Spa, yet he struggled to score points on occasion.

But the Prancing Horse was back. If only Schumacher had stuck to what he was good at rather than playing bumper cars, we'd be more inclined to look at it that way.

Serious opposition was thin on the

Maple treat: Villeneuve on the planet euphoria (far left) and niggling Michael Schumacher before they clashed in Jerez (below). The 1997 season was not only Renault's last, it also marked the 20th anniversary of its first race with the trend-setting turbo, with which engine wizard Bernard Dudot posed at Silverstone (above).

Desperately seeking Damon (right). Hakkinen (below) sustained several major blows, usually in the engine department. The Finn finally scored his first F1 success with a little help from his friends. Irvine's tactics in Japan earned him a rightful dousing of Moët (bottom).

But it wasn't enough to persuade him to stay. With a string of abortive transfer negotiations and irate team bosses in his wake, Hill jumped ship to a Jordan team that promised more than 1997 delivered.

Ireland's national outfit was not sufficiently consistent – though it was fast enough to challenge the establishment from time to time. Feisty youngsters Giancarlo Fisichella and Ralf Schumacher did the trick – Fisichella even leading at Hockenheim before being shaded by the almost bus pass-eligible Gerhard Berger.

This emotionally-charged success was the last of the Austrian's F1 career – and was the high point in Benetton's mediocre season, a campaign overshadowed by boardroom shenanigans during which the charismatic Flavio Briatore was replaced by the suave David Richards.

Multi-team investor Briatore also deferred to Alain Prost, the four-time world champion spending the year burdened by the hopes of the French populace when he took over the team formerly known as Ligier. They looked good, flattered by excellent tyres from F1 newcomer Bridgestone, but never recovered from an accident in Canada which left team leader Olivier Panis with broken legs.

The new Stewart team carried Bridgestone hopes too, the highlight being a sensational second at a wet Monaco courtesy of Rubens Barrichello. He never scaled such dizzy heights again, but by the season's end the team seemed as much a paddock fixture as Jackie Stewart's engaging rhetoric.

The other newcomer, Lola, didn't last long. It folded after one race which suggested that its leviathan contender needed a calendar to chart progress.

If nothing else, the failure of this great name demonstrated how highly pressurised F1 is these days. Never has it been so technically challenging, so commercially cut-throat, so demanding of its drivers.

Fortunately, it hasn't often been so entertaining either.